The Expressive Actor

"The study of acting should not begin with an exploration of feeling, perception, imagination, memories, intention, personalization, self-identification ... or even performance—but *physical action.*"

Michael Lugering's *The Expressive Actor* presents a foundational, preparatory training method, using movement to unlock the entire acting process. Its action-based perspective integrates voice, movement, and basic acting training into a unified approach.

A wealth of exercises and diagrams guide the reader through this internationally taught program, making it an ideal step-by-step course for both solo and classroom use.

Through this course, voice and body training becomes more than a simple skill-building activity—it is the central prerequisite to any actor training.

This new Routledge edition has been fully updated, to include:

- A revised prologue, further discussing the historical and philosophical grounding of The Lugering Method.
- A new introduction, with particular focus on the integrative nature of the method and how the book should be used.
- A new chapter defining integration in theory and practice.
- New developments, clarifications, and 12 new exercises.
- 6 new illustrative diagrams.

Michael Lugering is the founding director of the Expressive Actor, a non-profit arts organization committed to integrated methods of actor training, and a Full Professor at the University of Nevada, Las Vegas. He has taught master classes in acting, voice, movement and classical text throughout the US, Korea, and the UK.

The Expressive Actor

Integrated voice, movement, and acting training

Michael Lugering
Illustrations by Louis Kavouras

Routledge
Taylor & Francis Group
LONDON AND NEW YORK

Second edition published 2013
by Routledge
2 Park Square, Milton Park, Abingdon, Oxon OX14 4RN

Simultaneously published in the USA and Canada
by Routledge
711 Third Avenue, New York, NY 10017

Routledge is an imprint of the Taylor & Francis Group, an informa business

© 2013 Michael Lugering

The right of Michael Lugering to be identified as the author of the text has been asserted in accordance with sections 77 and 78 of the Copyright, Designs and Patents Act 1988.

All rights reserved. No part of this book may be reprinted or reproduced or utilised in any form or by any electronic, mechanical, or other means, now known or hereafter invented, including photocopying and recording, or in any information storage or retrieval system, without permission in writing from the publishers.

First edition published by Heinemann 2007

Trademark notice: Product or corporate names may be trademarks or registered trademarks, and are used only for identification and explanation without intent to infringe.

British Library Cataloguing in Publication Data
A catalogue record for this book is available from the British Library

Library of Congress Cataloguing in Publication Data
Lugering, Michael.
The expressive actor: integrated voice, movement and acting training / Michael Lugering.
p. cm.
Includes bibliographical references and index.
1. Acting. I. Title.
PN2061.L83 2012
792.02′8—dc23
2012009898

ISBN: 978-0-415-66930-6 (hbk)
ISBN: 978-0-415-66931-3 (pbk)
ISBN: 978-0-203-12521-2 (ebk)

Typeset in Baskerville
by Book Now Ltd, London

Printed and bound in Great Britain by
TJ International Ltd, Padstow, Cornwall

Contents

Figures

Acknowledgments

When I first began developing this method, I had no intentions of writing a book and now find myself somewhat remiss in remembering all the various resources and references that shaped my thinking and influenced my exploration. Consequently the business of acknowledging my indebtedness to others is somewhat difficult. I am indebted to many great philosophers, scholars, scientists, teachers, students, actors, and other theater artists. I have included a substantial bibliography at the end of the book for anyone interested in retracing at least part of my journey. In places in the text, I mention the names of authors and/or the title of books that have contributed to my thinking. However, I fear my obligation to others who are not referenced directly is often greater than might be gathered from the few references in the text.

With respect to indebtedness, I am most respectful of the enduring legacy of Stanislavski, in particular his Method of Physical Action, which shaped and influenced my discussion of expressive action presented here. I am equally indebted to Jerzy Grotowski, Michael Chekhov, Richard Schechner, to the aesthetic philosophy of Mark Johnson, F S. C. Northrop, Susanne K. Langer, John Dewey, David Best; as well as the psychological writings of Daniel Goleman, David Eagelman, Edward W. L. Smith, James I. Kepner, Daniel Kahneman, and Stanley Keleman. This second edition includes the discussion of recent advances in neuroscience by contemporary scientists Antonio Damasio, Daniel Wolpert, and Joseph LeDoux.

With respect to practical experience, my initial voice and body training with master teacher Kristin Linklater was invaluable and profound. Her influence and wisdom will be readily evident to students familiar with her work. Additionally, the time I spent at the Alexander Training Institute in Santa Monica, California remains a great resource. Invariably, I am reminded by others of the similarities between the physical method of training presented here and the movement vocabulary of Rudolf Laban. Though my practical and academic links to his work are minimal, I am flattered to be held in such great company.

Most importantly, I must acknowledge the work of Erick Hawkins and the Erick Hawkins Dance Company. The Voice and Body Exercises presented in this book are adaptations of many of the physical exercises, which comprise the Erick

Hawkins Dance Technique. Erick Hawkins was a master dancer, choreographer, and teacher. After a serious injury to his knee, he began to question the strenuous muscular approach to movement present in classical ballet and the popular modern dance technique espoused by his first wife Martha Graham. Working in his studio with his newly formed company, he began to develop a natural approach to movement that worked in harmony with the biomechanics of the human body. The Erick Hawkins Dance Technique is characterized by free-flowing movement patterns, economy, ease, and efficiency. Though I never met the late Erick Hawkins, I am deeply indebted to the Erick Hawkins Dance Company for their patience and graciousness during the time I studied with them in New York City. The improvisational studies presented in this book have their roots in the choreography classes of Lucia Dlugoszewski, the late wife of Erick Hawkins, who served as artistic director, choreographer, and composer during the time that I studied extensively with the company. In particular, I wish to thank my partner and collaborator Louis Kavouras, company member and principle dancer with the Erick Hawkins Dance Company, without whose guidance and direction this book and its many illustrations would not have been possible.

I must also thank the Board of Directors at the Expressive Actor, a 501 3(c), nonprofit organization (www.expressiveactor.org) that offers national and international workshops and training intensives, which promotes the sharing of this integrated method of actor training with others.

Additionally, I must thank my colleagues at the University of Nevada, Las Vegas in particular Phil Hubbard and Rayme Cornell; and the many fine students there who shared in the creation of this work. I am particularly grateful to Jonathan Shultz, Kristen Loree, Shelley Lynn, Joan Melton, Natalie Stewart, and Bonnie Raphael for their careful review of the content of this book. The faculty at the Expressive Actor who have committed to study this work and to teach it to others have my deepest appreciation. Finally, my editors: Talia Rodgers, Ben Piggott, and everyone who contributed to the publication of this book at Routledge have my deepest thanks.

Part I

Prologue

A

Introduction to the method

Premise

Date: 22 December 2009/Tuesday
Event: Public Television Broadcast
Title: *Charlie Rose: The Brain Series*
Guest: Daniel Wolpert, Cambridge University Neuroscientist

> Daniel Wolpert:
>
> I think you have to ask a very fundamental question: Why do we animals have brains? ...We have a brain for one reason and one reason only, and that's to produce adaptable and complex movement. There's no other reason to have evolved a brain … . So I'm really a movement chauvinist.
>
> There are many species who live very happy lives on our planet, do very well socially, but they don't need to move. So, the tree is a very nice example. It doesn't require complex movements. It hasn't developed a brain. But the clinching evidence for those who don't believe in this view … is the humble sea squirt. It is a very rudimentary animal, and it has a brain, a spinal cord, and it swims around in its juvenile life. And at some point in its life, it implants itself on a rock and never leaves the rock again. And the first thing it does upon implanting on that rock is to digest its own brain and nervous system for food. So once it doesn't need to move, it doesn't need that brain anymore. So I think … really—the brain is there for movement … .
>
> (*Charlie Rose: The Brain Series* 2009)

I, like the Cambridge University neuroscientist Daniel Wolpert, am a movement chauvinist. I believe movement can provide a foundation for unlocking the entire acting process.

The central premise of this book is that the study of acting should not begin with an exploration of feeling, perception, imagination, memories, intention, personalization, self-identification, script analysis, character, language, style, the ensemble or even performance—but *physical action*. It is not that these things are unimportant to the acting process, but as Daniel Wolpert asserts these things are secondary to physical action, arise from physical action and are components of physical action:

> So we need to remember that things like sensory processing, the perceptual system, memory, and cognitive processes are all important. But, they can only be important to drive action or suppress future actions. There's no point in laying down memories of childhood or perceiving the color of a rose if it doesn't leave you to do something different with your motor system later in life. So … from an evolutionary point of view, there would be no point in having the thinking processes, if they can't be expressed through action … . We cannot look at memory or perception [or any seemingly mental operation] in isolation from action … .
>
> (*Charlie Rose: The Brain Series* 2009)

This method seeks to reestablish the body's rightful seat at the table as the central participant in the actor's quest for the artful re-creation of human experience. The method presented is foundational and preparatory. It explores how meaning and understanding emerge from our sensorial and visceral connections to our bodies. Fundamentally, the method explores physical action as a means of reconnecting the natural links between the mind and the body that are often short-circuited in the "seemingly artificial" process of acting. While the mind and the body are unquestionably inseparable in daily living, the theatrical expression of the thoughts and feelings of characters other than ourselves often presents an insurmountable disconnect that can divide and separate the mind and body of the actor. The re-establishment of the natural connection between the mind and the body is the central goal of this integrated method of training.

Additionally, this specialized *action-based method* of training promises to integrate the seemingly disparate disciplines—voice, movement, and acting—in a unified method of study. The exercises are founded on a series of universal principles, which articulate the shared pattern and structure by which all thoughts and feelings find a physical life in the voice and body. These principles encompass specific directives for the integrated development of the actor's physical, vocal, and emotional instrument in the context of physical action. Moving, breathing, sounding, and speaking—all the components that make human expression possible—are not so much *nouns* or *things*, but rather, a series of *integrated actions* occurring simultaneously in the body. Moving is an action. Breathing is an action. Sounding is an action. Speaking is an action. A study of *how* each of these individual actions integrate in the service of the expression of thought and feeling is a specialized type of acting training in its own right and equally worthy of such a label. I assert that it is possible to develop a type of voice and body training—rooted in physical action—that is in essence a specialized type of actor training. This unique type of *action-based training* simultaneously prepares the body and voice for the expression of *thought and feeling* and the creation of *meaning and understanding* that are essential to the actor's storytelling process. From this perspective, voice and body training is not merely some isolated and arbitrary skill-building activity that is divorced or separated from the creative process, but an integrated component in a comprehensive acting curriculum.

Context

The idea that actor training could begin in the body is not a new or a revolutionary concept. The legacy of this training is echoed in the work of Stanislavski, Rudolf Laban, Michael Chekhov, Jerzi Grotowski, Peter Brook, Richard Schechner, Phillip B. Zarrilli, Anne Bogart, and others. However, despite the many notable proponents, in certain circles of training there remains a deep-seated resistance to physical methods of preparation. This resistance manifested itself most significantly in psychological realistic approaches to actor training in the United States, but vestiges of this prejudice remain pervasive and have proved difficult to overcome. The origins of this bias are not new, but centuries old—a systemic tendency to celebrate the *mind* over the *body;* and ultimately, intellectual methods of actor training over physical methods of actor training.

Underpinning this biased view are three traditional and controversial scientific and philosophical beliefs about the mind and the body:

"My body is not me."—the tendency to view our bodies as an object, something separate from and other than the person we think of as our self. In this view, the true nature or essence of a person exists solely because of mental activity. The body is viewed merely as a physical container that houses or holds the true spirit of a person. The process of self-identification and the concept of personhood exist without reference to physical experience.

The spotlight of human consciousness

Without question the mind and body are an indissoluble unit. However, the nature of human consciousness, human communication, and indeed, actor training often require that we direct our awareness towards one aspect of our integrated mind/body experience at a time. It is difficult for the conscious mind to be in two places at once. Consequently, some training approaches focus the *spotlight on the mind*—mental methods of acting training; and other training approaches focus the *spotlight on the body*—physical methods of acting training. Regardless, of where the "spotlight of human consciousness" might be focused in training, it is important to recognize that the mind and body are always functioning together as one. Without question, in the rehearsal room the actor needs the resources of both the mind and the body to create a meaningful artistic experience for the spectator.

"My emotions and feelings are mental events."—the tendency to view our emotions and feelings exclusively as isolated intellectual constructions, while overlooking the rich, full-bodied physical experience that make emotion and feeling possible.

"My emotions and feelings are irrational."—the tendency to view our emotions and feelings as interfering with the thinking process; rather than as foundational co-participants in the meaning-making, reasoning, and understanding process.

The result of these views is a swift theoretical undercurrent that reinforces the notion that the most valuable methods of acting training are intellectual and not physical—or as commonly stated *internal* and not *external.* There is, however, compelling contemporary scientific and philosophical research that questions these traditional views of the mind and body. I suggest that if these advances are fully digested they will lead to a reexamination and a radical new validation of physical methods of acting training.

I will step aside at this point and allow the words of two contemporary thinkers—the neuroscientist Antonio Damasio and the philosopher Mark Johnson to articulate a challenging alternative view, which underpins the philosophical foundation of this method:

"My mind and body are one"

Neuroscientist Antonio Damasio:

> The human brain and the rest of the body constitute an indissociable organism … . The organism interacts with the environment as an ensemble: the interaction is neither of the body alone nor the brain alone.
>
> (1994, xx–xxi)

Philosopher Mark Johnson:

> There is no radical mind/body separation. A person is not a mind and a body. There are not two "things" somehow mysteriously yoked together. What we call a "person" is a certain kind of bodily organism that has a brain operating within its body, a body that is continually interacting with aspects of its environment (material and social) in an ever-changing process of experience.
>
> (2007, 11)

"My emotions and feelings are an integrated mental and physical experience"

Neuroscientist Antonio Damasio:

> The essence of feeling may not be an elusive mental quality attached to an object, but the direct perception of a specific landscape: that of the body.
>
> (1994, xviii)

Philosopher Mark Johnson:

> … feeling is our felt awareness of something going on in our body.
>
> (2007, 65)

> There wouldn't be an emotion without a brain, a body and flesh and blood ….
>
> (2007, 67)

> Emotions are not merely cognitive structures, they are not merely brain processes, and they are not merely bodily responses. Rather emotions encompass all of these dimensions and more.
>
> (2007, 62)

"My emotions and feelings assist me in reasoning and thinking"

Neuroscientist Antonio Damasio:

> I … propose that reasoning may not be as pure as most of us think it is or wish it were, that emotions and feelings may not be intruders into the bastion of reason at all … . At their best, feelings point us in the proper direction, where we may put the instruments of logic to good use.
>
> (1994, xvi–xvii)

> Clearly, I never wished to set emotion against reason, but rather see emotion at least assisting with reason and at best holding a dialogue with it … . I view emotion as delivering cognitive information via feeling … .
>
> (1994, xiii)

Philosopher Mark Johnson:

> There is no cognition without emotion, even though we are often unaware of the emotional aspects of our thinking.
>
> (2007, 9)

The embodied mind

Ideas similar to those of Damasio and Johnson abound in contemporary neurological and cognitive science, philosophy, evolutionary epistemology, artificial intelligence, robotics, linguistics, and other disciplines. All around us, the traditional tendency to separate the integrated action of the mind and body is being challenged in what may be the most significant scientific and philosophical phenomena of our time—*embodied cognition*. Embodied cognition is a revolutionary way of thinking about human reasoning, which suggests that the content of the human mind—ideas, meaning, understanding, precepts, and principles—are shaped and developed through physical experience (*Internet Encyclopedia of Philosophy* [refereed], 8 July 2005).

Mark Johnson speaks of the *embodied mind* as follows:

> Meanings emerge, "from the bottom up" through increasingly complex levels of organic activity; they are not constructs of a disembodied mind.
>
> (2007, 10)

News of these ideas is beginning to trickle down into practical discussions about acting training. A new understanding of the important role the body plays in the feeling and thinking process is raising complex questions about how actors have studied in the past, while posing new opportunities for the future. We may soon arrive at a clearer place, where we can finally walk away from a centuries old dichotomy that has celebrated *thinking* over *sensing*, *thought* over *feeling*, *cognition* over *emotion*, *fact* over *value*, *knowledge* over *intuition* and essentially, the *mind* over the *body* (Johnson 2007, 7). These misperceptions have divided actors from their instruments—separating the *internal* and the *external*, the *organic* and the *technical*, the *artist* and the *craftsman*; and humorously, even the *Americans* from the *British*.

Implications for acting training

The concept of embodied cognition has profound practical implications for the actor:

If …

- the actor's body is not merely an object, a thing—a mere physical container that houses or holds a person, but an essential component in the process of self-identification and the concept of personhood;
- feeling and thinking and meaning and understanding are built on the scaffolding of the body;

… then it stands to reason that:

- the actor's basic technique could be taught via the body through physical action;
- the actor's physical and vocal training should have an equal seat at the table as co-participants in the acting process;

- the actor's emotional and mental preparation are foundationally physical in nature;
- the actor's quest to create meaning and understanding should be grounded in physical experience.

What is most important to recognize is that the foundations of *thinking and feeling* and *meaning and understanding* are physical. Whenever the actor works physically to create *meaning and understanding*, this physical work is fundamentally actor training. In this spirit, the best voice and movement teachers, of every kind and creed, have always been at their very core, acting teachers.

Coda

Despite notable exceptions, many contemporary actors tend to think their way into the characters that they play while often ignore and neglect their bodies. They analyze the script, concentrate, remember, daydream, and fantasize—all mental activities—in a quest for vivid and authentic human feeling. They use their intellect to create subtext, inner monologues, and character biographies. Above all, they attempt to believe in everything their characters do and say. It is important to recognize that *believing* something to be true is virtually synonymous with *thinking* something to be true. As Phillip B. Zarrilli rightly points out, "believing is devoid of any reference to the body; there is no assertion that believing needs to be embodied" (1995, 10). The contemporary actor often creates emotion and character through an act of sheer mental determination and willpower.

Without question, there are numerous benefits to these and other "seemingly" mental methods of preparation. However, an overemphasis on the intellect has led a generation of actors to neglect the important role that the body plays in the process of self-identification, the concept of personhood, and its foundational role in the creation of meaning and understanding.

All too often voice and body training is given second-class status. The appreciation of voice and body training is often limited to technical niceties such as the importance of standing up straight, breathing "properly," resonating "well," or speaking "clearly." It is wrong to assume that voice and body training is to the actor what learning to type might be to the writer. The physical properties of the voice and body are simultaneously rich physiological and psychological resources—co-participants in the feeling/thinking and the meaning/reasoning process.

It is important to remember that the *well-coordinated body* and the *well-coordinated mind* go hand in hand. The prerequisite technical skills required for successful mental and emotional expression and successful physical and vocal expression are one and the same. When a sophisticated level of integration is achieved, physical flexibility and dexterity is linked directly to emotional and mental flexibility and dexterity. When the body learns efficient and coordinated ways of moving and sounding, it simultaneously learns efficient and coordinated ways of thinking and feeling. In time, the body comes to be viewed as a rich mental and emotional playground—a malleable physical medium through which thought and feeling are experienced and organized.

The future of acting training requires a new understanding of technique. I suggest that there is a shared universal, human *physical experience* that is a direct product of years of human evolution. Each of us has a body that has evolved to interact with the world that surrounds us. This body is physiologically designed to assist us in making intellectual and emotional sense of our world through *physical action*. This integrated study of physical action has the potential to unite the actor's physical and psychological training. The next wave of actor training requires an integrated method that is too comprehensive to be labeled as either *psychological* or *physical*, *internal* or *external*, in which the content of acting, voice, and movement classes mixes, mingles, overlaps, and ideally becomes indistinguishable. The actor will not study the parts—voice, movement, acting—but a single integrated discipline—expression itself. In the not-too-distant future, acting teachers, voice teachers, movement teachers, and their students will work as a team, sharing a compatible philosophy of training, a shared set of principles and a common vocabulary. I mean this book as a step in this right direction.

B

Overview of the method

The heart of the method centers on the exploration of a highly specialized type of physical action that is enlisted in the direct service of the expression of thought and feeling. I call this unique type of physical action an *expressive action.* An expressive action is any physical action that embodies a thought and feeling.

Central to the study of expressive action, is the exploration of a *weight shift*—the physical redistribution of the body's weight that make movement and expression possible. The actors' ability to move and shift their weight appropriately and authentically lays the physical foundations for the creation of artistic truth. A weight shift is a natural manifestation of the process of living—when movement ceases so does life itself. In particular, the method focuses on specific *physical properties* that comprise the weight shift—its *energy*, *orientation*, *size*, *progression*, *flow*, *direction*, *speed*, *weight*, *control*, and *focus*. These physical properties unite to form what is called the *architecture of an expressive action*—the raw materials, which lay the physical foundation for the expression of *thought and feeling* and the creation of *meaning and understanding.*

Through the study of a *weight shift*, the actor's voice and body are simultaneously developed, strengthened, liberated and sensitized. In integrated acts of human expression, a weight shift corresponds with a *breath-shift*, which corresponds with a *sound-shift*, which corresponds with a *speech-shift*, which simultaneously correspond with a *thought/feeling-shift.* In this context, the actor's voice and movement training are not merely a set of prerequisite technical skills that when one day mastered must be "placed on top of the acting;" but rather, are viewed as co-participants in an integrated, action-based training process.

The exercises transcend any specific acting style, focusing on universal aspects of human communication present in all drama from Shakespeare to Simon, Wycherly to Wasserstein, and Molière to Mamet. The goal is an expressive actor ready for action, capable of a vivid, powerful, and artful expression of thought and feeling.

The exercises focus specifically on the collaboration between *actor* and *instrument*—between the individual and his or her body, breath and voice. The exercises do not comprehensively address the important collaboration that occurs between actors and directors in concert with a playscript. Also, detailed speech and language training, interpretation and analysis, character study and style, while important subjects, receive only a cursory treatment in these chapters. I hope to extend these ideas, concepts and principles presented here with a second book entitled *The Expressive Actor in Rehearsal.*

Technique

The technique consists of two distinct and related components: *Voice and Body Exercises* and *Improvisation.* These exercises are designed to build important prerequisite skills in movement, respiration, resonance, and range. Most importantly, they are designed to prepare the actor for integrated, full-bodied expressive action. These exercises help the actor integrate and organize a wide variety of emotional, mental, and physical sensations into meaningful forms of expression. They are designed to cultivate a healthy respect for impulse, spontaneity, and creativity while simultaneously expanding the actor's imagination and increasing expressive power.

The method fosters an intuitive approach to skill-building. The exercises begin with the repetition of a physical action and progress sequentially adding breath, then sound, and finally words and phrases in a process called *stacking.* The outcome is the sensuous, integrated expression of the body's most powerful thoughts and feelings. The exercises have proved to be an essential link in bridging the wide gap that so often separates traditional methods of voice, movement, and acting training. Through the exercises, the actor learns new forms of expression never thought possible and many of which he or she has never experienced in his or her own life. In an advanced study, specific exercises can be structured to address individual deficiencies and limitations. The goal is to develop an instrument that is flexible and dynamic and in direct contact with pure sensation.

Practical working vocabulary

Additionally, the technique provides the actor with a *practical working vocabulary* that accurately describes the physical experience of expressing a thought and feeling. In the method presented, the actor might describe a moment of performance as *charged, direct, light,* and *free* and another moment as *sharp, heavy,* and *withdrawn.* These physical properties have a comprehensive application and reference all aspects of the actor's craft—movement, breath, sound and language—all the integrated components that make the expression of thought and feeling possible.

These specialized terms are as useful to the actor as *tempo* and *meter* are to the musician, and *plié* and *leap* are to the dancer. It is important to recognize that the body is simultaneously a mental and emotional meaning-making center, and a technical hub for adjustments and adaptations that allows us to direct and shape our thoughts and feelings. The body is the means by which concrete emotional and mental experience is directly felt and immediately sensed. Additionally, the language of the body is specific and concrete and of great practical use to the actor. One of the reasons acting training has lagged behind dance and music training is that it has struggled to develop a practical working vocabulary that tangibly describes the physical experience of acting. Pianists recognize *forte*: (loud) or *pianissimo*: (very soft) not as mere technical manipulations, but as insightful psychological directives that must ultimately be incorporated into the working whole. Similarly, a dancer would never be offended by being reminded of the "truth" of the musical pulse. A detailed and precise physical vocabulary lies at the very heart of any serious technique. Most importantly, a detailed physical vocabulary lays the foundation for the creation of technical exercises. When the physical vocabulary is unclear and incomplete, the acting exercises and the training process becomes muddied and convoluted.

A practical working vocabulary and a corresponding set of exercises pave the way for a method of daily practice and preparation that are central to the training process. Actors need a method of daily practice similar to the musician's scales and the dancer's barre. These types of technical exercises can be practiced in a group, but most importantly without the assistance of others. Regretfully, many methods of actor training are not possible without a partner and sometimes even a teacher or a director. As a result actors tend to practice less frequently than other performing artists. The reason for this is that actor's often lack a practical working vocabulary that makes solo methods of preparation possible. Without a practical working vocabulary, the actor working alone is always in danger of the process becoming overly subjective and biased. When this happens the actor looses any reliable physical reference to steer and shape the process. Fortunately, a practical working vocabulary—comprised of terms such as *fast* or *slow*, *charged* or *released*, *heavy* or *light*—provide rational directives for productive solo exploration and development. They provide the actor with the confidence needed to work alone in the quest for the simultaneous perfection of both art and craft.

C

Introduction to the actor

Expression is the process of revealing through *physical action*—in movement, sound and words what one thinks and feels. Under the rubric of "expression," the traditionally disparate disciplines—acting, voice, and movement are synthesized. The study of expression roots all aspects of the actor's training in a human exploration of the universal process with which we express our thoughts and feelings. This exploration of expression has potential to unlock and unify the acting process.

There is an important distinction between having or experiencing a thought or feeling and expressing that thought or feeling. Everyone experiences thoughts and feelings that are deeply moving and fully committed. However, not everyone is able to reveal in movements, sounds, and words the rich mental and emotional content of those thoughts and feelings. There is nothing more frustrating than having a thought or feeling and not being able to find an appropriate and effective way to express it. Most of us would like to express ourselves better, and we genuinely admire individuals who seem to have mastered the art of doing so. Any act of expression—whether in a coffee shop, a classroom, a subway, a synagogue, a courtroom, or the back seat of a car—when executed skillfully can be said to be artful. Sometimes inspiration descends, and thoughts and feelings miraculously find their perfect and complete expression. At other times, we are not so lucky. Often we find ourselves mumbling and fumbling for an appropriate way to express ourselves. In moments of great passion, we are often at a total loss. Rarely does the caliber of our daily discourse possess the grace, skill, power, sensitivity, and ease characteristic of artful expression. As Aristotle said, "Anyone can become angry—that is easy. But to be angry with the right person, to the right degree, at the right time, for the right purpose, in the right way—that is not easy" (1996, 64). This is exactly what the actor is required to do: express the right feeling, with the right person, to the right degree, at the right time, for the right purpose, and in the right way. Actors are society's best models for the expression of life's most complex thoughts and feelings. Most characters in the best dramatic literature express themselves better than the average person. Playwrights do more than merely reveal human experience; they explain it, question it, challenge it and sometimes change it, often by empowering a character, even if for a single moment, with an almost supernatural gift of self-expression. This perfect organization of thinking, feeling, moving, breathing, sounding, and speaking is human expression at its best. This is not to suggest that there are not examples of disorganized and incoherent expression in some of the theates greatest plays. Actors are often called upon to move, speak, feel, and think in less than ideal ways. Surprisingly, creating characters that express themselves in inefficient, unnatural, and clumsy ways can be more difficult than creating characters that express themselves very well. In the theater, even inefficient, unnatural, and clumsy expression must be coherent and artful. A prerequisite for poorly expressing a thought and feeling on the stage is knowing how to express that thought and feeling masterfully.

The best acting often looks so spontaneous and effortless that it is easy to assume that no training or technical skill is required. Appearances are deceiving. Great actors, like great athletes, make the most sophisticated activities look easy because they have highly developed technical skills. This type of expertise strikes at the heart of what it means to be a great actor. It is the great dividing line that separates the professional from the amateur. To some degree, all actors bring to rehearsal and performance a somewhat limited and habitual method of expressing themselves. Conscientious actors recognize that there are certain types of emotional, mental, physical, and verbal expression readily at their disposal, while other types of expression remain elusive and inaccessible. Even actors who can express their personal thoughts and feelings with relative ease and grace often have trouble expressing the complex thoughts and feelings of the characters they portray. Without training and technique, even the most talented actors eventually find themselves holding the short end of the stick.

The road to fluid and flexible expression is a complex human journey. It involves exploration, discovery, discipline, self-respect, and patience. This journey begins with the belief that all human beings have the potential for dynamic, varied, and flexible expression that is capable of communicating every feeling, nuance, attitude, mood, and desire that can be experienced by the species. It requires the actor to imagine an ideal world—the possibility of perfect expression not limited by force of habit, physical deficiencies, psychological imbalances, personal idiosyncrasies, or immaturity.

The actor in training should begin focusing not on *what is* but rather on *what ought or could be* if the conditions were right. It is important to emphasize the possible rather than the actual. Ideally, the actor should not focus on what is wrong with the body or the voice, but on how the body and voice are designed to work right. Actors need to envision themselves in an ideal light—without the squeaky or husky voice, the awkward and gangly arms, the spindly and unstable legs, the tense jaw or shoulders, the fear of deep feeling or large expression. The pessimist is quick to question whether the ideal is reachable, easily conceding that certain limitations may be difficult to overcome. A negative approach limits growth and impedes progress. Actors interested in improving must remain optimistic.

This is not to suggest that a positive attitude will solve all problems at the expense of hard work. Indeed, the actor's road to flexible and varied expression can be long and arduous. Unfortunately, not all actors experience growth at the same rate. It can take as long as three years to significantly reorganize one's body structure. Even then, some deep-seated patterns and tensions are often not completely resolved. The mistake of the pessimist is to see the glass half empty. To embrace the ideal (and indeed technique itself), the actor must always maintain a positive outlook, celebrating the potential for and the process of change—slow or fast, steady or intermittent, accelerated or seemingly arrested. Each actor brings to the training a unique set of strengths and weaknesses. Consequently, each actor should move at his or her own pace. A healthy way of working requires maintaining an acceptable comfort level. A responsible approach strikes a healthy balance between challenging the body without abusing it—between pushing and pampering, disciplining and nurturing. Personality plays a strong role in the manner in which each individual approaches the work. Regardless of a person's particular disposition, there is a time to rest and a time to push ahead. The best learners seem to make these choices intuitively, never injuring or hurting themselves, while simultaneously reaching, exploring, and conquering new and uncharted territory.

The body is a creature of habit. It likes to do what it has been doing. Often when we ask the body to do something new, it puts up a struggle. Mental discipline, willpower, commitment, emotional fortitude, and physical tenacity are important for development and change. What often appears difficult and uncomfortable at first, with time becomes easy, familiar, and rewarding.

Part II

Principles of expressive action

Chapter 1

Expressive action

1.1 DEFINITION

This *action-based method* of actor training cannot begin with just any random, mechanical or arbitrary movement—but rather, a flexible, adaptable, specialized, and structured weight shift that makes human expression possible. I call this unique type of physical action an *expressive action*. An expressive action is any physical action that embodies a thought and feeling. *Scolding a child, confessing a mistake, standing your ground, turning your back on a friend, lying through your teeth, and screaming bloody murder* are good examples of expressive action. As Stanislavski stated, "in every physical action, unless it is purely mechanical, there is concealed some inner action, some feelings" (1961, 228).

- An expressive action is an integrated activity that reflects a synthesis of the *feeling, thinking,* and *doing* components of the human person.
- An expressive action is the smallest unit of human communication. They can be as small as a shrug of the shoulders, a disapproving look or a handshake. Regardless of their size, expressive actions can be quite simple or profoundly sophisticated. They span the entire compass of human experience and are capable of communicating every conceivable thought and feeling experienced by the species.
- An expressive action is commonly described in the infinitive verb form such as: "to bluff," "to amaze," "to hound" or "to sprout"—though the verbal label of an expressive action may take many forms.
- An expressive action, though rooted in action and activity, is not merely a physical task. Strictly speaking, closing a car door, flipping on a light switch, folding a newspaper and drinking a glass of wine are physical tasks, not expressive actions. However, it is possible to close a car door in a huff, flip on a light switch with trepidation, fold a newspaper sternly, and drink a glass of wine in celebration. In instances like this, these physical tasks could simultaneously be labeled expressive actions.
- Expressive actions are the building blocks of the actor's art and craft; not at all unlike what the brushstroke is to the painter, or the note is to the musician or the step to the dancer. They lie at the very heart of the actor's process.

Weight shift

A study of an expressive action begins with a *weight shift*. A weight shift is the process of moving the body or a part of the body from one place or position to another.

Process-oriented approach

A weight shift provides a practical study of the process with which we express our thoughts and feelings. It serves to focus the attention not so much on *why* we express ourselves but *how*. While greed, enthusiasm, pride, disgust, frustration, and joy are each expressed in different ways, the process with which these different thoughts and feelings find their physical life in the voice and body is universally consistent and readily identifiable. When focusing on a weight shift, the actor is not simply studying the expression of a single or specific thought and feeling, but also the universal and consistent pattern with which all thoughts and feelings receive their physical form regardless of context, content, situation, or circumstance. Fortunately, when actors become aware of the physical process with which they express a single thought and feeling, they simultaneously become aware of the universal physical process with which they express every thought and feeling. (A discussion of this universal process is discussed in detail in *Chapter 3: Physical properties*.)

Mind/body integration

A weight shift sits on the *threshold of human consciousness* providing a bridge between the *voluntary* and the *involuntary*, the *manual* and the *automatic* systems of the body. A *conscious* weight shift results in a host of *preconscious* or *semiconscious* neurological firings and endocrine secretions—changes in heart rate, respiration and numerous other subjective, preconscious physical sensations commonly associated with thinking and feeling. For the actor, it is a direct physical link to unlocking the psychological process. Weight shifts serve to integrate mind and body simultaneously making the actor on stage "whole"—an integrated functioning human being.

Simple expressive action

Select an action from the list below:

to beg	to warn	to apologize
to promise	to scold	to praise

Compose a simple but flexible piece of text for the action you have selected. (For example, for "to promise" you might compose: "I will never tell another lie.") Play your action several times, while delivering the piece of text. Notice your weight shifts. Rest. Repeat using other actions listed above or with other actions listed in Appendix II.

Sensation + impulse + action/form = expressive action

- An expressive action begins with a *sensation* or a group of sensations.
- If this sensation or a group of sensation generates enough energy, an *impulse* prompts the body to action. Legendary theater practitioner Jerzy Grotowski defined an impulse as an *in/push*—a push from inside, which results in an *out/push*—an outward movement that makes action possible (Richards 1995, 94). This impulsive quality of an expressive action creates the potential for reflexive and spontaneous human communication.
- This *action*—essentially, a weight shift or a series of interconnected weight shifts serves to define and characterize the expressive action. This is the substantive phase of the expressive action, characterized by the movement(s) generally associated with the process of expressing a thought and feeling. For example, reaching outward to assist someone in need, retreating inward to avoid a confrontation, motioning erratically and energetically to attract someone's attention or simply saying and waiving "hello" are several of the innumerable possibilities. Ultimately, the process is completed when an individual's thoughts and feelings find a representative physical, and sometimes, verbal *form* through *action*.

Passing sensations and acting on our sensations

It is important to make a distinction between *passing sensations* and the more complete process of *acting on our sensations*. Passing sensations are those sensory stimuli that fade in and out of our awareness without motivating us to expressive action. For example, as I type, the sound of the furnace, a glimpse of a car moving past the window and the growling of my stomach move freely in and out of my consciousness, but these passing sensations have not prompted or motivated me to expressive action. However, if I wave to the neighbor in the passing car, I will have acted on just one of the many sensations filtering through my consciousness and successfully executed an expressive action. Though both *passing sensations* and the process of *acting on our sensations* share the same phenomenology, it is important to make a technical distinction between the *experience of a thought and feeling* and the process of *expressing a thought and feeling* when defining expressive action (Kepner 1993, 15).

Idiomatic expressions

Each of the idiomatic expressions listed below describes an emotional experience in physical terms. Working with body-based idiomatic expressions of this type is a useful starting point for exploring the physical process of an expressive action: *sensation + impulse + action/form = expressive action*. In this exploration, the actor begins with a prompt, which creates a series of sensations in the body that creates an impulse for action that is then expressed in both a physical and verbal form. For example, the actor given the idiomatic expression "to be a pain in the neck" might begin by twisting, turning, stretching, and rubbing their neck with their hands. When these physical sensations culminate in a playable expressive action, the actor composes a piece of text on the spot. Such as: "You gotta be kidding me." or "Unbelievable" or "Can't you just let it go."

Step 1: Select an idiomatic expression from the list below.
Step 2: Allow the idiomatic expression to prompt you to physical action.
Step 3: Allow words to participate with the physical action.
Step 4: Repeat with other selected idiomatic expressions.

lose your head
save face
face up to
grit your teeth
give your eyeteeth
be a pain in the neck
shoulder a burden
twist someone's arm
get your nose out of joint
be nosey
can't stomach something
be a tight ass
get out of hand
turn the other cheek
be starry-eyed
have an ace up your sleeve
slap someone down
lower your sights
be a sight for sore eyes
have no balls
get pissed off
get choked up
shrug it off
be itching to do something
be able to breathe again
have your heart set
be full of hot air

have your nose in the air
roll in the aisles
run around in circles
have your tongue a-wagging
be empty-handed
get back on your feet
have your back to the wall
turn your back
bad-mouth
have a bad taste in your mouth
beat your brains out
bend over backward
be on bended knee
put your best foot forward
be too big for your britches
swallow a bitter pill
draw a blank
turn a blind eye
cry bloody murder
blow off steam
get the blues
talk a blue streak
feel it in your bones
dig in your heels
be bored stiff
beat your brains out
rack your brain
put on a brave face
hold your breath
bite the bullet
burst at the seams
bust a gut
button your lip
raise your eyebrows
get something off your chest
chew out
keep your chin up
have a chip on your shoulder
lick your chops
keep a civil tongue
have your head in the clouds
get cold feet
be hot under the collar
cool your heels
crack a smile
get the creeps

(Continued)

(Continued)

cross your heart
cross your fingers
get your dander up
be dead on your feet
turn a deaf ear
be tickled to death
throw your hands up
be driven up the wall
drop in your tracks
give someone the evil eye
prick up your ears
eat your heart out
have stars in your eyes
eye someone
keep a straight face
find it in your heart
be full of hot air
give a tongue-lashing
tear your hair out
sit on your hands
wash your hands of someone
bite someone's head off
stick your head in the sand
hold your head up
hold your tongue
jump out of your skin
keep a stiff upper lip
kick up your heels
laugh something off
stay on your toes
lie through your teeth
let your heart go out to
look down your noses
feel your blood run cold
quake in your boots
feel your mouth water
shoot your mouth off
don't believe your eyes

Describing expressive actions

Finding the right words to describe an expressive action is tricky. Unfortunately, the most vital and exciting expressive actions often defy precise verbal description. As the dance aestheticist David Best states: "the expressive meaning of an action, though a characteristic of the movement itself, cannot be explained purely in anatomical, physiological or other scientific terms." (1974, 65) Part of the difficulty in describing an expressive action is that an expressive action is simultaneously a physical, emotional, and mental experience. Most often, the limitations of language disallow us to describe in a single, simple sentence the totality of a physical, emotional, and mental experience. It can often take three or more sentences to adequately describe a complex expressive action: "I'm trembling! (body)." "You're scaring me! (feeling)." "I don't know why we are friends? (thinking)." Each of these individual statements, though limited in their verbal point of view, describe the experience of a single expressive action.

Additionally, we commonly associate certain expressive actions with specific physical, emotional, and mental states. For example "sparring" is physical, "debating" is mental and "lamenting" is emotional. Regardless of how we might choose to describe it, the expressive action is always an integrated *doing*, *feeling* and, *thinking* experience. Mark Johnson's asserts that when we label any aspect of our integrated physical, mental, or emotional experience that "we do this only reflectively and for the very specific purposes that we have in trying to make sense of our experience" (2007, 11). We label it *emotional* when we wish to stress the emotional aspects of our experience. We label it *physical* when we wish to stress the physical aspects of our experience. We label it *intellectual* when we wish to stress the intellectual aspect of our experience (Johnson 2007, 74). I suggest that in rehearsal, as in daily living, actors use the perspective that is most meaningful in the moment.

In the acting studio, the most popular method of describing an expressive action is to use an active verb: "to confess," "to bluff," "to tempt," or "to tease." A verb is preferred because it provides the actor with something specific to do and often roots the action in intention. While this is without question a useful way of describing an expressive action, it is certainly not the only way. For example, to say that a character is "huffing and puffing," "spinning like a top," or "tongue-wagging" is as descriptive as saying that a character wants "to defend" or "to protest." I have heard actors describe expressive actions with all manner of language, some of which borders on poetry: "as if for the last time," "without hesitation," or "never again." Any of these simple phrases, among countless others, can suggest, prompt, lead and describe an expressive action. Sometimes the best clues for what to call the expressive action are in the script. When Romeo describes Juliet at the masquerade ball, he states: "O, she doth teach the torches to burn bright (I.iv.)." Juliet is beaming and radiant. There is nothing wrong with calling her expressive action "torches burning bright." Sometimes the best labels for an expressive action are nonsensical—"to yuck 'n fluster," "to tick and tack," "to wee," "to gobbledygook." Sometimes idiomatic expressions are helpful—"to wear your heart on your sleeve," "to have a bee in your bonnet," or "to burst at the seams." Additionally, it is just as useful to describe an expressive action in physical terms such as *light*, *direct*, and *fast*. Sometimes expressive actions are referenced to blocking—"when I pick up the book" or "as I come down the stairs." In the end, it does not matter what we call the expressive action. An expressive action is an expressive action, quite simply, if it is expressive. The appropriateness of an expressive action should not be judged by the words used to describe it, but rather, the authentic expression of thought and feeling and meaning and understanding that it creates in the voice and body.

Classifying actions

Classifying expressive actions by category leads to a deeper understanding of the diverse and rich verbal perspective our vocabulary affords us when attempting to label an expressive action.

For each of the following categories, select an additional five actions from the list in Appendix II:

- *emotional actions:* an emotional state or condition (*to lament, to despair, to delight, to brood, to bristle*);
- *physical actions*: a physical action or movement (*to claw, to hobble, to knock, to dab, to slither*);
- *intellectual actions*: a mental activity or state (*to criticize, to debate, to hypothesize, to discriminate, to rationalize)*;
- *intentional actions*: a desire, want, goal, or need (*to avoid, to debate, to wish, to halt, to quiz*);
- *non-intentional actions*: passive, involuntary, or vegetative conditions (*to digress, to gawk, to sink, to tremble, to stagger)*;
- *manipulative actions*: deceptive or devious ways of controlling others (*to intimidate, to fib, to brainwash, to coerce, to mystify*);
- *repressive actions*: the controlling or restricting of thought and feeling (*to cap, to hold in, to cower, to bite your tongue, to bind*);
- *explosive actions*: violent or uncontrollable expression (*to explode, to vent, to boil, to lose it, to hit the ceiling*);
- *exaggerated actions*: the disingenuous overplaying or embellishing of a real or pretended thought and feeling (*to lie, to embellish, to brag, to flatter, to patronize*).

Compose a simple but flexible piece of text for each of the actions selected. Play your expressive action several times while delivering the piece of text.

Expressive actions in rehearsal

In rehearsal, it is often useful to name the specific expressive action being played. Labeling the action provides a point of reference and assists in structuring and creating a coherent journey for the character. This is not to suggest that every expressive action must be named, discussed, and analyzed. There are so many expressive actions in a single scene of a play that labeling them is all but impossible. Actors tend to label the important expressive actions, the expressive actions they are struggling with and the ones they discuss with other actors and the director.

Each expressive action that a character plays is like a single bead in a beautiful necklace. Just as many beads unite to create a necklace, many expressive actions unite to create the life of a character in a play. The job of the actor is ultimately to find a specific expressive action to play during each moment of performance. Just as a dancer learns the choreography step by step or a pianist learns the piece of music finger-sequence by finger-sequence, the actor also creates an authentic performance one expressive action at a time. The rehearsal process is largely the business of discovering expressive actions that work, testing them, changing them, and ultimately structuring them into a repeatable pattern. The script is a blueprint or road map to expressive action (Harrop 1992, 71). If the actor reads the blueprint well, the expressive actions played will simultaneously reveal thought and feeling, create meaning and understanding, forward the plot and define the character. In rehearsal, expressive actions sometimes spring forth spontaneously with little or no conscious effort; one is stacked upon another intuitively and instinctively. Others require technique, training, experimentation, experience, and the guidance of a gifted director.

Expressive actor and emotion

When working with expressive actions, the actor does not create the emotional life of the character by pursuing feeling directly but through outward physical action and activity. Any actor who has sat down with a playscript and attempted to make emotional notations in the margins—"sad," "shocked," "confused," "angry"—can readily attest to the methods shortcomings. Once having determined the desired feeling, the misguided actor manipulates the voice and body in any manner possible in an attempt to manufacture the authentic emotion. This often leads to a mechanical indication or manipulation of the body that is devoid of sincere feeling. The problem with this direct approach is that feelings cannot be conjured up at will and displayed on demand. Authentic feeling is best induced indirectly through the playing of an expressive action—desperation through acts of pleading and begging; love through acts of praising and cherishing; loss through acts of mourning and reflection. Ultimately, the art of acting lies not in the conscious recreation of a predetermined emotional state but in finding appropriate expressive actions that indirectly reveal emotion.

The trap of playing a feeling often occurs in big dramatic scenes, even for experienced actors, where the emotional stakes are usually very high. Consider a scene in which a mother mourns the loss of her child. The emotional demands are clear: the actor must demonstrate a passionate display of grief, loss, and desperation. But it is important not to become sidetracked and start to work for the emotional result. The actor should not begin by trying to conjure up a big sad feeling. Nor is it necessary to feel the emotion completely and fully at the first rehearsal. The desired feeling can only be created with time and exploration. The job of the actor is to create not one big feeling but many small and varied expressive actions that unite to form the larger display of grief. As the actor begins to find specific expressive actions to play in each moment of the scene, the feeling emerges indirectly and spontaneously. Many small expressive actions—"holding your heart," "pulling your hair," "questioning the facts," "cursing the gods," "wiping away your tears," "maintaining self-control," and "finding someone to blame"—unite to achieve the total affect of loss and devastation. The more specific and varied the expressive actions found, the clearer and more profound the feeling expressed. With each rehearsal, more specific and detailed expressive actions emerge. The actor works, consciously and unconsciously, to structure the expressive actions into a well-ordered whole. When the actor has found a detailed and specific expressive action for each moment in the scene, the larger display of grief becomes decidedly simpler. In the end, the result is a powerful display of feeling that is well structured, repeatable, and above all, authentic.

1.2 EXPRESSIVE ACTION IN CONTEXT

The term "action" has its deepest roots in the word "drama," which comes from the Greek word "dran" meaning "to do." Consequently actors, directors, theater critics, and scholars use the term "action" frequently and often somewhat differently. It is important to clarify the exact meaning and context of the term "expressive action" used here.

Expressive action and dramatic action

A clear understanding of *expressive action* requires the ability to distinguish it from the widely used term *dramatic action*. A play's dramatic action is comprised of all the individual actions that unite in creating the plot—Hamlet kills Polonius; Willy Loman commits suicide; Stanley rapes Blanche; Nora leaves Torvold; Peter Pan, Wendy, Michael, John and Tinkerbell fly to Nevernever Land. Dramatic action focuses on storytelling. Expressive actions, however, do not directly describe the action of the playscript; but rather, the actions that occur in the body of the actor. Expressive actions such as "to plead," "to tempt," and "to deny" articulate what the actor is *literally doing* in any given moment of the play. Through expressive action the actor fulfills the requirements of the play's dramatic action. Dramatic action is concerned with the artistic creation of the playwright, and expressive action is concerned with the artistic creation of the actor. The most important difference between dramatic action and expressive action is flexibility. Dramatic action is set specifically in the playscript and is relatively constant and unchanging. Expressive actions, however, can differ significantly from actor to actor and production to production.

Expressive action and objective

It is also important to make a distinction between an *expressive action* and the Stanislavski-based term *objective*. In contemporary acting circles, objectives are referred to in a variety of ways: "action," "motivation," "intention," "want," "need," "goal" and sometimes "spine." Regardless of the terminology, all are concerned with articulating the motivating force, which compels or prompts the character to execute the play's dramatic action. Most often objectives are stated in simple sentences that possess an active verb: "I want to make up for past mistakes." " I wish to better my position," or "I need to save myself from further humiliation." Objectives describe *why* a character behaves in a certain way. Expressive actions, on the other hand, such as "to scoff," "to berate," and "to assess," describe what the character is literally doing at a specific moment in the playscript. It is important to recognize that the expressive actions "to scoff," "to berate," "to assess" could be played to achieve any number of different objectives.

Most often, many expressive actions unite to help the character achieve a single objective. Consider a young boy whose objective is to go outside and play:

- *To beg* ("Please, please, Mom, can I go outside, please, please?") .
- *To abuse* ("You are so mean. I hate you. You never let me do anything.").
- *To negotiate* ("If you let me go outside, I promise I'll clean up my room and do my homework and always say 'please' and 'thank you'.")

If the young boy is successful, all of these smaller individual expressive actions will unite in helping him to persuade his mother to let him go outside.

Ultimately, an objective is a statement of the goal or the desired *result*, while an expressive action is a statement of *process*, articulating the means and methods with which the objective is fulfilled.

Lightning Round

The Lightning Round is designed to get you playing expressive actions impulsively and instinctively without thinking or making any predetermined decisions about the outcome.

Select 25–30 actions from the list in Appendix II. Write them on a blackboard or have a partner call them out to you. Allow the first verb on the list to prompt you to expressive action. Without deliberation, spontaneously compose a piece of text to accompany the action. Proceed directly without interruption to the next action on the list. Continue until all the actions have been explored. If at any point in the exploration, you draw a blank simply say, "pass" and move quickly on to the next action.

Chapter 2

First and second functions

2.1 DEFINITION

In the study of expressive action presented here a distinction is made between an *expressive action in its first function* and an *expressive action in its second function*. This discussion of an expressive action in the first and second function is intended to provide a comprehensive theoretical overview of the manner in which the body and the mind work together to structure thought and feeling into meaningful expressive action.

The terms *first function* and *second function* are borrowed from the philosopher F. S. C. Northrop (1946, 306–11). He asserts that there are two *simultaneous* ways of knowing and experiencing our world—a *sensing way* (first function) and a *thinking way* (second function). I first encountered these terms when I was studying choreography with the Erik Hawkins Dance Company. The company used them to describe two separate, yet seemingly simultaneous, "functions" of choreography—the physical and the intellectual. Northrop suggests that virtually anything could be known or understood from these two distinct perspectives. An expressive action can certainly be known or understood in these two distinct ways—a *sensing way* (first function*)* and a *thinking way* (second function). These different ways of knowing can also be distinguished by differentiating between *knowing how* (first function) and *knowing that* (second function). For example, I can *know that* I overslept and am late for work, and I can *know how* this late for work/overslept experience feels—my heart is racing, my movement hurried, and my focus scattered. We have two kinds of information: *intellectual data* and the *physical experience* of that data in our bodies. Most importantly, we need both *sensing information* (first function) and *thinking information* (second function) to create meaning and understanding, and ultimately, to make informed decisions. This is true in daily living and in rehearsal and performance. Actors need both *sensing information* and *thinking information* to create meaning and understanding, and additionally, to successfully direct and shape the creative process.

In life, and ideally in the theater, the first and second functional components of an expressive action are rightly integrated and seemingly inseparable. In the acting studio and in rehearsal, the process of exploring an expressive action often requires a particular *vantage point* with which to initiate and structure the exploration. This particular vantage point—either the first or second function—assists the actor in the process of understanding and describing an expressive action, which is the fundamental building block of the actor's craft.

Regretfully, F. S. C. Northrop is a profound thinker who is rarely mentioned in discussions of contemporary philosophy. His idea of the first and second function dates back to 1946 and was very forward reaching. It has currently received new-found credence in contemporary neuroscience and psychology.

Upstairs and downstairs brain

A deeper understanding of the first and second functions requires an investigation of the *upstairs and downstairs brain*. This will require a layman's overview of brain anatomy—a simple working definition of the *upstairs* (*high* and *new*) and the *down-stairs* (*low* and *old*) parts of the brain.

- *Defined*: The upstairs brain refers to the *neocortex*, and the downstairs brain refers to the *subcortex*.
- *Location*: The terms *high* and *low* refer to the physical location of these two parts of the brain. The higher brain structure is the *neocortex*, which is located above the *subcortex*, the lower brain structure.
- *Evolutionary history*: The terms *old* and *new* refer to the evolutionary history of the brain. The subcortex is the old, ancient brain that we share with reptiles and other less evolved living creatures. The neocortex is the newer, recent evolutionary edition found in all mammals but is most developed in humans.
- *Function*: The upstairs brain is the seat of thought, responsible for cognition, language, and other advanced mental processes. It is what we commonly refer to as our *intellect*. The downstairs brain is responsible for biological regulation, sensory perception, instincts, drives, emotions, feelings, and other bodily states. It is what we commonly refer to as our *instincts* and *intuition*.

Body states

For the actor, this upstairs/downstairs brain theory is experientially manifested in expressive action through *body states* (first function) and *mind states* (second function).

- *Body states* manifest themselves in chemical, neurological, and endocrine changes associated with qualities, moods, patterns, and structure that form the physical machinery of emotion and feeling. Body states receive their outward and physical expression through a weight shift or a series of integrated weight shifts. Body states make emotional communication possible. The human brain has a built-in structuring device that enables us to organize gestures, facial-expressions, postures, stances, and a host of vocal sounds into meaningful patterns of emotional expression.

Feelings are physical

Often we think of our feelings as merely a sequence of thoughts going on inside our brains and not as a physical and sensory experience occurring in our bodies. The feelings commonly thought of as residing in our heads are busily traveling through the whole body. As the psychologist Daniel Goleman states:

> With anger blood flows to the hands making it easier to grasp a weapon or strike a foe. With fear blood goes to the large skeletal muscles, such as the legs making it easer to flee. The lifting of the eyebrows in surprise allows the taking in of a larger visual sweep and also permits more light to the retina. (1995, 6–7)

The neuroscientist Antonio Damasio asserts that while emotion is impossible without some sort of cerebral activity, "the body is the main stage for emotion (1999, 287)" As David Best states, feeling is not simply some added ingredient mixed with or placed on top of our bodily movements but rather a by-product of the movement itself. There are not two separate things—a movement and a feeling—but one thing—a movement that possesses and contains feeling (1974, 54). It is useful to recognize that "the word *emotion* comes from the Latin e (out) and *movere* (to move): [meaning] to move outwards (Kepner 1993,16)." Idiomatic expressions like "sorehead," "lily-livered," "hair-raising," "choked up," "tight ass" and "blood-boiling" are a testament to the physical nature of our feelings.

Mind states

- *Mind states* manifest themselves in images—mental pictures that form the neural machinery for perception, memory, reasoning, and critical thinking. Mind states receive their outward, physical expression in words, phrases, and sentences. Mind states make sophisticated verbal communication possible. Language is essentially an intellectual activity, and words are the wrapper in which our thoughts are delivered.

Body states + mind states = meaning and understanding

We can now turn our attention to the integrated process with which *body states* (first function) and the *mind states* (second function) unite to create meaning and understanding. This involves the reexamination of some traditional views about the role body states play in the meaning-making process. Up until rather recently, it was widely thought that body states played no role in the cognitive process. Meaning and understanding were thought to be the sole product of the upstairs brain. This traditional view rested on a widely held assumption that the downstairs brain—the brain that governs the body process—its urges, instincts, sensations, emotions, and feelings could only cloud our thinking and muddy our judgment. The neuroscientist Antonio Damasio sums up, with skepticism, this traditional view:

> The old brain core handles basic biological regulation down in the basement, while up above the neocortex deliberates with wisdom and subtlety. Upstairs in the cortex there is reason and will power, while downstairs in the subcortex there is emotion and all the weak fleshy stuff.
>
> (1994, 128)

For sometime, Damasio himself thought this to be true until his research with brain impaired patients began to set the whole *upstairs/downstairs brain theory* on its heels:

> There was a brilliant corporate lawyer who, unfortunately, had a brain tumor. Luckily the tumor was diagnosed early and operated on successfully. But during the operation the surgeon had to cut circuits that connect key areas of the prefrontal cortex [upstairs], the brain's executive center, and the amygdala in the midbrain's area for emotion [downstairs].
>
> After the surgery there was a very puzzling clinical picture. On every test of IQ, memory, and attention, this lawyer was absolutely as smart as he had been before the surgery. But he couldn't do his job any more. He lost his job. He couldn't keep a job any more. His marriage broke up. He lost his house. He ended up living in his brother's spare bedroom and, in despair, he went to Damasio to find out what was wrong.
>
> At first Damasio was completely puzzled, because on every neurological test, the lawyer was fine. But the clue came when Damasio asked the lawyer, "When shall we have our next appointment?"
>
> It was then that Damasio realized the lawyer could give him the rational pros and cons of every hour for the next two weeks—but he didn't know which was the best. Damasio says that in order to make good decisions, we need to have feelings about our thoughts—and that lesions created during the surgery for the lawyer's tumor meant he could no longer connect his thoughts with the emotional pros and cons.
>
> (Goleman: 2011, Introduction)

Damasio asserts that:

> The apparatus of rationality traditionally presumed to be neocortical [upstairs], does not seem to work without that of biological regulation, traditionally

> presumed to be subcortical [downstairs]. Nature appears to have built the apparatus of rationality not just on top of the apparatus of biological regulation, but also from it and with it … . I believe both the upstairs and the downstairs: the neocrotex becomes engaged along with the older brain core, and rationality results from their concerted activity.
>
> (1994, 128)

Simply put, we need a *feeling body* (first function) and *thinking brain* (second function) to create meaning and understanding. Additionally, it appears that the foundations of higher reasoning are built upon lower and prior physical actions occurring in the body. Two decades of neuroscientific research by Antonio Damasio led him to the hypothesis "that emotions and feelings may not be intruders in the bastion of reason at all" (1994, xvi.). What Damasio's research suggests is that when an individual is emotionally impaired they are also mentally impaired. Our feelings assist us in making wise and well-informed decisions and without feelings we often make bad choices. Most importantly, reasoning, meaning, understanding, rationality, and cognition are not solely mental phenomena but simultaneously physical experiences.

Thoughts are physical

Often we think of our thoughts as merely a sequence of mental images flashing through our minds or as a string of words flowing from our lips; all the while overlooking the deeper sensorial and physical foundations of our thinking. As philosopher Mark Johnson rightly points out...

> ...meaning is grounded in bodily experience; it arises from our feeling of qualities, sensory patterns, movements, changes and emotional contours. Meaning is not limited only to those bodily engagements, but it always starts there and leads back to them. Meaning depends on our experiencing and assessing the qualities of a situation.
>
> (2007, 70)

Common sense instructs us that what we feel at any moment affects the way we think. If we change the physical qualities surrounding any particular situation, we simultaneously change the way we think about that situation. When we are agitated we might state: "I can't think straight." However, this fails to adequately address the complexity of the situation. The agitation is not somehow interfering or interrupting our thinking; the agitation is a physical property of the thinking process itself. It would be more accurate to state: "my thinking is agitated." "Thinking is action

(Johnson 2007, 78)," and the foundation of our thinking is physical. The action of our thoughts can be fast or slow, heavy or light, loud or soft, sharp or diffused—the physical properties of our thinking are as vast and as varied as the sensory world itself.

Furthermore, what we often consider abstract thinking, is predicated on our physical experience. For example, our cognitive understanding of "falling in love" is built upon the physical experience of the vulnerability and uncontrollability associated with "loosing one's footing." Similarly when we say that "a fence runs around the property," the concept of enclosure and containment is predicated upon our physical understanding of the experience of a runner's pathway. These metaphorical meanings are made possible by reoccurring physical patterns and structures occurring in our sensory motor experience that simultaneously inform our thinking process.

System 1 and system 2

Similar theories to those found in neuroscience have emerged since the 1990s in psychology in the exploration of what is called the "two modes of thinking"—called *System 1* and *System 2*, which conveniently correspond directly to the terms first and second function used here. Psychologist Daniel Kahneman in his book *Thinking, Fast and Slow* (2011, 20) defines the two systems as follows:

- *System 1* operates automatically and quickly, with little or no effort and no sense of voluntary control.
- *System 2* allocates attention to the effortful mental activities that demand it, including complex computations. The operations of System 2 are often associated with the subjective experience of agency, choice and concentration.

Simply put *System 1* is fast, reactive, and emotional. It is engaged automatically and involuntary when we seek to avoid the dangers of a falling tree branch. System 2 is slow, deliberate, methodical, and rational. The multiplication problem 17 × 24 is made possible by *System 2*.

Like the neuroscientist Antonio Damasio, Daniel Kahneman asserts both systems work together in a complex type of "push and pull" that make meaning and understanding possible:

> I describe System 1 as effortlessly originating impressions and feelings that are the main sources of the explicit beliefs and deliberate choices of System 2. The automatic operations of System 1 generate surprisingly complex patterns of ideas, but only the slower System 2 can construct thoughts in an orderly series of steps.
>
> (2011, 20–1)

Central to Kahneman's premise is the idea that meaning and understanding emerge in the System 1 first and then proceeds to System 2 for further processing:

> System 1 runs automatically and System 2 is normally in a comfortable low mode, in which only a fraction of its capacity is engaged. System 1 continually generates suggestions for System 2: impressions, intuitions, intentions, and feelings. If endorsed by System 2, impressions and intuitions turn into beliefs, and impulses turn into voluntary actions. When all goes smoothly, which is most of the time, System 2 adopts the suggestions of System 1 with little or no modification. You generally believe your impressions and act on your desires and that is fine—usually.
>
> (2011, 24–5)

Sometimes System 2 overrides the impulses and desires of System 1. Kahneman suggests this experience occurs when we tried to avoid looking at an oddly dressed couple in a restaurant, or any time we are faced with what is often called the "heart/head" dilemma—when our *gut* tells us one thing and *head* another (2011, 26).

How the body hides out

If the body plays such an important role in our decision-making process, why do we so often think of reasoning, meaning, and understanding as exclusively a mental experience? The nature of human consciousness most often requires that we direct our attention to one aspect of our integrated mind/body experience at a time. It seems that in a given moment, we often have a conscious awareness of either our physical or mental experience, but rarely both at the same time. This is because the nature of human consciousness makes it difficult for us to be present in two places at once. In our day-to-day activities, it is most common to lack an awareness of the important role our bodies plays in daily living and how it assists in creating meaning and understanding. Often we are so focused on the subject, reasons, and circumstances surrounding our feelings that we our unaware of their immediate physical presence. This common misperception is called *background disappearance* (Johnson 2007, 5). Background disappearance is a type of evolutionary censorship, which allows our physical sensations to fade into the background leaving us free to focus on conscious activities such as having a conversation, reading a book, or driving a car. Without a certain amount of background disappearance life as we know it would be almost impossible. We would be so busy tending to our bodies that we would have little time for anything else. As a result we are often intimately aware of the intellectual circumstances surrounding our feelings but not the bodily process, which makes them possible. Neuroscientist David Eagleman author of *Incognito: The Secret Life of the Brain* asserts that—"The conscious mind is not at the center of action in the brain; instead, it is far out on a distant edge, hearing but whispers of the activity" (2011a, 49). An added benefit of an acting technique founded on physical experience is its potential to bring background experiences into the foreground of the actor's consciousness.

Expressive action in the first and second function

Having laid the necessary framework, it is possible to outline the differences between an *expressive action in the first function* and an *expressive action in the second function*. The differences are multifaceted and are difficult to define in a simple sentence. Consequently, a comprehensive understanding is best gained by examining the subject from several vantage points. Figure 2.1 provides a multi-dimensional outline of the various differences between an expressive action in its first function and an expressive action in its second function:

FIRST FUNCTION	SECOND FUNCTION
Subcortex	Neocortex
Downstairs	Upstairs
Physical	Mental
Body States	Mind States
Doing	Saying
Feeling	Speaking
Intuition	Intellect
Nonverbal	Verbal
Sensing	Thinking
Movement	Language
System 1	System 2
Involuntary	Voluntary
Fast	Slow
Reactive	Deliberate
Emotional	Rational

Figure 2.1 First and second functions.

2.2 APPLICATION TO ACTING

An expressive action in the first function

The content of this book and the method of preparation presented here is concerned primarily with the physical process with which meaning and understanding are created in the body of the actor. Consequently, its focus is concerned with the creation of *body states* and the seemingly preconscious operations of *System 1.* The central premise is that if meaning and understanding "emerge from the bottom up"—from *body states* to *mind states,* from *System 1* to *System 2*—then actor training should likewise begin with an exploration of sensations, impulses, patterns, and structures that originate in the body before proceeding to the upstairs brain for higher processing. The most practical and reliable method for this intrinsically physical method of training is through the exploration of the tangible and physical *raw materials* that make expressive action possible. This exploration of the raw materials is an investigation of an *expressive action in the first function.*

Physical properties

Our study of an *expressive action in the first function* will focus directly on the physical sensations associated with a shift of weight. Every weight shift is comprised of a series of identifiable physical properties. These physical properties make expressive action possible. They are organized into two groups: the *Major physical properties of an expressive action* and the *Minor physical properties of an expressive action.*

Major physical properties of an expressive action

- *energy* (charge/release)
- *orientation* (contact/withdraw)
- *size* (expand/contract)
- *progression* (center/periphery)
- *flow* (free/bound).

Minor physical properties of an expressive action

- *direction* (direct/indirect)
- *speed* (fast/slow)
- *weight* (heavy/light)
- *control* (stable/unstable)
- *focus* (sharp/diffused).

(The major and minor physical properties will receive a thorough definition in *Chapter 3: Physical properties.*)

The many varied combinations and intensities of the mixing of these physical properties creates many varied combinations and intensities of sensations, impulses, urges, feelings, physical patterns and structures of thought and feeling and meaning, and understanding in the body of the actor.

These physical properties describe the actor's *direct and immediate felt-experience* when expressing a thought and feeling. The physical properties provide the actor with a practical method of describing and exploring an *expressive action in its first function*. For example if the expressive action is "to badger," its first functional properties might be *heavy*, *direct*, *charged*, and *sharp* depending on how the action is experienced in the body. If the expressive action is "to celebrate," its first functional properties might be *light, indirect, expansive*, and *free* depending on how the action is experienced in the body. These are important *first function facts* about the action. There are also *second function facts*. For the action "to badger" the second function facts might be "a desperate need to get your way" or "a compulsive need for power and control." Similarly, possible second function facts for the action "to celebrate" might be "to mark an important occasion" or "to acknowledge someone's accomplishments." The first function facts describe what the actor is physically and literarily doing in any given moment of a performance. The second function facts are vast and varied describing the circumstances, reasons, motivations, and justifications surrounding the actions. On the simplest level, a detail such as: "it is 2:00 pm on Tuesday" is a second function fact, while an actor standing with open arms (an *expansive* physical property) is a first function fact.

In sum, an exploration of an *expressive action in the first function* involves "turning a spotlight" on the sensations, qualities, feelings, patterns, and structures associated with a weight shift. This process involves directing the actor's sensory attention to the *immediacy of the present moment*. This goal is to put the actor in touch with the *physical circumstances* that make expressive action possible. By contrast, an exploration of an *expressive action in the second function* generally involves *turning a spotlight* on the *intellectual* circumstances or situation surrounding the expressive action, and the reason, justification, motivation, intent, and purpose of the expressive action. Much of this process involves an analysis and interpretation of the playscript. The first function is sensorial and intuitive. The second function is deductive and logical.

In rehearsal, actors have to make choices with respect to how to build a character, play a scene and tell the story. It is important to recognize that the intellectual decisions that actors make about a playscript are linked directly to the *feelings* that the playscript creates in their bodies. Consequently, actors need an awareness of the first functional, physical properties of an expressive action to assist in making these important interpretive decisions. Knowing that a section of the playscript elicits a *slow*, *indirect*, or *unstable* response in the body is as important as knowing that Hamlet has lost a father, lives in Denmark and has a relationship with Ophelia. Actors need both first functional and second functional facts readily at their disposal. The actor whose sole focus is on the intellectual facts surrounding the playscript, but has limited awareness of how these intellectual facts integrated with the physical facts, is at a decided disadvantage. The actor's job is not simply to make intellectual decisions in a vacuum, and then simply direct the body as if it were merely a machine to some predetermined outcome. Ideally, the integrated role of the mind/body in rehearsal is a two-way street. Information needs to travel simultaneously in both directions—from the *mind-to-the-body* and the *body-to-the-mind.* This is not to suggest that mind/body integration is a divided highway; but more accurately, a busy intersection in which mental and physical resources meet and intersect in a seemingly indissoluble meaning-making process. Contemporary acting theorist, Richard Schechner states it this way:

> When I talk of spirit or mind or feelings or psyche, I mean dimensions of the body. The body is an organism of endless adaptability. A knee can think, a finger can laugh, a belly cry, a brain walk, a buttock listen. All the body's sensory, intellectual and emotional functions can be performed by many organs. Changes in mood are reflected in changes in chemistry, blood pressure, breathing, pulse, vascular dilation, sweating, and so on; and many so-called involuntary activities can be trained and consciously controlled.
>
> (Schechner 1973, 132)

Foreign language film

Rent a foreign film in a language that you do not understand. Watch the film with the subtitles turned off. Without the assistance of language, you will be experiencing much of the film in the first function. See how much emotional and mental information you can glean by simply observing the body and listening to the sound of the speaker's voice.

Chapter 3

Physical properties

3.1 OVERVIEW

A study of an *expressive action in the first function* involves a type of experiential research into the physical properties that comprise an expressive action. The physical properties unite to form the building blocks that define the *architecture of an expressive action.* When the physical properties of an expressive action unite in a weight shift that embodies a thought and a feeling an expressive action is created. My understanding of the architecture of an expressive action is an assimilation and adaptation of the ideas of somatic psychologists James I. Kepner (1993), Edward W. L. Smith (1985), Jack Lee Rosenberg (1985), and the movement analysis method of Rudolf von Laban (1950/1971).

3.2 MAJOR AND MINOR PROPERTIES

Expressive actions are not unlike people in that there are certain *major physical properties* that all human beings share and certain *minor physical properties* specific and particular to each individual. Ideally, human beings have eyes, arms, legs, fingers, and the like. In addition to these major physical properties, there are other minor physical properties specific to each individual that make them unique and different. While human beings have two eyes, no two eyes are the same. This is true for a host of other secondary characteristics: weight, height, skin color, eye color, hairline, and so on. Similarly, expressive actions also have major physical properties—things that define their essential structure; and minor physical properties—things that define their secondary characteristics. The major physical properties form the physical foundation for the shared universal pattern and structure characteristic of all expressive actions. The minor physical properties serve indirectly to influence the functioning of the major properties.

Expressive cycle: major physical properties

The major physical properties of an expressive action unite in the *expressive cycle.* The expressive cycle is a blueprint outlining the manner in which all living

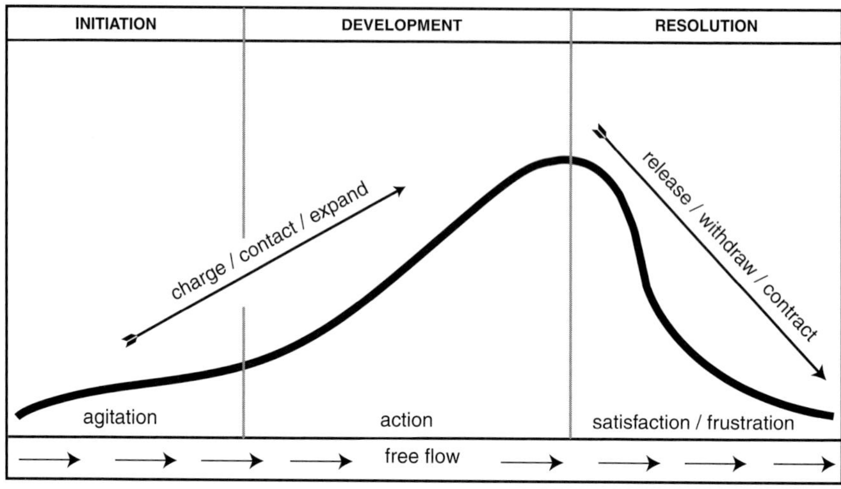

Figure 3.1 Expressive cycle.

creatures function and operate in their environment. The expressive cycle represents an organic and uniquely human type of *operating system*—a physical clearinghouse—that organizes and shapes the physical properties into meaningful expressive action. It is created by the five interrelated major physical properties—*energy, orientation, size, progression,* and *flow.* The expressive cycle is characterized by a wave-like action illustrating the progressive and orderly flow with which an expressive action begins, matures and subsides. As illustrated in Figure 3.1, each wave of the expressive cycle has a clearly defined beginning, middle and end representing one complete unit of living, which corresponds to the execution of one complete expressive action.

The wave-like action of the expressive cycle is experienced in three stages:

- The *initiation phase* is characterized by an internal imbalance or agitation, which prompts and prepares the body for action.
- The *development phase* is the substantive portion, characterized by outward action and physical activity.
- The *resolution phase* is characterized by feelings of satisfaction and gratification or frustration and discomfort, depending on whether the expressive action was successful or unsuccessful.

The sequential journey of the expressive cycle from start to finish, beginning to end—agitation to action, and finally to satisfaction or frustration—has intrinsic rhythmical properties that are similar to the ocean's waves. Each wave of the ocean has a clearly defined beginning, middle, and end. The wave rises, swells, crests, cascades, and finally subsides. The end of one wave is followed directly by the start of a new wave. Though each individual wave is a separate and unique event, when sequenced one right after another a rhythmical pattern emerges. Similarly, a series of successive waves of the expressive cycle sets up a rhythmical pattern that can be seen in the comings and goings of daily life. Saying "good morning," taking a sip of coffee, stretching the arms, and opening a newspaper are each individual and separate actions with a clearly defined beginning, middle, and end, yet when connected in a sequence they unite to form a larger rhythmical pattern of someone's morning ritual. Whether the seas of life be choppy or calm, the tides high or low, skillful expression rises, swells, crests, cascades, and falls with rhythmical harmony.

Phrasing

Practical work organizing expressive actions into rhythmical, structured movement patterns is called *phrasing*. Phrasing is essentially organizing a weight shift or a series of weight shifts that make up an expressive action into a single phrase that has a clearly defined beginning, middle, and end. Phrasing an expressive action is similar to phrasing any physical activity. Examining a series of simple physical actions will give you a clearer understanding of how an expressive action is organized into physical phrases. Select one of the following physical activities:

- pour a drink of water;
- scratch your head;
- turn a page of a newspaper;
- cross and uncross your legs;
- fold a letter;
- button a sweater.

Repeat the activity several times, taking a short rest or pause between each repetition. Allow the activity to become fluid and seamless, structuring it so that it has a clearly defined beginning, middle, and end. Where does the action begin in your body? How does the action escalate and develop? When does it diminish and dissolve? Repeat using the other physical activities listed above or any other physical activities you choose.

Energy: charge/release

Energy refers to the relative degree of physical and psychological vitality and power present in the body. A high level of energy is identified as a *charge*, a low level of energy as a *release*. Charge and release work as a team, making expressive action possible. When we reach out to shake someone's hand, the building up of energy necessary to extend the arm is identified as a charge. After completing the handshake, the return of the arm back to its resting position is identified as a release. The charge reflects the conscious, mobile, and active phase of the expressive cycle; the release reflects a letting go—a semiconscious, passive, "non-doing" that returns the body to a state of equilibrium and balance.

Orientation: contact/withdraw

Orientation refers to the directional force that motivates the action of the individual in the environment. An individual makes *contact* with the environment to fulfill specific physical and psychological needs and *withdraws* when these needs have been satisfied. A state of contact refers to an individual with a strong outward/external orientation. Similarly, a state of withdrawal refers to an individual with a strong inward/internal orientation. Contact and withdrawal work as a team, making expressive action possible. When we reach out to shake someone's hand, the process of extending the arm results in contact with the environment. After completing the handshake, the return of the arm back to its resting position results in a withdrawal from the environment. Outward observable interaction with the environment characterizes the contact phase of the expressive cycle, while the withdrawal phase is characterized by a period of internalization, reflection, assessment, and evaluation.

Size: expand/contract

Size refers to the physical range or volume of a movement. Changes in the size of the body are made possible by the bending and unbending of various joints. Movements that involve lengthening and elongating the body are *expanded.* Movements that involve folding or recoiling the body are *contracted.* Expansion and contraction work together in expressive action, moving the muscles and bones of the body in an almost infinite number of physical configurations that make expressive action possible. When we reach out to shake someone's hand, the process of extending the arm requires an expansion of the body. After completing the handshake, the return of the arm back to its resting position requires a contraction of the body.

Progression: center/periphery

Progression is the sequence or pathway of a movement through the body. The *center* of the body is the midsection, specifically the pelvis. The *periphery* of the body are the parts furthest away from the pelvis—the head, arms, hands, legs, and feet. An expressive action that begins with movement in the center of the body is a *centered action.* An expressive action that begins with movement on the periphery of the body is a *peripheral action.* Successful and fluid expressive action often requires that the center of the body and the parts on the periphery work together in an organized manner, creating movement that flows from the middle of the body (the center) outward into the appendages (the periphery).

Pelvic center and feeling

Initiating movement from the pelvis has important ramifications with respect to the expression of feeling. Feeling is a full-bodied experience that begins deep in the center of the body and travels outward to the periphery on waves of energy. When an actor initiates movement from the pelvis, feeling is carried outward on that movement from the center of the body to the periphery. This simultaneous outward movement of the physical and psychological is a central component of integrated expression and a useful directive for the actor seeking an authentic expression of the body's richest and most powerful feelings.

Flow: free/bound

Flow refers to the degree of resistance that the body experiences while moving. The flow of a movement may be classified as either *free* or *bound*. For example, water streaming from a faucet flows free without interruption or interference. However, if you put your hand over the faucet to block or stop its stream you would bind its flow. A free-flowing movement is spontaneous and efficient. Bound flow manifests itself in inefficient patterns of muscular holding. On one hand, an impulse to express a thought and feeling prompts the body to move in an outward direction, while a desire to repress the thought and feeling pulls the body in an inward direction. The result is a type of physical turmoil that reflects an individual literally pushing and pulling in two different directions at once. Just as rivers do not attempt to stop their water from moving downstream and wind does not try to stop itself from blowing, bound flow appears to work against the natural forces found in nature. While human beings are capable of binding their flow (and it is most certainly at times useful to do so), they do not thrive in physical environments where bound flow is the predominate pattern of movement. Bound flow manifests itself as a type of muscular resistance to the forward, advancing movement of life itself. The physical pattern of muscular holding associated with bound flow diminishes the impulsivity, spontaneity, and vitality associated with pleasurable living.

To free or not to free

Neuroscientist Daniel Wolpert reminds us that our survival is predicated on our ability to *free* the body's flow and to *bind* the body's flow—"to drive action or suppress future actions" (*Charlie Rose: The Brain Series* 2009)." In daily discourse, context and purpose should determine the flow of the body's movement. Free flowing movement patterns are rewarding, desirable and to be encouraged in life and certainly in actor training when and where appropriate. However, occasionally, binding the flow can be a useful method for making an important point or a gracious social survival tool. In negative social situations, sometimes the best approach is to simply "put up and shut up." In moderation, the regulation of an impulse can serve the greater good. However, the chronic muscular holding associated with bound flow often reflects a type of clinical repression that should ideally be treated by a trained psychologist. This condition occurs when bound flow is used consistently over time, is automatic and involuntary and often cannot be modified even with conscious effort. Similarly, free-flowing, impulsive, spontaneous actions can in the extremes be violent and uncontrollable. While they may be dynamic and exciting, they can be destructive. The explosive individual who has just run his fist through the wall and busted the furniture is doing nothing to solve his problems or to create positive alternatives to an already negative situation. Ultimately, useful and rewarding expression is not inwardly repressive or outwardly violent, but reflects a skillful coordination of the flow of the body that is genuine, dynamic, rewarding, and satisfying.

Essential structure and universal form

The major properties of an expressive action unite to create the *essential structure* that gives all expressive actions their characteristic *universal form*. Without the integrated and organized interaction of *energy*, *orientation*, *size*, *progression*, and *flow*, it is impossible to successfully structure a weight shift into a recognizable expressive action. It is important to recognize that it is possible to experience sensations in the body that never unite and organize themselves into an expressive action. For example, you can be very *withdrawn*, but never shape that introverted state into expressive action. Similarly, you can be very *charged*, but never shape that excitation into expressive action. When this occurs the actor simply experiences sensations, qualities, moods, and attitudes related to feeling, but never organizes and integrates these experiences into recognizable and communicative expressive action. The process of shaping sensation into meaningful expressive action requires the teamwork of each of the major properties of an expressive action—*energy*, *orientation*, *size*, *progression*, and *flow*.

Consequently, the major properties of an expressive action play a pivotal role in the actor's formative training. Initially, time must be spent developing a sensory appreciation of the expressive cycle. The actor must be able to *sense* the differences between *charge* and *release*, *contact* and *withdraw*, *expansion* and *contraction*—the differences between movement in the *center* of the body and movement on the *periphery*, the differences between *free* and *bound* flow. Additionally, the actor must *sense* how to unite, shape, and integrate these sensations into a wave-like movement that forms the physical foundation of an expressive action. This important sensory education is the hallmark of this action-based approach to actor training. Through integrated action and activity misdirected energies in the body are redirected to new and more appropriate patterns. When the major physical properties of expressive action find fluid integration in the expressive cycle, the physical foundations of expressive action have been realized in the body of the actor.

Simple physical task

To gain a clearer understanding of how the major properties of an expressive action work together via the expressive cycle, let's put them together in a simple physical task. Retrieve a book (real or imagined) from a high shelf. Repeat the action of retrieving the book several times. Allow the action to have a clearly delineated beginning, middle, and end: the initiation (agitation: the sensations associated with wanting the book); the development (action: retrieving the book); and the resolution (satisfaction: sensations associated with having the book). Now repeat the physical task several more times, exploring each of the major physical properties of an expressive action:

- *Energy: charge/release.* The act of reaching for the book provides the necessary power—*charge*. Bringing the book down from the shelf reverses the process—*release*.
- *Orientation: contact/withdraw.* An outward orientation directs you toward the book—*contact*. Bringing the book down from the shelf reverses the process and results in an inward orientation—*withdraw*.
- *Size: expand/contract.* Elongating and unbending various joints of the body make it possible to reach for the book—*expand*. Contracting and bending various joints of the body brings the book downward so it may be held and read—*contract*.
- *Progression: center/periphery.* First, allow the process of retrieving the book to be a full-bodied experience. This will involve a sequential journey of uninterrupted action from the *center* (pelvis) to the *periphery* (upward into the ribcage, shoulders, head, arms, and hands). This full-bodied experience is a *centered action*. Now, allow the process of retrieving the book to be an isolated experience. This will involve retrieving the book with a localized action of the arm and the shoulder. This localized experience is a *peripheral action*. What differences do you notice between the centered action and the peripheral action?
- *Flow: free/bound.* Begin by binding your flow. Notice how muscular tension interrupts and interferes with the efficiency of the action. Now, rest for a moment and then repeat the reaching action, allowing the entire process to flow freely. Release any tensions that inhibit fluidity, grace, and economy. What differences do you notice between the free action and the bound action?

(Continued)

(Continued)

Repeat several times. Become aware how each of these major physical properties contributes to the essential structure of the physical task.

Repeat the above exploration with other simple (real or imagined) physical tasks:

- pour a drink of water;
- scratch your head;
- cross and uncross your legs;
- fold a letter;
- button a sweater;
- open and close a door;
- change a light bulb.

You may have discovered in the exercise above that different expressive actions organize the expressive cycle in different ways. For example, some expressive actions *charge* before they *release*, while others *release* before they *charge*; some *contact* before they *withdraw*, while others *withdraw* before they *contact*; and so on. The wavelike action of the expressive cycle is a flexible structure capable of a great many modifications, adaptations, ebbs, and flows. Just as no two moments of life are repeatable, no two waves of the expressive cycle and no two expressive actions are ever the same.

Learning to participate with the ebb and flow of the expressive cycle is not something we necessarily teach the body to do, but rather something the body desires to do naturally. The goal in training is to learn not to interrupt or interfere with the natural flow of the expressive cycle. The body has been hardwired through years of evolution to instinctively *charge* and *release*, to *contact* and *withdraw*, to *expand* and *contract*, to move outward from the *center* to the *periphery* and to flow as intended. This process is natural and innate. For the actor, it involves learning to do what comes naturally without physical and/or psychological interference.

Living form

The major properties of an expressive action unite in the expressive cycle to create the experience of *living form* in the body of the actor. The term *living form* suggests quite simply that the performance of the actor is life-like, alive and living—that it exhibits the discernable physical properties associated with the state or condition of being alive (Langer 1957, 44–58). This identifiable physical condition is what is sometimes referenced when an actor's performance is described as "truthful," "believable," or "honest." An actor exhibiting living form appears to grow, change, and evolve naturally and organically as all living creatures do. The actor charges and releases, expands and contracts, contacts and withdraws in an organic, natural progressive and orderly flow that is authentic and immediately identifiable as human. Each movement is harmonic and rhythmic, punctuated by a clearly differentiated beginning, middle, and end. This "physical truthfulness" is the embodiment of living form. The concept of living form makes explicit that *truthful acting* is not just a product of an inner commitment or mental affirmation; but simultaneously, a richly structured physical experience that can be created and trained via the body. As Modern Dance master Martha Graham famously states: "The body does not lie." For the actor, the skillful embodiment of the expressive cycle provides an immediate and direct link to an authentic performance.

Physical properties in performance

The following critiques of an actor's performance are based upon a practical understanding of the major properties of an expressive action:

- Your expressive actions seem under-charged for the high stakes and risky behavior that your character is making in this scene. You seem to lack the physical and psychological *energy* and vitality demanded by the scene.
- Your physical tensions disallow your character to participate with the *release* of emotional, mental, and physical energies that are essential to the organic and spontaneous expression of genuine feeling.
- Your expressive actions lack a clearly defined *beginning*, *middle*, and *end*.
- You seem unable to find clearly definable points of *contact* with which to direct your physical, vocal, mental, and emotional energies. What specifically in each moment of this scene is your character making *contact* with? When and why does the character *withdraw*?
- Your character seems trapped in a state of emotional and physical *withdrawal* that is indulgent, manipulative and seemingly despondent. Where does your character want to reach out into the environment to change it or shape it?
- You seem to interrupt the *release* phase of the expressive cycle. You are working too hard. Can you find places to do less and simply participate with the passive phase of the expressive action?
- Physical tensions in your body interrupt your character's ability to freely *expand* and *contract*.

- In binding your *flow*, you bind the thought and feeling you are attempting to express.
- You initiate all of your expressive actions on the *periphery* of the body. By starting on the outside of the action, you lose the essential deep connection with your *center*. This leads to a type of mugging, indicating, miming and manipulation of the body that distorts organic and integrated expression.

Additionally, the minor properties of an expressive action (*direction*, *speed*, *weight*, *control*, and *focus*) provide additional objective and practical directives for critiquing an actor's performance.

Minor physical properties

The minor physical properties of an expressive action—*direction*, *speed*, *weight*, *control*, and *focus*—describe additional conditions, factors, or circumstances that affect the quality and character of the expressive action and play a secondary, yet important role in further defining it.

Direction: direct/indirect

Direction refers to the relative straight or curved quality of an expressive action. For example, "to scold" may be classified as a *direct* expressive action, "to fidget," an *indirect* one.

Speed: fast/slow

Speed refers to the relative rate or pace of an expressive action. For example, "to scurry" may be classified as a *fast* expressive action, "to plod," a *slow* one.

Weight: heavy/light

Weight refers to the relative degree of lightness and heaviness of an expressive action. For example, "to sulk" may be classified as a *heavy* expressive action, "to tiptoe," a *light* one.

Control: stable/unstable

Control refers to the relative degree of stability or instability of an expressive action. For example, "to stand your ground" may be classified as a *stable* expressive action, "to swagger," an *unstable* one.

Focus: sharp/diffused

Focus refers to the relative degree of ocular (eye) intensity of an expressive action. For example, "to stare" may be classified as a *sharp* expressive action, "to daydream," a *diffused* one.

Minor properties

Select an expressive action from the list below:

- to beg;
- to warn;
- to apologize;
- to promise;
- to scold;
- to praise.

Compose a simple but flexible piece of text for the selected expressive action. (For example, for the expressive action "to promise" you might compose: "I will never tell another lie.") Play your expressive action several times while delivering the piece of text. Rest. Repeat your expressive action while exploring each of the minor properties of an expressive action: *direct/indirect*, *fast/slow*, *heavy/light*, *stable/unstable*, *sharp/diffused*. Become aware of the manner in which each of these minor properties affects the quality and character of the expressive action. Repeat using the other actions listed above or other actions in Appendix II.

3.3 EXPRESSIVE CONTINUUM

Each of the ten physical properties (*energy*, *orientation*, *size*, *progression*, *flow*, *direction*, *speed*, *weight*, *control*, and *focus*) unite in the creation of an expressive action. For example, all expressive actions have an energy, a direction, a flow, a weight, and so on. However, in each expressive action the ten physical properties are present in varying degrees on a type of sliding scale illustrated in the *expressive continuum* (see Figure 3.2). For example, certain expressive actions are more charged than others, while others might be more released; some may have a stronger point of contact, while others are more withdrawn, some may have a sharp focus, while others are more diffused. Regardless of the degree, it is important to remember that what expands must eventually contract, that what charges must ultimately be released, that a period of contact will be followed by a period of withdrawal, that an individual moving fast will eventually slow down, that a sharp focus will eventually become more diffused.

An expressive action can be revealed in an infinite number of ways—actors with the most physical dexterity have the greatest expressive potential. Integrating and organizing the physical properties of the expressive action is like mixing paint on a palette. When skillfully combined they can reveal or express almost anything. However, just as the unskilled mixing of paint ultimately results in undifferentiated shades of brown and gray, a poor mixing of the physical properties can result in the undifferentiated expression of thought and feeling.

EXPRESSIVE CONTINUUM	
PROPERTY	SENSORY ELEMENTS
Energy	Charge←--→Release
Orientation	Contact ←--------------------------------------→Withdraw
Size	Expand ←---------------------------------------→Contract
Progression	Center ←--------------------------------------→Periphery
Flow	Free←--→Bound
Direction	Direct←---→Indirect
Speed	Fast←---→Slow
Weight	Light←---→Heavy
Control	Stable←--→Unstable
Focus	Sharp←--→Diffused

Figure 3.2 Expressive continuum.

Physical foundations of meaning and understanding

The physical properties of an expressive action lay the physical foundations for meaning and understanding. In this respect, *fast* has a different meaning from *slow*, *heavy* a different meaning from *light*, *direct* a different meaning from *indirect*. Different thoughts and feelings are expressed by integrating the physical properties in different ways. For example, the expressive action "to mope" typically mingles *release*, *withdraw*, *indirect*, and *slow* physical properties. The expressive action "to pester," by contrast, typically mingles *charge*, *contact*, *direct*, and *fast* physical properties. These physical properties are the physical form of our thoughts and feelings.

Voice and body

The physical properties that make up an expressive action are not limited to bodily movement but are applied to the breath and voice as well. When playing an integrated expressive action, any physical shift in the body—*speed*, *weight*, *flow*, *focus*, *direction* for example—should ideally result in corresponding and relational shifts in the management of the breath and the tonal quality of the voice.

The physical properties of an expressive action reflect broad categories of sensation that assist the actor in classifying and expressing thought and feeling. However, they can only be used to describe an expressive action that we see or experience. We cannot take a specific mental and emotional state such as sadness, joy, anger or frustration and insist that this particular experience is always *slow*, *heavy*, *direct*, *charged*, or *sharp*. For purposes of instruction, the list below identifies specific mental and emotional states commonly associated with specific physical properties. The list is general, broad, inexact, theoretical, and in no way definitive. It merely illustrates the essential link between physical sensation and emotional and mental experience. It may also provide a deeper understanding of the terminology used in the expressive continuum.

- *charge*: spirited, energetic, lively, animated, forceful, intense;
- *release*: easygoing, serene, relaxed, lethargic, sluggish, lackadaisical;
- *contact*: sociable, involved, outgoing, intrusive, extroverted, interfering;
- *withdraw*: introspective, reflective, contemplative, unsociable, distant, detached;
- *expand*: welcoming, accessible, available, overreaching, intrusive, meddlesome;
- *contract*: intimate, confidential, private, insignificant, diminutive, repressive;
- *center*: solid, stable, authentic, immovable, settled, static;
- *periphery*: versatile, adaptable, lighthearted, superficial, flighty, frivolous;
- *free*: liberated, spontaneous, natural, impulsive, irrepressible, imprudent;
- *bound*: cautious, circumspect, prudent, repressed, controlled, inhibited;
- *direct*: clear, assiduous, straightforward, abrupt, curt, blunt;
- *indirect*: versatile, affable, flexible, erratic, wishy-washy, disingenuous;
- *fast*: swift, smart, efficient, impulsive, hasty, reckless;
- *slow*: careful, thorough, prudent, lazy, slow-witted, sluggish;
- *heavy*: solid, serious, solemn, sullen, glum, depressed;
- *light*: cheerful, lighthearted, optimistic, flighty, giddy, frivolous;
- *stable*: secure, solid, steadfast, stubborn, strong-willed, bullheaded;
- *unstable*: spontaneous, variable, fluctuating, unsteady, dizzy, shaky;
- *sharp*: penetrating, cutting, acerbic, shrill, strident, harsh;
- *diffused*: vague, distant, mysterious, dull, fuzzy, confusing.

There is nothing intrinsically positive or negative about any of these mental and emotional states. There is a time to be animated and a time to be distant, a time to be interfering and a time to be detached, a time to be accessible and a time to be confidential, a time for stability and a time for adaptability, a time for impulsivity and a time for caution. Similarly, there is a time to be fast and a time to be slow, a time to be indirect and a time to be direct, and so on.

From mental/emotional state to expressive action

Select several mental/emotional states from the list above. Take *spontaneous* for example. Allow your flow to become *free*. (*Spontaneous* is a mental/emotional state an associated with *free flow* in the above list.) With time and exploration, allow the *free* physical sensations in your body to integrate into a playable expressive action. When ready, compose a piece of text on the spot such as: "Yippee!" or "I win, I win!" or "You gotta be kidding!" Repeat with other emotional/mental states of your own choosing.

Embodiment of feeling

The actor experiences the *embodiment of a feeling* when the physical properties become directly felt and immediately sensed when playing an expressive action. When this occurs, feeling finds a physical form in the body. Feelings are often thought of as some type of uncontrollable, unshaped overflow of human excitement and not as structured and organized physical patterns occurring in the body. To the contrary, the physical *form of feeling* can be found within us and all around us—even in unpredictable places. In fact, the physical form of a feeling is so imprinted on our consciousness that we often infer feeling in places where actual feelings do not exist. For example, a jagged red line pounding across a computer screen might appear angry or hostile; while a pink, yellow, and baby-blue line dancing across the computer screen in harmonious, explosive jumps might appear joyous and celebratory. The philosopher Susanne K. Langer (1942/1993, 123) states that when she was a young child, the heavy, dark, and intricate chairs in her grandmother's living room appeared to her as stern and ominous. Of course, chairs in the living room and colored lines on a computer screen are inanimate objects incapable of feeling anything. Nonetheless, their physical form in some manner suggests a feeling. Similarly, the physical properties—*slow, sharp, charged, indirect, unstable*—unite in the body of the actor to create a unique, yet similar form of feeling.

Our perception of the physical form of a feeling is so instinctual and automatic that our conscious mind often fails to recognize these forms even when they are right in front of us. Gilbert Ryle (1949, 16) cites an example of a foreign visitor who is taken on a tour of Cambridge University: the lecture halls, the dormitories, the classrooms, the laboratories, the library, the playing field, the chapel—the whole campus. At the end of the tour, he asks: "This is all very good, but where is the university?" What he has failed to recognize is that in examining the classrooms, the library, and the laboratories in front of him, he has in fact seen the university. It is just as illogical to examine the piercing eyes, clinched teeth, tight lips, and stilled breath of a person fuming with anger and say, "I see all of this, but where is the anger?" Feeling and bodily movement are inseparable. Asking how the feeling got into the body is not unlike asking how the fruit got into the apple, the wind into the hurricane, or the fire into the sun. When the body moves, we experience our feelings, and through movement, we give form to our feelings.

Embodiment of thought

Similarly, the actor experiences the *embodiment of a thought* when the physical properties become directly felt and immediately sensed when playing an expressive action. As with feeling, this occurs when our thoughts find a physical form in the body. Thoughts are often perceived of as ideas bouncing around in the mind or a string of words strung together in sentences, and not tangible physical forms flowing through the whole body. When we say things such as, "my thoughts are muddy," "she's as sharp as a tack" or "his thoughts were reeling," we are intuitively acknowledging our understanding of the physical embodiment of the thinking process.

The physical foundations of meaning found in the words, phrases, and sentences that reveal the content of our thoughts are most readily apparent in poetry. Poetry is a special type of language that exploits and luxuriates in the physical properties of words and sounds. It is a heightened type of language that likes to flex its physical muscle. For example, the "o" vowel has dark and heavy resonant properties. The "e" vowel has brighter and lighter resonant properties. The consonants "p," "t," "k" have a popping quality, while the consonants "b," "d," "g" have a banging quality. "Ss" and "shs" hiss along, while "zs" and "ms" like to buzz. Language is innately physical, and poets capitalize on these physical properties to create meaning and understanding. Perhaps the most effective literary device for evoking feeling is rhythm. Some lines race and soar with a dynamic immediacy, while others move with a slow deliberateness that has a very different physical effect. Rhyme, alliteration, assonance, diction, structure, imagery, allusions, symbols, metaphors, and a host of other literary and rhetorical devices all have a powerful physical effect. Most importantly, Mark Johnson asserts that there is no "radical difference between poetry and our more mundane linguistic practices" (2007, 224). Johnson further asserts that:

> All of poetry ever written stands as a testimony to this fact of embodied meaning. Beneath and within what is said is the vast richness of what is meant, and this meaning pulsates with corporal significance.
>
> (2007, 219)

Subtext

Actors commonly identify a similar type of "meaning beneath the words" that they use as *subtext*. *Subtext* is defined as the inner thoughts of the character that are seemingly hidden beneath the text. Some actors actually write down the hidden and interior thoughts of their character with pen and paper. Subtext is a useful exercise only if it creates a physical experience in the body of the actor. When this occurs the "sense" of things in the actor's mind, is integrated with the "sense" of things in the body. Most importantly, this embodiment of the thought is not merely a series of movements or sensations that somehow happen to be accompanying the thinking process, but are in fact the physical raw materials of the thinking process itself. Change the sensations in the body, and the subtextual meaning of the text will change as well.

Figure 3.3 shows three different possible subtextual meanings for the words "I love you." It also suggests several physical properties that represent the physical embodiment of the subtext via expressive action.

(Continued)

TEXT	SUBTEXT	PHYSICAL PROPERTIES
"I love you."	"Do you love me?"	*contact/sharp/direct*
"I love You."	"I'm not sure I love you."	*bound/contract/diffused*
"I love You."	"I don't love you."	*release/ withdrawn/slow*

Figure 3.3 Subtext and expressive action.

The waltz

Write each of the major properties of an expressive action on a chalkboard or a large sheet of paper. Begin to move around the room in a simple waltz-like fashion counting aloud 1–2–3. 1–2–3. 1–2–3. When the movement and the counting are comfortably integrated in your body, begin to move through each of the physical properties counting aloud as follows while making the corresponding physical adjustment to the waltz-like action:

Charge–2–3/Release–2–3. Contact–2–3/Withdraw–2–3. Contract–2–3/Expand–2–3. Center–2–3/Periphery–2–3. Free–2–3/Bound–2–3. Direct–2–3/Indirect–2–3. Fast–2–3/Slow–2–3. Heavy–2–3/Light–2–3. Stable–2–3/Unstable–2–3. Sharp–2–3/Diffused–2–3.

Repeat several times focusing on integrating the rhythm, sensation, and movement.

What are you doing?

Select a physical property from the expressive continuum (*light, withdrawn, expansive, bound, etc.*). Explore the selected physical property as you walk around the room. For example, if you selected *slow*, begin to move around the room slowly. Allow the physical action to develop into an imagined mental and emotional experience. When this level of physical, mental, and emotional integration has been achieved, answer the question: "What are you doing?" Possible answers might include sneaking, accusing, turning the other cheek, standing my ground, minding my own business, daydreaming—or any language you can think of to describe the expressive action. The exact language is immaterial as long as it is descriptive of an expressive action that embodies thought and feeling. Repeat the exploration with numerous other physical properties.

Stacking

Explore working with several physical properties of an expressive action simultaneously. For example, select any three physical properties such as: *free*, *stable*, and *light*. Begin moving around the room in a *free* manner. When you are ready, add (or *stack*) *stable* and begin moving in a *free* and *stable* manner. When you are ready, add (or *stack*) *light* and begin moving in a *free*, *stable*, and *light* manner. Develop this *free*, *stable*, and *light* movement into a playable expressive action. Compose a simple but flexible piece of text for the expressive action you have created. Repeat the stacking exercise several more times exploring different physical properties.

Part III

Principles of integration

Chapter 4

Integration

4.1 CONTEXT

Traditionally, the diligent acting student travels from movement class to voice class to acting class, often with limited formal instruction in how these seemingly isolated disciplines work together. It is important to recognize that a detailed examination of individual parts does not always render a clear view of the working whole. Imagine learning to ride a bicycle one part at a time—practising peddling one day, balance the next, followed by a day of steering. Just as the line of a mountain range can only be understood by moving away from it and standing too close to a painting can distort its full effect (Best 1974, 96), an isolated study of voice, movement, and acting often fails to render a comprehensive understanding of the whole. Skills learned in isolation often remain isolated.

Isolation invariably leads to compartmentalization. The compartmentalization of the actor's training has led to a somewhat punitive approach to voice and body training that has focused on fixing problems in specific parts of the body: shallow breathing, a tight jaw, held shoulders, a misaligned spine, lazy articulators, a weak center, and so on. Real progress and growth requires a global understanding of how these seemingly problem parts work together. Regretfully, an unexpected by-product of this part-by-part approach is often the development of a less-than-healthy relationship with the body. Invariably when one part of the body is singled out and chastised, a negative relationship with that part develops. This only serves to further disenfranchise the pesky part and makes the desired integration all the more difficult. Psychologist James I. Kepner states:

> We do not so easily get rid of parts of ourselves merely by unlearning them. Worse, however, is the possibility of so over-learning the new, good habit that the original conflict becomes inaccessible beneath a thick layer of secondary repression. I have seen this repeatedly in devotees of various training arts, such as dance, athletics (particularly weight lifting), and the martial arts. Such people have often so assiduously worked to counter their bad habits that the original feelings and expressions are driven far below the surface. These

> clients have to spend much time undoing their overlearned good habits before they can restore connection with the self- expressions that led to the tensions and distorted postural holdings.
>
> (1993, 63)

The ability to coordinate the body, breath, and voice in the context of fluid human expression is a highly complex process that cannot be tackled piecemeal. Ultimately, the goal is not to simply build new, or seemingly more desirable, skills through a series of isolated physical and vocal calisthenics; nor is the goal to simply "transcend" the body. As Mark Johnson states:

> There are disturbing overtones to the dream of "freeing oneself from the body," as if this would actually be a good thing to strive for! It reinforces the dangerous idea, so deeply rooted in Western culture, that purity of mind entails rising above one's bodily nature.
>
> (2007, 7)

The purpose of integrated acting training is to create an environment in which the experience of the body, breath, voice, and speech of the actor unite in physical action to create meaningful experience. Integration is predicated on physical action, occurs through physical action and is foundationally a study of physical action. Through an exploration of integrated physical action, interfering and inappropriate energies are simultaneously released and redirected into new and more appropriate physical patterns. In training, as in everyday life, integration often happens without our knowing it. While the hip-joint is being limbered, the diaphragm receives a more complete inhalation, while the resonating space is being expanded, the ribs are simultaneously receiving a stretch that strengthens the breathing musculature ... and so on ... all the while the seemingly disparate parts are simultaneously trained to express every conceivable thought and the full compass of human feeling.

Integration

Integrate is defined as to join two or more objects, to make something part of a larger whole, or to become joined or combined in this way. It is a mistake to assume that the concept of *integrated actor training* suggests that by some miraculous means movement, breath, voice, speech, and acting all become one thing rather than a combined set of individual parts working together. The individual parts are always there (and can be identified separately). They simply unite together in physical action for a common purpose. Figure 4.1 illustrates the specific role individual parts of the body play in integrated expression.

While I believe that integration is something that the brain is hard-wired to do. I also believe that integration of any particular activity is also a learned experience. A baby is born with the propensity for integration; and uses this innate potential to learn to nurse, to crawl, to walk, and finally to talk. Throughout life,

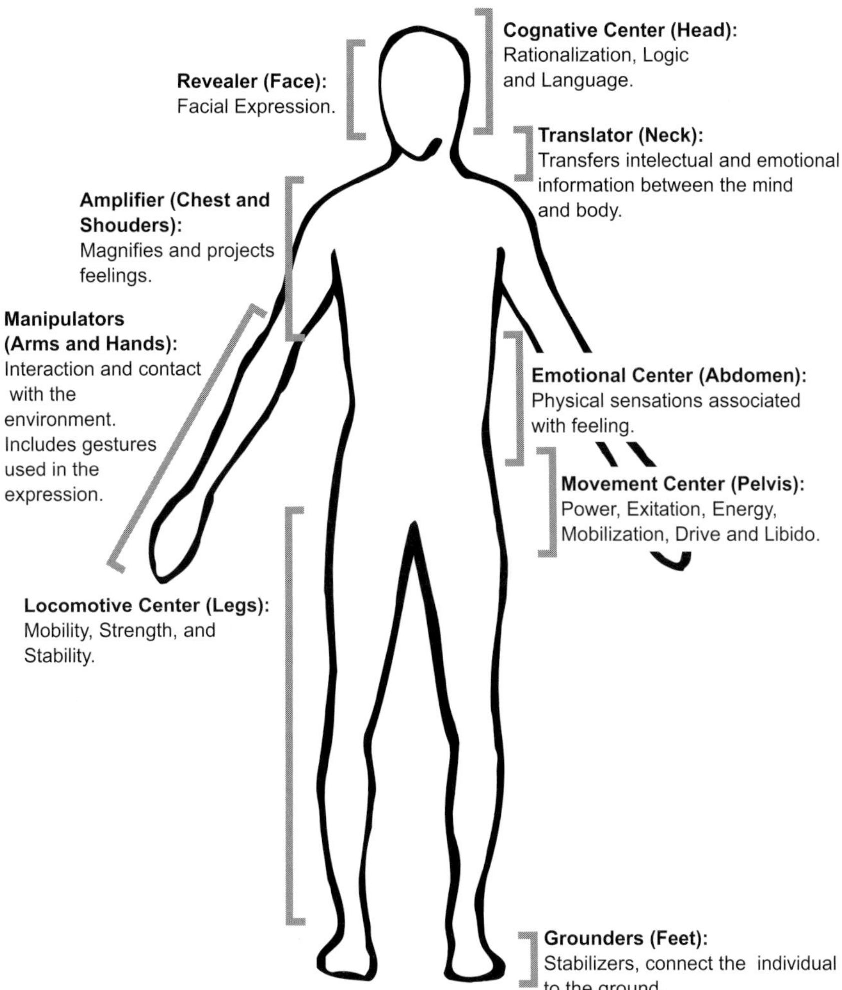

Figure 4.1 Integrated expression.

the ability to integrate and organize new and different actions continues. Anytime that we learn to do something new, undoubtedly, our mind and body have learned to integrate a new experience. We admire athletes, artists, singers, and other performers who have learned a highly specialized type of integration that is spectacularly human and captivating. Most certainly, the ability to express the thoughts and feelings of others in front of a live audience or a camera, as an actor does, with skill, passion, clarity, and good taste is also a highly specialized process of integration that is at the same time both natural and learned.

Integrating the actor's training is a comprehensive undertaking. The solution is more complex than simply combining arbitrarily selected vocal exercises with arbitrarily selected movement exercises. There has to be an understanding of how each of these seemingly disparate parts unite and work together to make expression possible. Integration is predicated on the following:

1. A conscious awareness of the reason and purpose that the individual parts are "becoming joined or combined." It is important to know what specific task you are attempting to integrate. For example, a golf swing and tennis swing are different actions, and when done well both require a different type of integrated full-bodied action. However, an integrated golfer may not have an integrated tennis game. This is precisely why the subject of this book is *expressive action.* Expressive action—a study of the integration of the body, breath, voice, and speech in the service of the expression of thought and feeling—is the reason and purpose that the individual parts of the actor's instrument are joined and combined. This type of specificity is essential to integration.
2. A working philosophy and a set of operational principles about how the individual parts are to be joined or combined. In this particular study, this will involve an experiential understanding of the following:
   - *Architecture of an expressive action*: As defined in Chapter 3, the architecture of an expressive action describes the physical raw materials that unite in the body of the actor to express thought and feeling.
   - *Hierarchy of an expressive action*: The hierarchy of an expressive action, is outlined in the next section. It describes the process of integration with which the body, breath, voice, and speech unite to make expressive action possible.

4.2 HIERARCHY OF AN EXPRESSIVE ACTION

The hierarchy of an expressive action is a theory and a set of operational principles describing how the body, breath, voice, and speech work together in integrated expressive action.

Centers and spaces

An understanding of the *hierarchy of expressive action* requires the definition of the terms *center* and *space.* The term *center* (central hub) refers to the place of origin or point of initiation of an action. The term *space* refers to the perceivable places in which the actions from the center can be most directly felt and sensed in the body (see Figure 4.2).

- **Moving center**: Pelvis—in particular the *ball-and-socket-joint* where the leg is inserted into the pelvis.

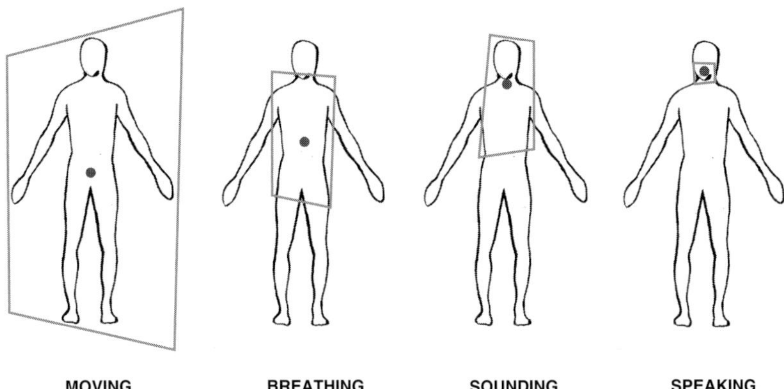

Figure 4.2 Centers and spaces.

- **Moving space**: Extends downward from the pelvis through the legs and feet and upward from the pelvis through the torso, shoulders, arms, hands, and head—the whole body from the soles of your feet to the top of your head. It includes all the movements that occur in all the various joints of the body.
- **Breathing center**: Diaphragm—located in the middle of the torso in and around the lower portion of the breastbone.
- **Breathing space**: Extends downward to the pubic bone and upward to the collarbone. It includes the movements in the torso and abdomen where the action of the breath can be sensed most directly.
- **Sounding center**: Larynx or voice box, where the vocal folds are housed.
- **Sounding space**: Extends from the larynx downward into the chest and upward to the very top of the head. It includes the places in the body where vocal resonance can be sensed most directly.
- **Speaking center**: Mouth.
- **Speaking space**: Extends from the oral cavity forward to include the teeth and lips and downward to include the throat. It includes all the moveable parts of the mouth and throat that make speaking possible—most certainly the tongue.

In the previous section, we discovered that all expressive actions share a set of physical properties—an *energy*, *orientation*, *size*, *progression*, *flow*, *direction*, *speed*, *weight*, *control*, and *focus*. Importantly, the physical properties that unite in making expressive action possible are the same physical properties that unite to make moving, breathing, sounding, and speaking possible. Like each expressive action, the moving, breathing, sounding, and speaking centers of the body also *charge* and *release*, *contact* and *withdraw*, *expand* and *contract* with various *progressions*, *flows*, *directions*, *speeds*, *weights*, *controls*, and *focuses*.

Sensory-based training

The method of physical and vocal development presented here is sensorial. The approach does not focus directly on learning to move specific muscles and/or bones that make moving, breathing, sounding, and speaking possible, but rather on the physical sensations in the body that make these actions possible. Similarly, the exploration is not primarily an intellectual question of *how do I move, breathe, sound, and speak*, but rather an experiential exploration of *how it feels to move, breathe, sound, and speak*. The principles that guide this study are not directives such as: "My diaphragm initiates inhalation." "My abdominal muscles manage exhalation;" but rather, "I feel my belly expanding." "I feel my belly contracting."

These sensory-based directives seek to place the actor in conscious touch with the seemingly innate, preconscious physical process that makes all motor learning possible. These sensory explorations of the physical properties have immeasurable benefits for the actor in training, eliminating the need to develop a separate vocabulary and method for movement, voice, speech, and acting training. Most importantly, voice and body training rooted in an exploration of the physical properties builds important skills in alignment, breathing, resonance, and range, while simultaneously preparing the actor to play expressive actions.

Hierachy of an expressive action

The process of integration—the *hierarchy of an expressive action*—begins with a weight shift in the pelvis. This weight shift provides a type of physical and sensory blueprint that is then echoed throughout each of the centers of the body. A weight shift in the pelvis sends out waves of physical sensations, patterns, and structures that reverberate through the entire body. When this happens, the physical properties associated with the weight shift in the *moving center*—its *energy*, *orientation*, *direction*, *weight* for example—travel upward and are imprinted and transferred to the *breathing center*, which then travel further upward and are imprinted and transferred to the *sounding center*, which then travel further upwards and are imprinted and transferred to the *speaking center*. Integration occurs when each of the body centers receives and accepts the physical properties being transferred. The hierarchy of an expressive action is a type of mutually beneficial collaboration between each of the respective body centers that is based on the giving, receiving, and sharing of the physical properties. When this occurs, all of the centers of the body work together participating in a common and integrated experience. The harmonizing action of the weight shift in the pelvis ensures appropriate sensory communication among all of the respective centers of the body. The result is a full-bodied, integrated expressive action. This coordinated and procedural progression of the physical properties makes integration possible.

Overlap, size and position

The hierarchy of an expressive action is made possible because of three important conditions that influence the integrated functioning of the body centers:

- **Overlap**: There is a great deal of overlap in the moving, breathing, sounding and speaking spaces (see Figure 4.2). Consequently, there is the potential for a great deal of influence and interplay between each of the respective body centers. It is important to recognize that the breathing, sounding and speaking spaces are housed within the moving space, and that the sounding and speaking spaces are housed within the breathing space, and that the speaking space is housed within the sounding space.
- **Size**: With respect to size, the larger spaces have the potential to influence the action of the smaller spaces.
- **Position**: With respect to position, the lower spaces have the potential to influence the action of the spaces above them.

These principles reflect a very simple, common sense understanding of how the body centers and spaces work together when we express ourselves. Logic would suggest that overlapping structures would influence and affect each other, and that smaller structures housed within larger structures would be influenced by the structures in which they dwell. It also stands to reason that larger structures have the potential to influence smaller structures. Additionally, in a very practical understanding of how the body works, the actions in the higher centers of the body are built upon and influenced by prior actions occurring in the lower centers of the body. When all of this happens in a harmonious and well-orchestrated manner, integration is the direct result. Most importantly, all the various centers of the body are intricately interconnected and instinctually desire to work together to facilitate integrated human activity.

In everyday life, the interaction of the body's centers and spaces might look something like this:

> Let's imagine that there is a knock at the door. A television spokesperson has come to award you a sweepstake in the amount of ten million dollars. Immediately, an impulse fires and sends a signal, which sets your entire body in motion. You are jumping up and down. This energetic, fast, unstable, free-flowing movement envelops your breathing system. Your breath is deep, spontaneous, powerful and fast. The jumping action of your body tosses your voice into the upper reaches of your vocal range. Finally, all of these sensations manifest themselves in a spontaneous, full-bodied scream: "I'm rich! I'm rich! I'm rich!"

Voice training

The hierarchy of the body is evidenced in voice training of all types. Voice training often begins with movement training. The stabilizing and grounding of the legs and feet and the alignment of the spine, central to voice training, are all actions that have their deepest roots in the pelvis (*moving center*). The voice teacher's directive that posture and alignment training are essential to healthy vocal technique demonstrates a conscious or unconscious understanding of the hierarchy of the body. Additionally, making sound is all but impossible without the *lower* action of the lungs (*breathing center*) that sends the breath upward and through the vocal folds. Similarly, speaking is reduced to a forced whisper without the *lower* action of the vocal folds (*sounding center*).

Pelvic center

The hierarchy of an expressive action is predicated upon a weight shift in the pelvis—the *moving center*. The foundations of this integrated acting technique begins with learning to initiate physical action from the movement center, which makes integration possible. An integrated action requires that all the various parts of the body participate in the action. When the muscles and bones of the pelvis move, all the other muscles and joints of the body, barring tensions or postural misalignments, naturally move in harmony with the pelvis. The pelvis has special integrative powers that serve to organize and coordinate the action of the whole body. When this larger and stronger structure leads, other body structures naturally follow its lead. No other part of the body is in the position or has the power to provide a similar efficient, coordinated and integrated experience.

This is not to suggest that all movements must be large and pronounced to be integrated. To the contrary, an actor with strong movement skills is capable of maintaining a deep connection to the pelvis even while executing small and delicate actions. In fact, the best actors can maintain a precise and subtle connection to the pelvic center that is often not immediately obvious to the untrained observer. I suggest that many of the best film actors do this all the time. Additionally, this is not to suggest that all movement or that all human expression must begin in the pelvis. Many smaller, less committed, commonplace expressive actions can be experienced with a localized movement of the head or an isolated waive of the arm. However, our most powerful and most important thoughts and feelings are most often full-bodied experiences, requiring the integrating and organizing action of the pelvis to guide and direct their complete expression. Isolated and localized physical actions are less powerful and less committed than their full-bodied counterparts. Furthermore, actors that can integrate movement from the pelvic center have little difficulty organizing localized movement in the outreaches of their bodies. It seems that actors who have learned to move their whole bodies in an integrated manner are able to perform "seemingly" isolated movements with their arms, hands, head, legs, and feet with even greater ease and efficiency.

The body has its respective centers: The heart is the circulatory center. The lungs the respiratory center. The nose the olfactory center and so on. Each center is designed to perform its specific function. This allows for an integrated, orchestration of a series of complex and efficient bodily actions. In fact, when one center misguidedly assumes the responsibility of another center—for example, when movement is initiated and coordinated in the shoulders and head and not the pelvis (*moving center*), or when breathing is initiated and coordinated in the upper chest and not the diaphragm (*breathing center*)—stress and strain on the entire body is the direct result of this misguided effort.

Many basic acting problems can be solved quite practically by encouraging the actor to take all the weight shifts that are necessary and appropriate. Tensions in the performance environment can sometimes interrupt the body's natural impulse to move. When this occurs the actor's instrument becomes fixed or arrested in a motionless and stationary pattern of holding that is contrary to authentic and natural human behavior. A weight shift from the pelvic center is a simple and direct method of initiating and directing expressive action. Additionally, each time the body's weight is shifted and redistributed; the body simultaneously re-centers itself in preparation for new and varied expressive action. This on-going organization and corresponding reorganization of physical action is essential to the organic process characteristic of "truthful living."

Integration and freedom

While freedom and ease in the body are often a prerequisite for integration, it is incorrect to assume that freedom and integration are experientially one and the same. It is possible to bind the body, to bind the breath, to bind the sound, and to bind speech all at the same time. When this occurs, the person is most certainly bound, but is also most certainly integrated. All of the various bound parts of the body are unified in an integrated, full-bodied action. Neuroscientist Daniel Wolpert reminds us that our survival is predicated on our ability to *free* the body's flow and to *bind* the body's flow—"to drive action or suppress future actions" (*Charlie Rose: The Brain Series* 2009).

It is important to recognize that these freeing and binding actions occur in daily living as well as in the performance environment. While integrated full-bodied, bound flow is probably not a pleasant or rewarding experience, sometimes survival requires that we hold onto every piece of ourselves for dear life. This integrated and intentional action of the whole person is a decidedly different experience from isolated pockets of muscular tension that often hover under the radar on a preconscious level, disallowing and interfering with the intended expression of the individual.

Integration: like begets like

Integration is made possible when the actions in each of the various parts of the body or sections of the body work together sharing a common purpose and a related sensory experience. The exact manner in which the physical properties in each of the various centers of the body interact is variable, adaptable, and impossible to fully describe or to predict with certainty. Human expression is decidedly sophisticated. However, a general operational principle can be identified that reveals how the hierarchy of an expressive action is made possible: *like begets like.* For example, a charge in the body often leads to a charge in the breath and voice. Similarly, an *expansion* in the body often leads to an *expansion* of the lungs and vocal tract, and a *heavy* body often leads to *heavy* breathing, *heavy* vocal tones, and *heavy* speaking patterns.

This occurs in theater as well as in daily living. At the end of *The Death of a Salesman* when Linda Loman is at the grave side of her husband Willy she states, "We're free. We're free." In this moment she experiences a full-bodied sense of freedom affecting equally every center of her body. Similarly, in *Richard III* before Hasting is to be beheaded he states, "Woe, Woe for England, not a wit for me." The weight and severity of the situation creates an integrated sense of heaviness in his body, breath voice, and speech.

Isolation: like does not beget like

I am not suggesting that all human expression, in life or in art, is an integrated endeavor. It is possible, and common, for a part of the body or section of the body to segregate or separate itself from the action of the rest of the body. When this occurs, the independently operating part is said to be *isolated from*, rather than *integrated with* the rest of the body. The reasons for this isolation are also complicated and often cannot be satisfactorily explained. An obvious, and often too pat, explanation is unnecessary muscular tensions that serve to hold or fix a certain body part in an inflexible and uncooperative position.

Sometimes stress and conflict create isolated patterns of muscular holding. Additionally, acts of deception and misrepresentation can manifest themselves in isolated patterns of physical action. Sometimes when we engage in "double talk"—when we mean one thing and say another—we split ourselves into two separate parts. It seems that when we hold back the truth, we also hold back a part of our body as well. It seems we often isolate parts of ourselves when we are desperate and vulnerable and sometimes when we are up to no good. Isolated patterns of this type are innumerable, and these examples are, perhaps, too simplistic for the complex interplay of conflicting physical actions that are possible. Nevertheless, it can often be hard to get all the parts working together for the greater good—*like does not beget like*—and instinctively we know that something is not right.

Most importantly actors must be empowered to choose isolated patterns of expression where and when appropriate. Perhaps, the disloyal and deceptive Iago lies to Othello with a strong *charge* in his voice, but a disparate and eerie *release* in his body. Perhaps, Medea prepares to kill her children with a controlled and *stable* voice and an *unstable* and frenetic body. Surprisingly many of the best actors perform these disparate actions of body and voice with great freedom and ease, giving them all the more an eerie and foreboding quality.

Within every human person, there is a need for balance, homeostasis, and a desire for integration. The surest sign of imbalance is a breakdown in the integrated function of the human person. When we isolate a part of ourselves, we inevitably feel less "whole." When we do so, we lose a piece of ourselves that desires to be restored. This important human need for integration and restoration propels us forward and prompts new acts of expression rooted in the desire for adaptation, readjustment and change that hopefully result in healing, rather than a further disassociation and isolation from our authentic self.

Just because you can doesn't mean you should

Master modern dancer Erik Hawkins often reminded his dancers that an "error consists in believing that because it [isolation] is possible that it is desirable" (1964, 65), or as he commonly put it "just because you can doesn't mean you should." This is a useful directive for actors as well. While actors most certainly can choose isolated patterns of physical action, it is always important to ask if they are necessary and appropriate.

Isolated movement patterns often violate the natural design of our bodies and can be stressful and unhealthy. Consider the un-integrated experience of slipping and falling. In this unfortunate instance, some parts of the body seem to have fallen away from other parts of the body. The result is a breakdown in the whole system that catapults us to the ground. Similar discordant experiences occur when we try to stay awake when we need sleep, or when we try to walk and talk straight while inebriated. In situations such as these, a certain degree of integration was lost and the body is always a little worse for the wear.

Just because you can doesn't mean it's easy

On the other hand, some isolated physical actions maybe harmless and very intriguing, but often they are anything but easy. When I was in high school I had an eccentric friend who would play one song on the piano while he sang another song. The result was two isolated and seemingly discordant actions. It was a natural oddity—a kind of musical, solar eclipse—something you just did not see everyday. *Like most certainly did not beget like.* My friend worked for hours, days on end to develop this ability. It was extremely difficult because it worked against the body's natural desire for integration. Isolated patterns of physical expression can be decidedly difficult to master. I had several other musical friends who also spent many hours trying to accomplish the same feat, but each of them met with unsatisfactory results. It seems this acquired act of isolation was as unique and as brilliantly peculiar as my high school friend.

In training, the initial and primary focus should center on developing integrated patterns of self-expression. When an embodied experience of integration is fully felt, it is possible to explore isolated patterns of self-expression. Ultimately, actors are required to express themselves as people do in daily living—in integrated and isolated patterns. The emphasis on integration in training is not to set up arbitrary "standards of correctness" or to foster a particular "aesthetic bias." Rather, the goal is to develop flexibility. Isolated patterns of holding locked in the actor's instrument are roadblocks to expressive potential. When integrated methods of expression are fully experienced and embodied, isolated modes of expression should be explored. It seems that the experienced actor who can get all the parts working together can learn to isolate when necessary. This skilled actor possesses an efficient, natural understanding of the integrated functioning of the whole person. This sense of *wholeness* and *oneness* is an important prerequisite in the artistic quest for truth, naturalness, and authentic human expression highly valued in many styles of acting.

Arm circles

Stand in the middle of the room. Stretch both arms out to the sides at shoulder height. Begin to turn each arm in a circular motion. Circle both arms fast. Circle both arms slow. This is an integrated action. *Like begets like.* Now, circle one arm fast and the other arm slow. These arms are working in isolation. Now, switch and circle the opposite arm fast and the opposite arm slow. *Like does not beget like.* Which action is easier and appears to work with the natural design of your body? Which action is more difficult and appears to work against the natural design of your body?

Whispering/shouting/running

Explore each of the following:

Whispering while tiptoeing—like begets like
Whispering while stomping—like does not beget like

Shouting while jumping up and down—like begets like
Shouting while resting and reclining—like does not beget like

Running while counting from 1–20 very quickly—like begets like
Running while counting from 1–20 very slowly—like does not beget like

Which actions are easier and appear to work with the natural design of your body? Which actions are more difficult and appear to work against the natural design of your body?

4.3 BODY STRUCTURE

James I. Kepner defines *body structure* as "the way we shape ourselves and have been shaped by our life experience" (1993, 48). Body structure refers to the organization of the whole body—bones, muscles, tissue, organs, and all. It is in the actor's body structure that the physical properties of an expressive action live, reside, and are ultimately expressed. A person with a *flexible body structure* possesses the necessary vocal and physical dexterity to shape any thought or feeling, no matter how powerful or intense, into meaningful expressive action. In a flexible body structure, the right muscles are always engaged at the right time to perform the right action. Most importantly a flexible body structure is a prerequisite for integrated expressive action. A *flexible body structure* has unfettered access to all of the physical properties of an expressive action, and can organize them in an infinite variety of ways. It can *charge* and *release,* it can move *fast* or *slow, heavy* or *light, stably* or *unstably*. The body is not arrested in a chronic physical state or a predisposed physical condition, but flexible and highly adaptable.

Barring biological defect, everyone shares a universal body structure that is by design intended to be flexible and adaptable. Childhood is characterized by great physical and vocal flexibility, spontaneity and vitality. Over time, however, the relatively limited and repetitive physical demands of contemporary adult living cause the once flexible body of the child to lose its dexterity, adaptability, and even its spontaneity and vitality. In time, certain physical and vocal patterns become frozen and fixed in the musculature of the body, limiting the possibility of varied and flexible expression. In today's sedentary culture, a somewhat fixed body structure can be acquired as early as adolescence.

Fixed body structures are characterized by modes of expression that:

- are consistently used over time;
- are automatic or involuntary; and
- can only be modified through conscious effort.

Fixed body structures develop for three reasons:

- chronic muscular tension;
- imbalances in strength and flexibility; and/or
- a static and inflexible personality.

In a fixed body structure, there are partialities and preferences for certain physical properties and prejudices towards other physical properties. The principle of *like begets like* applies to body structures as well. For example, a fast moving person has a fast body structure and often prefers to play fast expressive actions. This fast moving person can have difficulty organizing slow expressive actions in their fast body structure. There are certain physical sensations, qualities, and properties that naturally and easily integrate with certain body structures and other physical, sensations, qualities, and properties that do not integrate naturally or easily with certain body structures. Additionally, it is possible to have great flexibility in one area; and yet, have great inflexibility in others.

Because the actor may be called upon to express any and every human emotion, a technical means of maintaining a flexible body structure is essential. Every actor, to one degree or another, brings to the training process a series of preferences, limitations or imbalances that can be deeply seated in the body's structure. Certain individuals are highly *charged* and *fast*, others *stable* and *slow*, some are *bound* and *contracted*—the possibilities are numerous and vary greatly from individual to individual. The difficulty with these preferences is that they limit the actor's expressive potential, setting up a kind of *physical interference*, which disallows varied and flexible expression.

The process of developing a flexible body structure can be a complicated personal journey. Sometimes a person with a fixed body structure has a deep-seated, conscious or unconscious, resistance to certain physical properties that are seemingly incompatible with their body structure. This resistance can often lead to feelings of frustration, discomfort, fear, or even exasperation. Work on developing a flexible body structure often requires a redefining of *who we think we are* and *how we perceive ourselves*. The process involves embracing and celebrating new and unfamiliar sensations, physical patterns, and structures that may seem foreign and unfamiliar. The *voice and body exercises* and the *improvisations* presented in this book are designed to develop a flexible body structure—an integrated place of human departure that provides balance, dexterity and flexibility.

4.4 THE STACKING PROCESS

First and second function improvisation

In the acting studio, the improvisatory process used to explore the *body centers* and the *hierarchy of an expressive action* is called *stacking*. The stacking process is a technical method designed to create the sensory experience associated with playing an integrated expressive action. The improvisations presented in the stacking process involve a unique type of research in which the primary focus is placed on the physical, and not the mental, properties of an expressive action. This type of exploration is called *improvisation in the first function* (see Chapter 2). The easiest way to explain this method of improvisation is to contrast it with its counterpart—*improvisation in the second function.*

Improvisation in the second function

Suppose you are given the following set of circumstances:

You have overslept. You are late for work for the third time this week. You cannot find your car keys. Go.

If, after thinking for a moment, you begin to search frantically for your car keys, you are taking the second functional approach, exploring expressive action through an intellectual analysis of the relevant circumstances. The mind prompts or motivates your body to integrated expressive action.

Improvisation in the first function

Stacking is a type of physical research in which each body center is explored sequentially from the moving center, to the breathing center, to the sounding center, to the speaking center. In this manner, the *improvisation* builds an expressive action "from the ground up," progressing sequentially through four stages: they begin with a *weight shift(s)* (1), which collaborates with a corresponding *breath-shift* (2), which collaborates with a corresponding *sound-shift* (3), which collaborates with a corresponding *speech-shift* (4). Paradoxically when all assembled, these shifting-actions appear to happen *in that order and all at once.* Stacking is a method of training in which through the exploration of physical action the moving, breathing, sounding, and speaking centers become integrated and fully embodied.

Suppose you are asked to move in an empty space in the following manner:

- *energy*: charge
- *speed*: fast
- *direction*: indirect

These directives to physical action initiate the stacking process. If, without conscious deliberation or planning, you begin to move quickly around the room in many directions a *charged, fast, indirect* manner, you are taking a *first-functional approach.* The body prompts and motivates you to integrated expressive action. The physical properties of the weight shift (*charge, fast* and *indirect*) have put you in touch with the physical foundations of meaning and understanding. As the stacking process continues, you might be asked to allow the breath to integrate with the physical action with the exploration of *sighing* and *hissing* sounds. Then sound might be integrated on any combination of vowel and consonants sounds. Later someone asks, "*What are you doing?*" and you respond, "*I'm searching for my car keys!*" The last stage of the stacking process typically involves an exploration of words and phrases. In the training process, the action of each of the respective body centers are stacked one on top the other in a harmonious, accommodating, and coordinated manner. The outcome is the organized, sensuous, and integrated expression of thought and feeling.

This first-functional approach to improvisation is the reverse of what might typically go on in acting classes and rehearsals. Most often the actor begins with the language provided by the playwright and looks for an expressive action appropriate for the text. A great deal can be learned about expressive action and language by working the other way around. It is important to recognize that language probably began with primitive sound and movement explorations. Actors benefit immeasurably from an exploration of expressive action in a pre-speech world. Working without words returns the actor to primordial and reflexive methods of communication that are visceral and full-bodied. The actor is asked to begin by *feeling and sensing*, rather than by *thinking and saying*. Jumping too quickly to words can often short circuit the body leaving a superficial connection to the physical truth. The ultimate goal is to *allow the body to speak* along with the brain:

> Gesture [weight shift] is older than words, and in the actor's dramatic creation, too, it must be their herald … . Anyone who starts with the words and then hunts for the appropriate gesture [weight shift] to accompany them, lies to the face of art and nature both.
>
> (Langer 1953, 316)

This type of first-functional improvisation is a practical method of exploring the central theme of this book: the foundations, the very beginning of meaning and understanding itself are physical. As Philosopher Mark Johnson reminds us "meanings emerge from the bottom up" (2007, 12):

> The core idea is that our meaning is based, first, on our sensorimotor experience, our feelings, our visceral connections to our world; and, second, on various imaginative capacities for using sensorimotor processes to understand abstract concepts.
>
> (2007, 12)

Paradoxically and most certainly counter-intuitively, this body-based method of improvisation is in natural alignment with the body and the mind's cooperative engagement in the cognitive process.

Typically, when improvising in the first function, you will be asked to explore, develop and repeat a single expressive action multiple times. You will not be asked to group a series of expressive actions into a larger context or story. Initially, you will not be asked to answer such questions as, "*Who am I? Where am I? What do I want?*" or to deliberately investigate the intellectual aspects of the action: "*My character is adopted. My character is afraid. My character is a habitual liar.*" Rather you will be encouraged to explore the action physically without predetermined analysis, interpretation, or justification. By directing your awareness to the physical, you will be encouraged to focus on the sensory life of the expressive action: Does my body feel *heavy* or *light*? Am I moving *fast* or *slow*? Does my body *expand* or *contract*? Am I *charging* or *releasing*? Free of character, scenario, situation, and circumstance, the process of expression is explored *in and of itself and for its own sake*. Emphasis is placed on spontaneity, exploration, structure, form, technique, and execution. The goal is to develop a specific set of physical resources that lead, prompt, and motivate expressive action.

Improvising in this manner is like *falling in love in the abstract*. The gentleman who falls in love in the abstract loves the sound of the woman's voice, the color of her hair, the twinkle in her eye—all her physical attributes—without any intellectual knowledge of who she is or where she came from. Similarly, when improvising in the first function, the actor falls in love with the expressive action in the abstract—its *weight*, *direction*, *flow*, *energy*, and *size*—all the physical properties that give it its unique form and character. When improvising in this abstract manner, you are not exploring a specific expressive action linked to a specific character, time or place but a universal expressive action that transcends character, time, and place. The expressive action is simply played *in and of itself and for its own sake*.

When you direct your attention to your physical experience, however, you cannot simply turn off your brain and make it quit thinking. As soon as you begin your physical exploration, your mind will begin thinking, rationalizing, and organizing the expressive action into some type of logical and meaningful human experience. Context emerges spontaneously because of the expressive action itself, not from any predetermined analysis or plan. Sometimes the physical sensations created will remind you of past events. Other times, the intellect suggests possible scenarios that transcend personal experience. Inherent within all of us is a built-in type of physical and emotional memory that is more powerful, clear, and profound than we may have previously thought. An expressive action has a mystical and transformative narrative power. When an expressive action is played *in and of itself and for its own sake*, meaning and context emerge naturally and effortlessly.

Typically, if you can play an expressive action in the first function, you'll have little problem translating, adjusting, or modifying the expressive action to meet the needs of a specific character in a play. The adjustments needed to play the same expressive action in Shaw, Shakespeare, Churchill, or Mamet are relatively easy to make. Furthermore, because all expressive actions have a universal structure (they all *charge* and *release*, *contact* and *withdraw*, *expand* and *contract*) when you learn to play one expressive action, your body and voice are simultaneously being programmed to play all expressive actions.

These improvisations have proved to be an essential link in bridging the wide gap that so often separates traditional methods of voice, movement, and acting training. With repetition and practice, you will begin to view your body as a rich mental, physical, and psychological playground. Many times your body will prompt you to undertake new and unfamiliar expressive actions that were previously unthinkable. In an advanced study, specific improvisations can be structured to address individual limitations that unlock the actor's expressive potential.

Part IV

Stacking

Chapter 5

Introduction to stacking

In this section *Part IV: Stacking*, the moving, breathing, sounding, and speaking centers and spaces are each explored sequentially in four separate chapters. Each individual chapter will explore the action of each body center in four steps:

Step 1: preliminaries—provides an initial experiential type of introduction to the each body center being explored. In this first-step exploration, you will be asked to explore each body center with limited explanation of either purpose or the process. It may feel a little like jumping in head first, but the intent is to create a physical experience that is not directed from the outset by the intellect. The goal in the preliminaries is to see how it *feels* first. Trust that intellectual explanations and justifications will follow in subsequent steps of the exploration. The *preliminaries* emphasize a reoccurring theme of this book, the importance of sometimes emphasizing *sensing* before *thinking*, *feeling* before *thought*, *intuition* before *knowledge* and the *body* before the *mind* in the acting process.

Step 2: principles—provides a technical discussion of each body center respectively, covering as appropriate related topics such as: anatomy, physiology, respiration, phonation, resonance, range, and other related practical matters within the context of the *physical properties*. The principles describe the manner in which *energy*, *orientation*, *size*, *progression*, and *flow*—the *major properties of an expressive action*—affect and shape the action of the body, breath, voice, and speech. A series of corresponding exploration/exercises accompany the discussion of the principles providing a type of experiential anatomy course in which the actor is placed in direct contact with the physical sensations that make expression possible.

Step 3: technique—provides a technical exploration of each body center through a series of *voice and body exercises* designed to build through integrated physical action corresponding skills in movement, respiration, phonation, resonance, range. These voice and body exercises form the foundation of the actor's basic training. In the course of a typical technique class the actor moves from lying, to sitting, to standing, and to upright locomotive movement in a series of integrated moving, sighing, hissing, and sounding actions that are abstract, physical representations of the *essence of an expressive action*. Each exercise possesses the physical architecture of an expressive action, mirroring their universal pattern and form. In this sense, all the voice and body exercises *charge* and *release*, *contact* and *withdraw* and *flow freely* from the *center* to the *periphery*. The voice and body exercises are intended to become a part of the actor's daily practice.

While it is possible to skip this foundational step and jump ahead to the improvisational studies, the actor who does so is in danger of omitting an essential component of the training. An experiential knowledge of the anatomical workings of the actor's instrument are an important part of any comprehensive method of training, and a central demarcation between the amateur and the professional. Without this knowledge, the actor is a little like the local musician who can play the piano well-enough but to his detriment and the stifling of his true potential cannot read a lick of music.

Creating your own exercises

There is no single set of codified exercises that comprise this method; but rather, the exercises are simply a practical extension of the principles. Any exercise that charges and releases, expands and contracts, contacts and withdraws in a free flowing matter are useful and acceptable. When the principles are fully understood, it is possible to create new, different, and inventive exercises of your own that transcend the ones suggested in this book.

Step 4: improvisation—The i*mprovisations* outlined in this step involve a fully realized investigation of each body center in the context of expressive action. Using the stacking process, you will build a *barre*—beginning with a physical action and then adding breath, sound, and speech respectively. The barre is comprised of a series of 20 expressive actions committed to memory and played one right after the other in a single exercise. Each of the 20 selected expressive actions explores each physical property—*charge*, *release*, *fast*, *slow*, etc. The process of building a barre—and the exploration of all the sensations that unite to create it—will lay a foundation for unlocking the physical fundamentals of the acting process.

The term *barre* is derived from the *ballet barre*, which is a handrail fixed to the wall in a dance studio at which the ballet dancer practices. The term *ballet barre* also references a series of steps or movements that are committed to memory and are practiced daily as a method of solo preparation. Similarly, the expressive actor's barre is a series of expressive actions committed to memory and practiced daily as a method of solo preparation. Like the ballet barre, the actor's barre is designed to become a part of the actor's daily workout.

Technique vs. improvisation

There are essentially two goals in training: the *potential* and the *possible*. The voice and body exercises seek to access the actor's *potential* by developing the body, breath, voice, and speech of the actor in the direct service of human expression. The improvisations seek to explore all the *possible* varied and vast methods of human expression. Without technique, actors have difficulty accessing their true *potential*. Without improvisation, actors have difficulty accessing all that is *possible*.

An important difference between *technique* and *improvisation* is one of intent. The voice and body exercises that form the technical foundation of this method seek to foster integrated and free-flowing patterns of human expression. In improvisation, on the other hand, anything is possible. Isolated movement patterns, bound flow, and inefficiency are welcomed and rewarded appropriately appearing in the improvisations as they do in daily living.

Chapter 6

Moving

STEP 1: PRELIMINARIES

The investigation of the moving center begins with the preliminary improvisations, which are located in *Chapter 11: Preliminaries*. At this first stage of the stacking process, you will only explore the movement component of the improvisations. In each of the improvisations, this (■) icon indicates the movement component intended for exploration. After completing the moving component of the preliminary improvisations, return to *Step 2: Principles* located below.

STEP 2: PRINCIPLES

This experiential approach to the principles of moving is a practical investigation of the *action of the body*. It is rooted in an exploration of the physical sensations that make moving possible. Its primary focus centers on how the body *charges* and *releases*, *contacts* and *withdraws*, *expands* and *contracts* in a *free flowing* manner from the *center* of the body outward to the *periphery*.

Movement is essentially a series of *weight shifts*. We learn to move efficiently when we learn to shift our weight efficiently. Weight shifts are made possible because the human body is a *segmented structure* (see Figure 6.1). Each body segment is connected to another body segment by a series of joints. When a joint is bent or flexed, lengthened or extended, rotated or turned, the body's weight is redistributed. Pointing the foot, bending the knee, turning the head, and shifting the hips are all examples of weight shifts.

There are two types of weight shifts: *isolated* and *integrated*. Isolated weight shifts involve moving one body segment at a time. They occur when one segment of the body is set apart from the other body segments and moved alone or independently. Tapping the foot, shaking the head, and shrugging the shoulders are examples of isolated weight shifts. By contrast, integrated weight shifts occur when multiple body segments move together in unison and harmony. The vast majority of all human movement involves some type of integrated weight shift. Picking up a pencil, opening a window, hugging a friend, or simply walking each involves the integrated movement of many body segments.

Because integrated weight shifts require a more sophisticated redistribution of body's weight, movement training typically concentrates on integrated weight shifts.

Thoughts and feelings/movement and stillness

Integrated weight shifts are central to the expression of powerful and important thoughts and feelings. We think and feel with our whole body, not in isolated sections, parts, or segments. An integrated weight shift corresponds directly to a shift in thought and feeling. Larger thoughts and feelings are expressed through larger weight shifts, smaller thoughts and feelings through smaller weight shifts. The statement *"a weight shifts corresponds directly to a shifts in thought and feeling"* often raises questions about the expressive power of *stillness*. Big thoughts and feelings that simmer underneath the surface in perfect stillness are in the strictest sense not being expressed but rather contained or maintained by an individual who is practicing a great deal of self control. While this arresting and regulatory act undoubtedly contains thought and feeling, it is inaccurate to suggest in the strictest sense that these thoughts and feeling are being adequately expressed. *Expression is the process of giving form to our thoughts and feelings.* This form making activity is not possible without physical action. Granted, stillness can be quite captivating and powerful and when used appropriately is, without question a viable dramatic choice for the actor.

Isolating and integrating

Wave hello to an imaginary friend. Like any movement, this is not possible without a weight shift, either *isolated* or *integrated*. First, use an isolated weight shift. Keeping your pelvis, torso, shoulders, and head relatively uninvolved, lift only your arm and hand to wave hello to your friend. Your goal is to separate the action of your arm from the rest of your body. Your arm moves independently with seemingly no connection to the rest of your body. Repeat several times. Now, wave hello using an integrated weight shift. Allow the action to begin deep in the center of your body. Allow your whole body to become involved. Experience the waving action from the soles of your feet to the top of your head. Repeat several times. The larger movement associated with an integrated weight shift corresponds to a greater sense of commitment, intensity, and feeling.

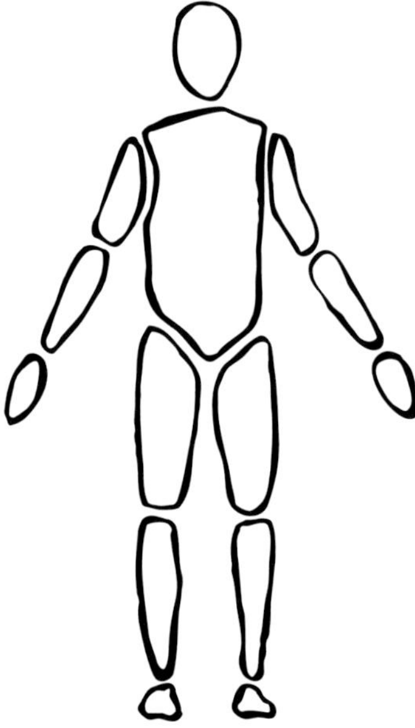

Figure 6.1 Segmented structure.

Movement progression: center/periphery

Center

The natural progression of movement begins in the pelvis—the geographical *center* of the body (see Figure 6.2)—and flows outward to the *periphery* into the arms, legs, hands, feet, and head. Three factors make the pelvis the ideal place to initiate movement:

1 It has the heaviest bones. Ideally, this heavier body segment assumes primary responsibility for moving other, lighter body segments.
2 It has the largest joints. Stress, strain, and tension in the smaller joints of the body is eliminated when the energy for movement is initiated and coordinated from this larger joint.
3 It has the strongest muscles. Efficiency dictates that the strongest muscles should do the largest share of the work.

It is natural and logical that a weight shift in the pelvis would be an ideal place to begin physical activity. Common sense suggests that leading with the pelvis is more efficient, pleasant, and advantageous than leading with the shoulders, head, rib-cage, legs, or feet. No matter which direction we desire to move—bending down to touch the toes or reaching the hands and arms up over the head—the

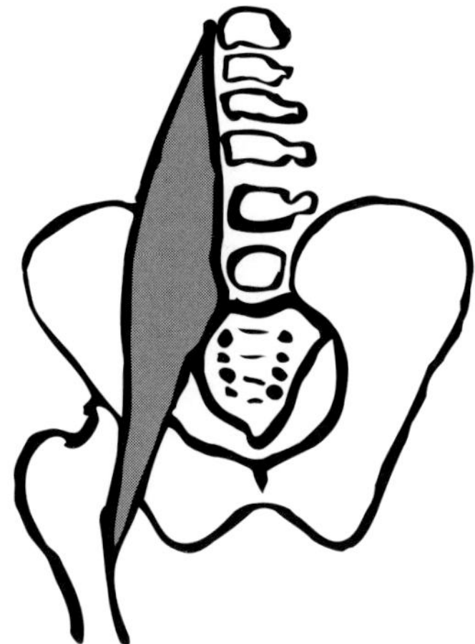

Figure 6.2 Pelvic center.

journey is more fluid, efficient, and integrated when the action is initiated from the pelvis.

Acting from the pelvic center

When an actor initiates movement from the pelvis, the experience of a thought and feeling is re-directed deeper and deeper into the body. As a result, the actor's mental and emotional experience becomes more *full-bodied* and more *embodied*—resulting in increased spontaneity, intensity, and vitality. For the actor, initiating movement from the pelvis is a physical method of raising the psychological stakes in performance.

Thigh socket

The prerequisite for initiating a movement from the pelvis is strength, flexibility, and freedom in the *thigh socket*—essentially the hip joint, the point where the upper leg attaches to the pelvis. This joint is commonly referred to as the *ball and socket joint*. The process of restructuring the body's movement patterns begins by initiating all movement with a weight shift in the pelvis. In practice, this involves directing one's attention to the place where the ball and socket meet and encouraging movement from this most important *central hinge*. In the beginning of training, a centered weight shift can be obvious, over-pronounced and laborious because muscles located deep in the center of the body can be difficult to coordinate. However, in time and with training, inefficient weight shifts give way to smaller, subtler, even semiconscious ones. Eventually it is possible to initiate movement from the pelvis with such subtlety and economy that it is almost imperceptible.

There are two basic ways in which the ball and socket joint moves:

1 The *ball moves in the socket* when we move our legs from the ball and socket joint. For example, when standing upright if you lift your leg upwards toward your chest, you are moving the ball in the socket.
2 The *socket moves over the ball* when we move the torso from the ball and socket joint. For example, when standing upright if you bend over from the pelvic center and not simply from your waist, you are moving the socket over the ball.

A movement of the *ball in the socket* moves the *lower half* of the body. A movement of the *socket over the ball* moves the *upper half* of the body. In this manner, the movement of the ball and socket joint plays a pivotal role in coordinating the integrated physical action of the upper and lower halves of the body. Learning to perform these two basic movements independently and simultaneously with the legs and feet (lower half of the body) and torso and head (upper half of the body) in varying configurations and rotations is a fundamental requirement for *centered movement.*

Creasing/de-creasing

A useful directive when learning to initiate movement from the ball and socket joint is to *crease and decrease in the thigh socket.* The ability to crease and decrease in the thigh socket is a concept similar to that of folding and unfolding a sheet of paper. When a piece of paper is folded in half, a crease is formed in the center. Similarly, as the torso and head fold downward towards the legs and feet, a crease is created in the thigh socket (*socket moves over the ball*). Similarly, as the legs are folded upwards towards the torso, a crease is created in.the thigh socket (*ball moves in the socket*). Experiencing a creasing and decreasing action in the thigh-socket ensures that movement is being initiated from the pelvic center. When movement is initiated from the waist, rib cage, shoulders, or head and not the pelvis, the result is invariably a loss of integration and functional efficiency.

In integrated movement patterns, the creasing and decreasing action in the thigh socket is always accompanied by two related and corresponding actions:

1 an upward and downward (or a downward and upward) pelvic tilt;
2 an arching and rounding (or a rounding and un-rounding) of the lumbar spine.

These tilting, arching, and rounding actions may be performed in any order that facilitates the purpose and direction of the movement intended.

These three central actions—the creasing and decreasing the thigh socket, the upward and downward tilt of the pelvis, and the arching and rounding of the spine form the foundation of this integrated movement technique. These harmonious and corresponding actions send out waves of momentous energy that flow outward from the pelvic center to the periphery—the arms, legs, hands, feet, and head. When these integrated actions occur, the body's core is organized to simultaneously support the body and to perform physical action.

Moving the ball in the socket

Egg-lying position: Lie on your back. Allow your knees to bend by folding your legs in and upward toward your chest. As the legs fold into the chest, gently grasp the knees with your hands. Allow your whole spine to lengthen and widen into the floor. You should not feel as if you are holding your legs in the air, but rather that they are stabilized and supported from the pelvis. Encourage the sensation of your legs floating or hovering above your pelvis. (This position is called an *egg-lying position* because the body is in an oval shape like that of an egg.)

Initiate a gentle rocking action in your pelvis by *creasing* and *decreasing* your thigh sockets. This creasing and decreasing action in the thigh socket is created by moving your bent knees inward toward your chest (*crease*) and then outward away from your chest (*decrease*). When you perform this action, you are moving the *ball in the socket*. Allow this repetitive rocking action to be quite rhythmical. Your arms do not need to assist in this gentle rocking action. Encourage freedom and flexibility in your thigh sockets. As you crease and decrease in the thigh socket, allow your pelvis to tilt upward and downward as your lumbar spine arches and rounds. Allow this centered movement to radiate through your whole body. Relieve any unnecessary muscular tension that is keeping the energy of your body from flowing freely from the center to the periphery. Rest. Repeat this gentle rocking action until your lumbar spine and thigh sockets feel loose and limber, and your whole body is rocking on the floor in response to the action of your pelvis.

Periphery: torso, legs, feet, arms, hands, and head

The pelvis is like the engine of a train; when it moves, all the other smaller body segments, like boxcars, follow its lead. The pelvis paves the way for integrated movement patterns from the *center* to the *periphery*. A weight shift in the pelvis progresses sequentially in a wavelike action. This wavelike action proceeds simultaneously in both an upward and downward direction:

- *upper-body sequence*: pelvis + torso + arm/hand + head.
- *lower-body sequence*: pelvis + knee + ankle + foot.

In integrated full-bodied physical action, the pelvis provides the *primary* power for movement, while the torso, legs, arms, and head provide the *secondary* function of *guiding and directing* the movement of the body in space. Stress and strain occur when the muscles and the bones located on the periphery of the body are wrongly engaged to do the strenuous work that should ideally be performed by the pelvis. The right muscles must be asked to perform the right tasks. It is important to allow the periphery of the body to be carried and supported from the pelvis. In this manner, the center leads and the periphery follows.

Tasseling and boomeranging

The connection that the legs, arms, and head share with the pelvic center during integrated movement is the physical experience *tasseling* and *boomeranging*.

Tasseling

When the body is tasseling, the legs, arms, and head maintain a strong sympathetic connection to the pelvic center. The experience of tasseling, as the name suggest, involves allowing the legs, arms, and head to dangle and swing from the spine and the pelvis like a "tassel" that dangles and swings from a moving drapery. This dangling and swinging action creates integrated, full-bodied patterns of physical action. When this occurs, the legs, arms, and head respond to both the rising and falling action of the pelvis and the arching and rounding action of the spine. Excessive tension in the legs, arms, and head can serve to disconnect the overly tense appendage from the center of the body. When actively engaging the legs, arms, and head to guide and direct the body in space or to execute a gesture, the goal is to be able to perform these peripheral actions without loosing the "tassel-like" connection to the spine and pelvic center. This ability to move the periphery in concert with the center is a central characteristic of integrated physical action.

Boomeranging

The purpose of boomeranging is to develop a natural pathway of movement and support for the arms and/or legs while moving and gesturing. A boomerang is a toy that when tossed travels away from the person who tossed it, and then returns back again to the person who tossed it. The legs and arms share a reciprocal physical relationship with the pelvis. Their similar boomerang-like journey begins with an integrated movement in the *center* (pelvis) that travels outward through the body to the *periphery* (arms and legs); and then "boomerangs" back again to the *center* (pelvis.) For example, a momentous action of the pelvis tosses the resting arm out and away from the center to perform a gesture. After having completed the intended gesture, the arm returns once again to its resting position near the center of the body. The arm's journey away from the center is active (*charge*), and the arm's journey back to center is passive (*release*). When boomeranging, it is essential that the action of the pelvis provide the primary support and power for the movement of the arms and legs. Again, excessive tension can interrupt the natural boomeranging action isolating the appendages from the support and power of the pelvis.

Tasseling and boomeranging arms

Begin by standing in a stationary position. Swing your pelvis from side to side. Allow your arms to respond to the action of your pelvis. Your arms will move up and away from your body and back down near the pelvic center as you swing from side to side. (This action is similar to a young schoolchild who stands and swings his/her lunchbox and book bag from side to side.) Begin to move around the room while performing this swinging action. As you bend and unbend your legs, sense your pelvis rising upwards away from the earth (*charge*) and falling back downward toward the earth (*release*). Allow your spine to round (*contract*) and un-round (*expand*). Initially, do not try to make your arms do anything, simply allow them to respond like tassels to the rounding and un-rounding, rising and falling action of your spine and pelvis. Sense your arms actively boomeranging out and away from center (*charge*) and passively falling back to center again (*release*) as the pelvis swings your arms. Allow your arms and shoulders to maintain a deep connection to the momentous action of your spine and pelvis. When you sense a clear tasseling and boomeranging connection between the arms and the spine and pelvis, begin to engage your arms in a series of gestures—pointing, waving, shoving, gathering etc. Perform each of these gesturing actions without loosing the tasseling and boomeranging connection to the pelvis.

Movement size: expand/contract

Modifications or changes in the body's *size* are created through the bending and unbending of various joints, which results in relative changes in the degree of *expansion* and *contraction* experienced in the body. Ideally, each joint of the body should enjoy a free and uninterrupted range of motion so that all the joints can expand and contract efficiently. For this to occur, the muscles of the body must be both strong and flexible. Weak muscles have difficulty contracting; tight muscles have difficulty expanding.

Spine

In general, the average person's wrists, ankles, elbows, knees, and feet are strong and flexible enough to perform a wide array of physical actions. It is relatively easy to bend and unbend the smaller joints of the body. However, the expansion and contraction of the spine is the largest and most complex movement the body makes. Consequently, it is important to learn to expand and contract the spine efficiently. The expansion and contraction of the spine is integral to almost every smaller movement that the body makes. When the spine is expanding and contracting properly, the other muscles and joints in the body tend to follow its lead. Individuals with a strong and flexible spine invariably experience adequate levels of strength and flexibility in the rest of the muscles and joints of the body.

One reason expanding and contracting the spine can be difficult is that the architecture of the spine is complex and generally misunderstood. The most common misconception is to view the spine as a stiff, inflexible structure like that of a broomstick or a metal rod. Rather, the spine is a flexible series of connected bones (vertebrae)—24 interconnected joints that unite to form the lumbar, thoracic, and cervical curves of the spinal column. These curves provide a natural distribution of the body's weight supporting the torso, shoulder, arms, and head when upright. Additionally, the vertebrae allow the spine to expand and contract (see Figure 6.3).

The moving spine

In movement training, the spine is often addressed in the context of good or bad posture. Consequently, the ability to hold the spine vertical and upright is often celebrated at the expense of its other important kinetic properties. The spine is not simply designed to keep the body erect and upright but to expand and contract—to bend and rotate, twist and turn, with great flexibility and in a variety of combinations. When attempting to improve the use of the spine, the essential question is not, *"Where should I place or hold my spine in space?"* but, *"How should I move my spine through space?"* Rigorous movement disciplines such as dance, the martial arts, and many sports spend little time discussing vertical alignment or posture. The physical demands of these disciplines indirectly improve the alignment of the spine. A spine that can expand and contract efficiently and economically—that can bend, turn, twist, and rotate finds itself in correct alignment by default.

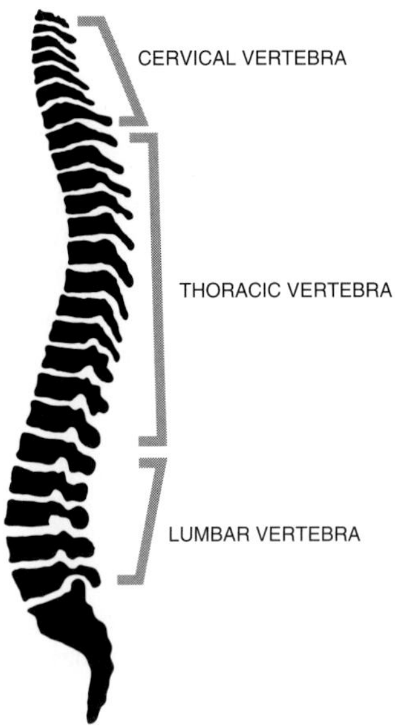

Figure 6.3 Spine.

The spine is designed to transfer the weight of the head, shoulders, arms, and rib cage downward into the pelvis. This downward transfer of weight is facilitated by the vertebrae of the spine, which become larger and stronger as they progress lower and lower into the body. The pelvis—the base of the spine—is strategically positioned to support and carry the weight of the entire upper body. Its bowl-like shape serves as a type of cradle, which not only supports and carries the weight of the upper body but also absorbs and cushions shock and stress during strenuous activity.

When the spine is expanded (upright and vertical), the weight of the upper body is transferred into the pelvis through a relatively straight vertical pathway. However, as the spine contracts, this straight vertical pathway becomes curved or rounded. The ability to round and un-round (*contract* and *expand*) the spine without interrupting the fluid flow of weight downward into the pelvis is essential to integrated and efficient movement.

Once again, a creasing and decreasing action in the thigh socket—the movement of *the ball over the socket*, coordinates this fluid downward transfer of weight, which contracts and expands the spine. This creasing and decreasing action in the thigh socket is always accompanied by two related and corresponding actions:

1 a downward and corresponding upward pelvic tilt;
2 a rounding and corresponding un-rounding of the lumbar spine.

These three actions when performed together unite to contract and expand the spine. A creasing action in the thigh socket tilts the pelvis downward and rounds the spine (*contract*), and a decreasing action in the thigh socket tilts the pelvis upward and un-rounds the spine (*expand*) (see Figure 6.4). Learning to crease and decrease the thigh socket efficiently ensures that the spine will expand and contract freely and naturally—that all the interconnected vertebrae will move in unison and harmoniously with one another, creating a fluid and uninterrupted pathway of movement and support.

Moving the socket over the ball

Diamond sit position: Begin in a seated position on the floor. Bend your legs at the knees and allow the soles of your feet to touch each other so that your legs and feet form a diamond shape. Allow your spine to float into a vertical and upright position without slouching downward or reaching upward.

Initiate a looping action by creasing and decreasing your thigh socket several times. Creasing your thigh socket tilts your pelvis downward, rounding your spine over your legs and feet—a *contraction* (see Figure 6.4). Decreasing your thigh socket tilts your pelvis upward, un-rounding your spine—an *expansion*. This creasing and decreasing action unite to create a looping action in the upper body. The looping action is performed in a fluid and circular pattern, not as an isolated up-and-down movement in which the upper body is systematically raised and lowered over the legs and feet. Encourage the sensation of your upper body being suspended from your pelvis and hovering out over your legs and feet rather than collapsing downward toward the floor. A sense of freedom and ease in the thigh socket facilitates the fluid expansion and contraction of the spine. Repeat this looping action several more times.

Movement energy: charge/release

Having a direct connection to the pelvis—the body's power center, the spine is the body central conduit for energy and support. The vitality of the spine is maintained by balancing the contrasting sensations of *charge* and *release* that create the energy flow in the spine. In this manner, it is useful to sense the energy from the pelvis *charging* up the front of your spine and *releasing* down the back of your spine. This complete circuit of charging and releasing energy creates a type of poise that suspends the spine out of the pelvis upward and away from the earth.

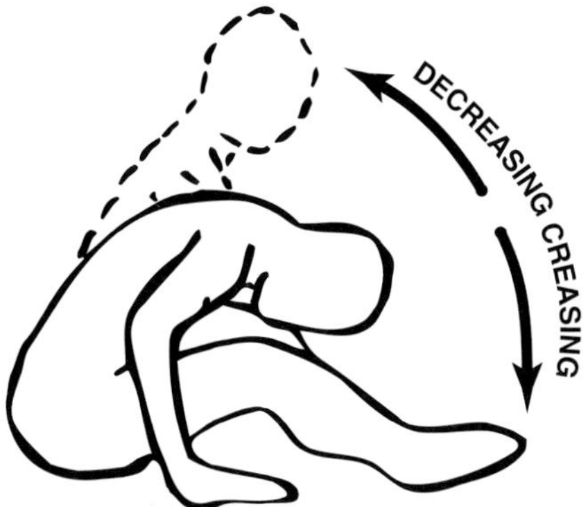

Figure 6.4 Creasing/decreasing.

This flow of charging and releasing energy cycles continuously in two directions:

1 *up the front of the spine* from the front of the pubic bone to the top of the spine; and
2 *down the back of the spine* from the base of the skull to the tailbone.

When this uninterrupted flow of energy is not blocked through injury or tension, it serves to unite the *emotional center* located in the lower half of the body with the *intellectual center* located in the head. This integration of the head and the tail via the spine provides an essential physical pathway for the integrated functioning of the mind and body (Rosen 1995, 50–1). While this *up the front* and *down the back* flow of energy is readily sensed in upright positions, it is important to recognize that this same flow of energy occurs when the spine is rounding, rotating, flexing, and spiraling.

Movement pathway

A weight shift is not possible without a corresponding building up (*charge*) and letting go (*release*) of *energy*. Learning to move efficiently in space involves organizing a charging and releasing action in the pelvis. This involves working *with* and *against* the forces of gravity. When we move in space, a *charge* propels or pushes the body up and away from the earth on a wave of momentous energy. After the charging action has run its course, the body passively *releases* and moves in a downward direction back toward the earth completing the wave of momentous energy. Efficient movement is a finely orchestrated dance between the forces of conscious muscle action (*charge*) and passive muscle action (*release*).

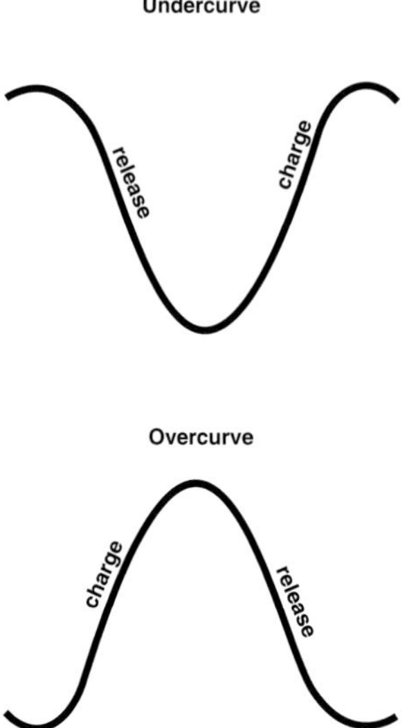

Figure 6.5 Undercurve and overcurve.

There are two specific pathways that describe the flow of energy when moving through space: *undercurve movement pathways* and *overcurve movement pathways* (see Figure 6.5). In undercurve movement pathways, the body *releases* before it *charges*. In overcurve movement pathways, the body *charges* before it *releases*. Regardless of the order of the charging and releasing action, in every phrase of movement there is time for activity and passivity, doing and non-doing, action and inaction—*charge* and *release*. Efficient movement involves participating freely with overcurve and undercurve movement pathways.

Punching and bowling

Undercurve movement pathways: Rolling an imaginary bowling ball down the alley involves an undercurve movement pathway that *releases* before it *charges*. Typically, a good bowler initiates the rolling action from the pelvis, using the weight of the entire body to propel the ball down the alley. Taking a few steps forward as the ball leaves your hand is essential to experiencing a full-bodied release and charge in the pelvis. Notice as you throw the ball how your body releases downward toward the earth before it charges up and away from the earth. Repeat this throwing action several more times. Focus your attention on the contrasting sensation of *release* and *charge* created by the undercurve movement pathway of the pelvis.

Overcurve movement pathway: Throwing an imaginary punch involves an overcurve movement pathway that *charges* before it *releases*. Typically, a good fighter throws a punch from the pelvis, using the weight of the entire body to knockout his opponent. Throw a pretend punch several times. Taking a few steps forward as the punch is thrown is essential to experiencing a full-bodied *charge* and *release* in the pelvis. Notice as you throw the punch how your body charges up and away from the earth before it releases downward toward the earth. Repeat this punching action several times. Focus on the contrasting sensation of *charge* and *release* created by the overcurve movement pathway of the pelvis.

Tension and relaxation

The terms *charge* and *release* must not be confused with the more common terms *tension* and *relaxation*. The physical experience of a *charge* is very different from the physical experience of *tension*. When the body experiences an increased charge, the buildup of energy is spontaneous, involuntary, and generally infectious. It travels from the center of the body outward to the periphery in uninterrupted waves of excitement. Tension, on the other hand, interrupts spontaneity and stifles the free flow of energy in the body. Tension is caused by the conscious or unconscious tightening of muscles. Unlike a charge, which is a full-bodied experience, tension is typically a localized and isolated phenomenon. Tension can occur almost anywhere—the head, shoulders, hands, neck, jaw, forehead, and feet. A charge is a type of positive body energy that facilitates expressive action; tension is a type of negative body energy that inhibits or blocks expressive action.

Similarly, relaxation refers to an overall decrease in the level of energy in the whole body. Relaxation is commonly associated with sleepiness, lethargy, and heaviness. Release, on the other hand, is not so much a condition, state, or mood, but a letting go of the prerequisite physical, emotional, and mental energy that makes movement possible. Release is actually a by-product of the charge. When the body charges, by design it eventually must release. Release is essentially a reaction to the prior charging action of the body. It is not the generalized sensation of letting go experienced after a hard day's work, when on vacation, while sipping a cocktail or having a massage, but a phase in the cyclical process of an integrated and organized movement. An individual in a very relaxed state and an individual bustling with boundless energy are both charging and releasing in relatively equal measure as they respond to the ebb and flow of life.

Movement orientation: contact/withdraw

Orientation refers to the directional forces that motivate the movement of the individual in the environment. A forward and advancing outward movement reflects an individual in *contact* with the environment. Reciprocally, an inward and retreating movement reflects an individual *withdrawing* from the environment. Ideally, an individual makes contact with the environment to fulfill physical or psychological needs and withdraws when these needs have been satisfied. Because the body cannot move in an inward and outward direction at the same time, the efficiency and authenticity of any movement is improved when the mover has a clear understanding of when the body makes *contact* with the environment and when the body *withdraws* from the environment. Identifying the logical pattern of contact and withdrawal is an essential first step when analyzing the structure of any human movement.

Movement flow: free/bound

Free flowing movement patterns allow for each part of the body to integrate in full-bodied physical action. Responsible movement training fosters free flowing patterns of movement that create an ideal physical environment for the expression of thought and feeling. The free flow of energy in the body produces an expansion in the connective tissue. This allows for greater flexibility, dexterity, and range of motion in all the joints. When the flow of energy in the body is bound, muscular tension inhibits the body's movement. The "held" part of the body is unable to participate freely in the expression of thought and feeling. Bound flow is a repressive or regulatory action that distorts natural and spontaneous behavior.

The problem

Pockets of muscular tensions that bind the body's flow:

- contracting the back of the neck;
- clenching the jaw;
- tightening the tongue;
- constricting the throat;
- lifting the shoulders and rib cage;
- tensing the hands and fingers;
- holding in the muscles of the abdomen;
- locking the pelvis;
- tightening the buttocks;
- gripping the upper legs (quadriceps);
- locking the knees;
- clenching or gripping the fingers or toes.

The solution

When working to free the body, the goal is not simply to relax the held part, but rather, to encourage the held part to participate in the larger charging and releasing, contacting and withdrawing, expanding and contracting action that facilitates the movement of the whole body from the center to the periphery.

Bound flow occurs when one part(s) of the body is:

- *charging* when it ideally should be *releasing*;
- *contracting* when it ideally should be *expanding*;
- making *contact* when it ideally should be *withdrawing*.

Any of these misdirected actions disallow the body to flow freely from the *center* to the *periphery*.

In this manner, the body is freed through integrated action and activity, rather than through creating isolated inactive pockets of passivity and relaxation.

Coda: stability

The ability to move the body is not possible without *stability*. Increases in mental and emotional energy must be stabilized if the content of our thoughts and feelings are to receive fluid expression. In integrated expression, *stabilization always precedes mobilization.* One of the reasons that newborns have limited mobility—the inability to get up and walk across the room—is because they lack the prerequisite stability that makes movement possible. *Stability* is defined as the state or quality of being stable. It is also defined as the capacity to return to equilibrium or balance after that equilibrium or balance has been displaced. Stability requires a complex organization of muscular control that transcends simplistic labels such as *tense* or *relaxed*. A stable body is neither *tense* nor *relaxed*, but reflects a sophisticated degree of control that facilitates freedom and mobility. An over tense body lacks freedom and spontaneity; an over relaxed body lacks steadiness and dependability. Finding the correct balance is an artful kinesthetic dance.

Freedom and control

As a child my younger sister was a great tree climber. She could stabilize herself on even the most narrow of branches. She had great control. Consequently, she was free to climb quicker, higher, and further away from the trunk. As she moved from branch to branch, she momentarily relinquished control only to regain it when she arrived at the next branch. Her control provided her with the freedom to climb to the treetop. Because I was unwilling to give up control, I remained lower and closer to the tree's trunk. My tree climbing experiences were less rewarding than my sister's. Like tree climbing, expression is a cyclical journey. It involves a delicate balance between *freedom* and *control*. Freedom provides expression with spontaneity and life. Control provides expression with clarity, form, and order. *Freedom* and *control* are not polar opposites, but two essential components linked directly in varying degrees in all types of human activity.

When upright, the legs and feet are responsible for stabilizing and mobilizing the entire body. Developing stability is largely the business of learning to stand solidly on your own two legs and feet. To the detriment of support, contemporary living has left us more sedentary than at any other time in history. Unlike our ancestors, we spend little time standing on our two legs and feet. We increasingly depend on counter-tops, furniture, and handrails for stability. All this leaning, slouching, resting, and reclining has led to atrophy in the muscles of the legs and feet, which stabilize the body. Paved roads and sidewalks allow for smooth and easy walking. Before such level terrain, the possibility of an unexpected fall or a sprained ankle required that the traveler be more alive, present, and physical in directing and stabilizing the legs and feet.

Increased stability is aided by an understanding of the *grounding of the feet* and *alignment of the leg.*

Grounding the feet

The foot plays a primary role in securing us to the ground. *Grounding the feet* can be likened to the roots of a tree, which spread outward to balance and stabilize the trunk, branches, and foliage above. Similarly, our feet serve to anchor us to the ground below. The idiomatic expressions: "he is well grounded," "her feet are securely planted" and "sure footed," suggest our intuitive understanding of this important stabilizing connection with the earth. Similarly, the idiomatic expressions: "caught up," "hung up," or "having your head up in the clouds" are illustrative of individuals who apparently have lost touch with the solid ground beneath them. Individuals with an inadequate sense of the ground have a poor base for physical action, which interrupts balance and coordination and impedes mobility. A telltale sign of the improper grounding of the feet manifests itself in the gripping and holding of the muscles of the foot. Typically, the muscles of the arch of the foot are tense and the toes are scrunched and gripping the floor beneath for support. This excessive muscular effort is usually a last ditch attempt to restore stability to the body. The greatest support in the feet is achieved when the bones of the feet lengthen and embrace the floor beneath them.

Triangular base of support

When the weight of the body is equally distributed over the feet, a *triangular base of support* is created between the ball of the big toe, the ball of the little toe and the ball of the heel (see Figure 6.6). This triangular base of support forms a type of *tripod* that helps to stabilize and ground the legs and feet. Movement of the foot off the ground in any direction heel, ball toe or toe, ball, heel always involves navigating and coordinating this triangular base of support.

Figure 6.6 Triangular base of support.

Standing your ground

Stand upright with your legs about shoulder width apart. Allow your arms to rest comfortably at your sides. Feel the ball of your heel, the ball of your big toe, and the ball of your little toe grounding you to the floor. Allow the weight of your body to be evenly distributed over your feet. Slowly lean forward. Notice that if you lean too far forward, you lose your stabilizing connection to the floor. Your legs tense, your heels reach up off the floor and your toes begin to grip the floor. Rest. Slowly lean backward. Notice that if you lean too far backward, you also lose your stabilizing connection to the floor. Rest. Repeat leaning to the right and then to the left, becoming aware of when you lose your stabilizing connection to the floor. Rest. Now begin to make a circular movement by leaning forward, then to the right side, then backward, then to the left side and finally back to forward again. Circle around to the right several more times. Each time allow the circle to become smaller and smaller. Continue allowing the circle to become larger and larger. Notice if at anytime you lose your stabilizing connection to the floor. Rest. Repeat circling in the opposite direction.

Leg alignment

The legs are said to be in proper alignment when the hip, knee, and ankle joints work in harmony with each other. Problems with *leg alignment* occur when the knees and ankles fall inward or outward. When the knees fall out of alignment, an individual is said to be either *knocked kneed* or *bow legged* (see Figure 6.7). A similar condition occurs when the ankles fall inward or outward. This is often called *pronation* (inward rotation) or *supination* (outward rotation) (see Figure 6.8). Proper leg alignment leads to more stable physical action. The better the leg alignment, the greater the support in the whole body and the less stress and strain on the ligaments, tendons, and the hip, knee and ankle joints.

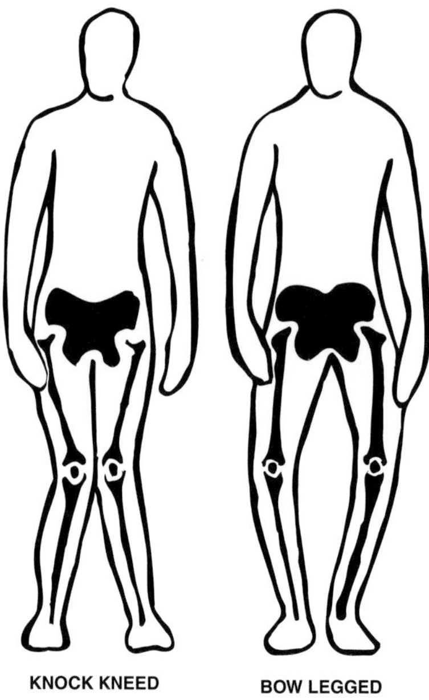

Figure 6.7 Knock kneed/bow legged.

Hierarchy of the leg

The *hierarchy of the leg* is a useful concept in illustrating the coordinated action of the hip, knee, and ankle joints during proper leg alignment. It suggests that the larger joints should assume a greater responsibility for organizing and coordinating movement than the smaller joints. The hierarchy of the leg is maintained when all movement in the lower half of the body is initiated from the thigh socket and not from the knee and ankle joints. Initiating the movement of the legs and feet from the thigh socket, allows the pelvis to assume primary responsibility for transferring the body's weight downward. When this occurs, the weight of the upper body is first suspended in the pelvis and then transferred into the legs and feet in a stable and coordinated effort. In practice, coordinating the hierarchy of the leg requires cultivating a sense of the weight of the upper body being suspended by the pelvis "above" or "over" the legs and feet. This is in contrast to the sensation of allowing the weight of the upper body to "fall" or "drop" into the legs and feet. A telltale sign of a loss of the necessary suspension in the pelvis is demonstrated by the sound of heavy heels pounding the floor. The sensation of the pelvis being suspended over the legs and feet ensures proper leg alignment and the fluid and efficient functioning of the hip, knee, and ankle joints.

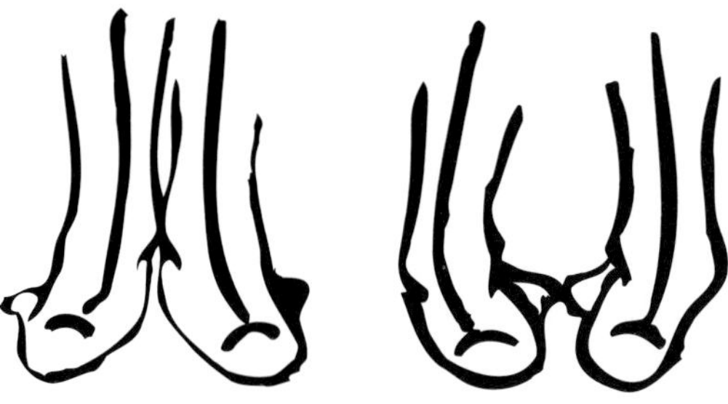

Figure 6.8 Pronation/supination.

Aligning your legs

Stand upright with your legs about shoulder width apart. Allow your arms to rest comfortably at your sides. Lower your pelvis towards the floor and then raise your pelvis away from the floor, by bending and unbending your knees in a comfortable *plié-like action*. Rest and repeat. Each time you lower your pelvis, observe the alignment of your knees and ankles. Maintain the *hierarchy of the leg*. Discourage the knees or ankles from falling inward or outward. The knees should move forward directly over the feet. Rest. Repeat the *plié-like action* with one leg and foot in parallel and one leg and foot rotated outward at a 45 degree angle. Repeat the *plié-like action* with the opposite leg and foot in parallel and the other leg and foot rotated outward at a 45 degree angle. We naturally rotate one leg and foot outward any time we desire to change directions or walk in a circle. It is not usually necessary for actors to practice this *plié-like action* with both legs and feet in rotation. This is typically a dance movement and is only present in more stylized patterns of movement.

STEP 3: TECHNIQUE

We can now put the principles of movement into practice by exploring the voice and body exercises located in Chapter 12. At this first stage of the stacking process, you will only explore the movement component of the exercises; breath, sound, and speech will be added later. In each of the voice and body exercises, this (■) indicates the movement component intended for exploration. After completing the movement component, return to the next section: *Step 4: Improvisation*.

STEP 4: IMPROVISATION

Movement work

The *Movement work* that comprises the stacking process involves the exploration of three related components:

1 prompt
2 phrasing
3 physical properties.

Prompt

A typical improvisation begins with a specific *prompt*, which serves as a physical point of departure. Sometimes the actor is given a physical property as a prompt such as: *indirect*, *charged*, or *diffused*. Commonly, prompts are stated in the form of a verb: "to praise," "to tease," "to demean," or "to accept." (An extensive list of actions is provided in Appendix II.) A great variety of other types of prompts may be used, including idiomatic expressions: "to give someone the evil eye," "to cry bloody murder," or "to keep a stiff upper lip." Any point of departure is acceptable, so long as it suggests a clear physical action that prompts the integrated expression of thought and feeling.

Let's look at an example. I give Steve the prompt "to bang." He accepts the prompt, stands and wanders around the room for a few moments looking perplexed, clearly trying to think of something to do. I ask, "Does the prompt motivate you to any type of physical action?" Steve looks more confused and thinks for a while longer. Then he turns around quickly, looks at the door, and asks, "Who's there?" I have Steve repeat this activity several times and then ask, "What just happened?" He replies, "Someone banged on the door, and I was just checking to see if anyone was there." I respond, "You have just played the expressive action 'to check,' not 'to bang.' You were checking, not banging. The door was banging. Can you bang?"

I tell Steve he is thinking too much. He has intellectually scripted a door-banging scenario, but hasn't explored the prompt physically. Steve looks perplexed: "So what do I do?" I respond, "Why don't you begin to move around the room, and when you're ready allow the banging action to happen in your body and go from there. The banging you are looking for is a physical action that embodies thought and feeling." Steve seems encouraged. He begins to walk around the room. Eventually, with a fair amount of force, Steve runs into the wall. I smile and tell him to continue but not to hurt himself. Steve runs into the wall several more times. Now the movement does appear to embody thought and feeling. Steve is frustrated and distraught each time he bangs into the wall. This is an important first step in the exploration. Steve is well on his way to finding a playable expressive action.

"What are you doing?" I ask. Steve responds defiantly, "I'm banging into a wall." "Yes," I say, "you are literally banging into a wall. Can you think of the wall as a metaphor for a type of human behavior?" He responds, "Yes, it's like I'm beating my head against the wall." "Very good, but do you need a wall to do that?" I ask. He says no and begins to walk around the room. Eventually, he stops, lifts up both hands near his face, and calls out, "I can't take this anymore." I ask him to repeat the action several times. He does. I tell Steve he has successfully played an expressive action. He smiles and asks, "But did I play the expressive action 'to bang'?"

I'm somewhat confused: "Didn't you?" He responds, "Well, I said I was beating my head against the wall, not banging." "Does it matter?" I ask. He says, "I guess not." I explain that as long as we arrive at a physical action that embodies thought and feeling, the improvisation has been successful.

Steve has successfully taken the journey from prompt to expressive action. In time and with experience, this process will become quicker and less labored. Steve is just beginning to learn the ins-and-outs of improvising in the first function. It is important to remember that the prompt is not the expressive action but rather a starting point that leads to expressive action. It stimulates the actor to expressive action; it doesn't dictate or prescribe a specific result.

Different actors respond differently to different prompts. Oftentimes, two actors can take the same prompt and arrive at two completely different expressive actions. Sometimes the prompts are successful; sometimes they are less successful. What stimulates the imagination of one actor often does not stimulate the imagination of another. What is important is that the prompt motivate the actor to some type of physical action. In time and with consistent practice, most actors can take almost any prompt and allow it to lead and direct them to a playable expressive action.

Moving barre: the prompt

Pair an action from the list located in Appendix II with each of the 20 physical properties of an expressive action. For example:

- **energy**: charge: *to bark*/release: *to fumble*;
- **orientation**: contact: *to meddle*/withdraw: *to cower*;
- **size**: expand: *to radiate*/contract: *to sag*;
- **progression**: center: *to wallow*/periphery: *to pester*;
- **flow**: free: *to cruise*/bound: *to gnash*;
- **direction**: direct: *to drill*/indirect: *to amble*;
- **speed**: fast: *to lash*/slow: *to linger*;
- **weight**: heavy: *to ram*/ light: *to flitter*;
- **control**: stable: *to thrust*/unstable: *to fumble*;
- **focus**: sharp: *to glare*/diffused: *to zone out*.

Explore each prompt you have selected physically.

Phrasing

Once the prompt has motivated the actor to a playable expressive action, attention can be turned to phrasing. This is very similar to the verbal phrasing of a sentence. A well-phrased sentence progresses naturally and fluidly—word-by-word—toward the verbal expression of a complete thought and feeling.

Figure 6.9 Wave.

Similarly, an expressive action progresses naturally and fluidly—weight shift by weight shift—toward the physical expression of a complete thought and feeling. Work on phrasing is largely work on rhythm: the progressive and orderly flow with which an expressive action begins, develops, and subsides. When an expressive action is well phrased, it has a rich rhythmical life. Phrasing is essentially organizing a weight shift or a series of weight shifts into a single phrase that has a clearly defined beginning, middle, and end. We are very aware of how a sentence begins and ends on the page but less aware of how a thought and a feeling begins and ends in the body. *When and where does the movement begin? How does it develop and mature? When and how does it resolve, end, or fade away?* These are the essential physical questions to be explored in the body when working on phrasing.

Ultimately, successful phrasing occurs when a series of expressive actions are strung together one right after the other in a seamless, fluid, and uninterrupted manner. Ideally, each expressive action should flow naturally and rhythmically into the next like a series of consecutive waves of the ocean. Scientists describe the two essential points on a wave as the *crest* (the high point) and the *trough* (the low point) (see Figure 6.9). Learning to sequence one expressive action after another is largely learning to ride the crest and rest in the trough, to balance the seamless sequence of activity and passivity, doing and non-doing, motion and rest—the natural ebb and flow of life. Like the waves of the ocean, expressive actions do not always come in regular intervals. Some days the tides are choppy and quick, other times the swells are long and slow with much time in between one wave and the next.

Lets look at phrasing in action. Sonya has received a prompt and has explored it physically. She is now ready to work on phrasing. I ask her to repeat her expressive action several times. She does. She is clearly having trouble with phrasing. She starts and stops in an arbitrary manner that looks more like an exercise than natural human behavior. I say, "Your rhythm seems very choppy. Can you structure each expressive action in your body so that it has a clearly organized beginning, middle, and end?"

Sonya responds, "I know what the expressive action is. I sense it and feel it. I just have difficulty organizing it."

I say, "Each expressive action has its own rhythmical life, but finding this life will require some exploration in your own body. The rhythm of an expressive action is similar to the rhythm of your breath. There is a need for breath. The breath comes. The breath goes. There is a rest. And the whole cycle repeats. The expressive action should come and go in the same way." She plays her expressive action several more times. I suggest she is rushing.

Sonya says, "It is like I just get nervous and I end the expressive action before it has completely resolved and then I feel like I should be doing something, and I start again before I am ready."

"Give the expressive action all the time that it needs," I reply. "Direct your attention to how the expressive action begins and ends. Often when an expressive action begins and ends naturally, everything else seems to fall into place."

Sonya asks, "How does an expressive action begin and end?"

I suggest this is a difficult question to answer, but I provide the following suggestions to help her. "With respect to initiating the action, does the impulse for expressive action spring from something that is going on inside you—*withdraw*—or is it motivated by something going on outside of you—*contact*?" Sonya says the motivation for her expressive action is prompted by a series of internal sensations. I suggest that she attend to these sensations before initiating the expressive action. "You seem to start the expressive action arbitrarily and mechanically. Can you wait for an impulse to begin?"

"Yes, but how long can I wait?" she asks.

"Until the impulse for a new action comes."

"How do I know it will come?"

"New impulses always come. Just like your next breath always comes. Your job is simple. Wait and direct your attention toward your internal sensations until you feel the desire to express yourself. Now, with respect to ending the action, does it turn off rather quickly like flipping off a light switch, or does it fade away more slowly like turning down a dimmer switch on a chandelier?" Sonya states it turns off quickly. "Great, so when you're finished, you're finished. Do not linger or second-guess the end of your action. When you are finished, let it go. Then rest and repeat the expressive action again." She plays her expressive action several more times. The rhythm and the phrasing are much improved

Moving barre: phrasing

Using the prompts from the previous barre exploration, you can now begin to explore the phrasing of each of the expressive actions selected. Repeat each expressive action several times, taking a short rest or pause in between each repetition. Allow each expressive action to become fluid and seamless, structuring it so that it has a clearly defined beginning, middle, and end. *Where does the action begin in your body? How does the action escalate and develop? When does it diminish and resolve?*

Physical properties

Having developed a playable, well-phrased and repeatable expressive action, the next step is to investigate the physical properties that define its essential structure.

Jan is playing the expressive action "to snap." She has received the prompt and organized it into a well-phrased expressive action. The expressive action looks something like this: she gets a disgusted grimace on her face and quickly turns her head in a snapping-like manner.

Progression: center/periphery

I ask Jan to play her action several times. She does. I observe that the lower half of her body is stationary and disconnected. Jan simply turns her head and snaps. Everything from the head down is immobile. I ask, "Where in your body do you feel the action is centered?"

Jan pauses and responds, "In my pelvis."

I suspect she thinks that is what I want to hear, that like a good and conscientious student she wants to please. "Are you sure?" I ask. I ask her to repeat the expressive action several times. She does and then says: "The action is centered in my head."

This is an important discovery. "Yes," I say, "is it possible that your whole body could snap and not just your head?" She says yes and repeats the expressive action. This time the movement begins in her pelvis, and her whole body seems to snap. The expressive action is full-bodied, more committed, and the size of the thought and feeling being expressed is more powerful. Jan repeats this centered action several times. She asks, "Which is right?"

I respond, "They are both right. The body organizes thought and feeling in many ways. In general, important, committed, and spontaneous expression engages the whole body and moves outward from the pelvis to the head, arms, hands, legs, and feet. Less committed and less important expressive actions are sometimes played primarily on the periphery. Sometimes, tensions in the body can also interfere with the natural progression of an expressive action." I ask her to play the expressive action several more times, alternating between centering the action in the pelvis and centering the action in her head. She does. I ask her what she has discovered.

"They're both real. The centered one is just more intense and powerful."

Flow: free/bound

I respond, "Is there any difference in the flow of these expressive actions? Is one more *free* or *bound* than the other?"

Jan knows the answer to this question immediately. "When the expressive action is centered in my head, I tend to hold the rest of my body back. I feel tenser. It's like I don't want my whole body to do anything, because it seems so rude. When I move from my center, my whole body follows and plays the expressive action. I really "snap," and it's intense. Which is right?"

I tell her, "Just be you. It is only pretend. We can be rude when improvising and not worry about the consequences. Both options have a unique place in the larger context of human expression. If it is important to you not to be rude, I suspect the expressive action centered in your head is best. However, if you really want to make your point and communicate the depth and richness of your thoughts and feelings, the expressive action centered in your pelvis that flows freely through your whole body is probably your best bet."

Size: expand/contract

Jan repeats the expressive action again, alternating between centering it in her pelvis and centering it in her head. I now direct her attention to the relative degree of expansion and contraction in her body. "What did you discover?"

"My body expands as I express myself and contracts when I am finished. When I expand, my left arm reaches out like I am trying to push someone away."

"Is there a difference when the action is centered in your pelvis and when it's centered in your head?"

"Yes. When the expressive action is centered in my head, tension keeps my body from expanding like it does when the expressive action begins in my center."

Energy: charge/release

"Is any of this related to the manner in which the energy charges and releases in your body?" I ask.

"Yes, it seems all connected. When I expand, the energy in my body charges, and when I contract, the energy in my body releases, but when my body is tense and I am holding back, I do not feel I release as much. It seems like I kinda hold the feeling when I hold my muscles, and I feel kinda frustrated."

"So freely expressing the feeling is more pleasurable?"

Jan giggles. "Yes, but it is such a negative feeling, I would not have thought so."

"I think we always feel better—at least on some level—when we express our thoughts and feelings, regardless of whether we perceive them as positive or negative."

Orientation: contact/withdraw

"Talk to me about contact and withdraw," I say.

"That is very simple. I contact when I express myself and withdraw when I'm finished"

"Very good," I say, "I think it's just that simple. The expressive action 'to snap' has very strong contact. However, other expressive actions like 'to shy away', 'to cower,' or 'to retreat' might be organized very differently Sometimes we express ourselves when we make contact, and other times we express ourselves when we withdraw."

I ask, "Can you tell me something about the action in the first function?"

"Yes. It is very fast, sharp, direct, and stable, but mostly has really strong contact . . . and I would not say it's heavy, but it certainly is not light."

Rather quickly Jan was able to identify how the minor physical properties—*direction*, *speed*, *weight*, *control*, and *focus*—affect the quality and character of the expressive action "to snap."

Moving barre: physical properties

Continuing to develop your barre, you can now begin to explore the physical properties of each of the expressive actions selected:

- **Energy**: Where do I feel a *charge* in my body? Where do I feel *release*?
- **Orientation**: When do I *contact* the outside world? When do I *withdraw*?
- **Size**: When does my body *expand*? When does my body *contract*?
- **Progression**: Where is the action located in my body—in the *center* or the *periphery*? How does the action progress from the *center* of my body to the *periphery*?
- **Flow**: Is the action *free* or *bound*? Am I holding myself back or letting myself go?

The minor properties: *direction*: direct/indirect; *speed*: fast/slow; *weight*: heavy/light; *control*: stable/unstable; *focus*: sharp/diffused should also be investigated.

A dozen suggestions

The following suggestions, though not absolute rules, have proved useful when improvising in the first function:

1 Work in an empty space without props, furniture, or costumes. The body should be the sole means and method of expression.
2 Remember that there is a fundamental difference between repeating a movement and playing an expressive action. Each time an expressive action is repeated, although the quality of the movement should be somewhat similar, the expressive action itself is always varied and flexible. Just as no two moments in life are the same, no two expressive actions are the same.
3 Avoid playing physical states, such as tired, drunk, dizzy, or stoned. These physical states are not expressive actions. However, physical states may affect the manner in which you play an expressive action.
4 Avoid playing emotional states, such as sadness, joy, or anger. Feeling must always be the indirect result of the expressive action.
5 Avoid miming absent objects. Car doors, apples, toothpicks, and playing cards are not an essential component of any expressive action and are unnecessary in improvisation.

6 Avoid actions that require a partner, such as handshakes, punching, caressing, or tickling. While these actions certainly contain and reveal thought and feeling, they can only be practiced effectively with a partner. (However, it is useful to direct your expressive action toward an imaginary "listener," in much the same way you would when auditioning or performing a monologue.)
7 Do only what is essential—avoid any unnecessary movement or gestures. Streamline the expressive action. You only need the activity that is "essential" for the expression of thought and feeling. Extraneous movement or vocal activity only creates interference and muddies the character of the expressive action.
8 Finish your business—play your expressive action completely. Continue to play the expressive action until the thought and feeling has been fully expressed. For example, if you are "pleading," continue "to plead" until your message has been heard. If you are warning, continue "to warn" until the warning has been heeded. This helps ensure that your actions have a clearly defined beginning, middle, and end.
9 Complete all weight shifts—don't become entangled in incomplete or muddied physical action. When the movement of the body is clarified, thought and feeling are also clarified.
10 Look for universal expressive actions that have been played in all times by all people in all places.
11 Move first, think second. It is not necessary to have any preconceived mental notions about how to play any given expressive action. Simply explore the expressive action in your body. This type of nonintellectual exploration is similar to a musician playing with musical notes to create a melody or a dancer playing with movement to create a piece of choreography. The process is intuitive and experiential.
12 Have fun. Playfulness is key. A spirit of play sets up a creative, impulsive, environment for improvisation.

Chapter 7

Breathing

STEP 1: PRELIMINARIES

The investigation of the breathing center begins with the preliminary improvisations located in *Chapter 11: Preliminaries*. At this second stage of the stacking process, you will explore how your breath unites with movement in integrated expressive action. In each of the improvisations, this (●) icon indicates the breathing component intended for exploration. It will be useful to repeat the entire stacking process—starting with movement (■) and then adding or stacking the breath (●). After completing the breathing component of the preliminary improvisations, return to *Step 2: Principles* located below.

STAGE 2: PRINCIPLES

This experiential approach to the principles of breathing is a practical investigation of the *action of the breath*. It is rooted in an exploration of the physical sensations that make breathing possible. Its primary focus centers on how the breath *charges* and *releases*, *contacts* and *withdraws*, *expands* and *contracts* in a *free flowing* manner from the *center* of the body outward to the *periphery*.

The breath provides the framework and the foundation for sound. Efficient and coordinated breathing paves the way for a strong, free, resonant voice. The breath is a type of highway on which the voice travels. The role of the breath is to stabilize the voice of the speaker. The breath is being managed optimally when an appropriate degree of pressure in the breath stream vibrates the vocal folds and propels the voice forward into the mouth and throat, so that the lips, teeth, tongue, and jaw can shape the sound into meaningful words, phrases, and sentences. If the pressure in the breath stream is insufficient, weak or erratic, the voice loses its power and clarity.

The purpose of breath training is to develop flexibility, dexterity, strength, control, and freedom in the muscles that make breathing possible. A telltale sign of faulty breath management is excessive muscular tension. When this occurs, the muscles of the throat, tongue, jaw, neck, shoulders, and rib cage desperately attempt to supply, bolster, and stabilize an unsteady and weak breath stream. The body fights the breath, and the breath fights the body. Inhalation is forced, audible, and overtly muscular. Exhalation is strained, pressed, and congested.

While most people have little trouble with breath management in daily life, the rigorous demands of acting in large spaces, over long periods of time, in highly challenging physical and emotional situations, places special demands on the actor's voice. Without specialized training, the actor often strains and pushes the voice in a desperate attempt to express large and powerful feelings (or simply to be heard in the back row of the theater). Taken to extremes, this pushing and straining can lead to vocal problems requiring medical attention. Even less severe vocal stress is physically debilitating and aesthetically unsatisfying. A voice that is pushed or forced is not only tired and strained but lacks range, flexibility, and a complexity of tone that is essential to the nuanced expression of thought and feeling.

Two groups of muscles make breath management possible:

1 muscles of inspiration—the breathing-in muscles;
2 muscles of expiration—the breathing-out muscles.

Typically, faulty breath management occurs for two reasons:

1 insufficient inhalation; and/or
2 a poorly managed exhalation.

The primary muscle of inspiration is the *diaphragm*. This dome-shaped muscle located in the middle of the body separates the chest from the abdomen. The diaphragm is attached to the lungs, and during inhalation moves downward toward the abdomen. This downward movement increases the volume of the lungs, causing the air pressure in the lungs to decrease, creating a type of vacuum, which draws the breath into the lungs. Another important but secondary group of inspiratory muscles are the intercostals, which are located between the ribs and assist the diaphragm by expanding the rib cage during inhalation. The primary muscles of expiration are a group of inner abdominal muscles located above and below the navel on the front and the sides of the body. During active expiration, these muscles instinctively draw the abdomen in, increasing the pressure in the breath stream, thus providing stability for the outgoing breath (see Figure 7.1).

How the "breathing-in" and "breathing-out" muscles work together to make sound possible is a complicated scientific subject. All I can safely say here is that successful breath management involves varying degrees of activity and passivity in the muscles of inspiration and expiration. These muscles work with and against each other to stabilize the flow of the outgoing breath. Successful breath management is made possible by a gradual transfer of energy from the muscles of inspiration to the muscles of expiration, creating

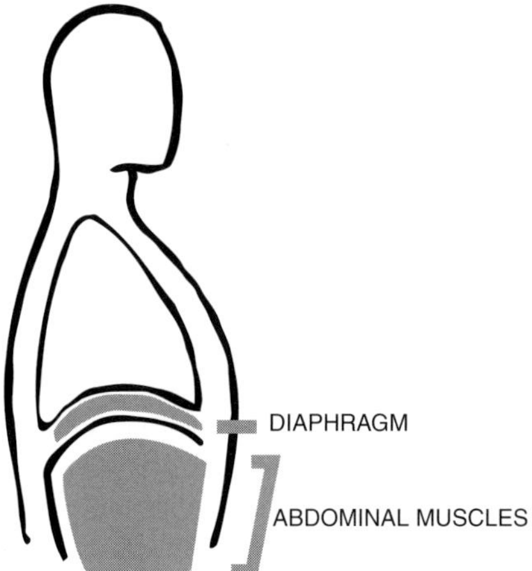

Figure 7.1 Breathing musculature.

a balance of tension, which provides just enough pressure to suspend the breath and stabilize the tone.

Natural breathing rhythm

It is useful to begin the exploration of the breathing process with a focus on the natural rhythm of the breath. The foundation of successful breath management springs from the natural rhythm of the breath. The natural rhythm of the breath is relatively simple: the breath comes, the breath goes, there is a slight pause, a new breath comes and goes, as the pattern repeats. The natural rhythm of the breath is often compared with the rise and fall of ocean waves. Each breath, like each wave of the ocean, is punctuated with a clearly defined beginning, middle, and end. Whether the quality of your breathing is calm and serene or rough and tumultuous, whether you are at rest or at play, whether you are expressing complex thoughts or insignificant banter, deep feelings or ambivalent retorts, long sentences or short phrases, whispering or shouting—the essential rhythm of your breath is consistent and universal. There is always an inhalation followed by an exhalation. Sensing the breath in the context of *receiving*, *giving*, and *resting* promotes a free, effortless, rhythmic approach to managing your incoming and outgoing breath. Central to the idea of giving and receiving is recognizing that the act of inhalation and exhalation are inextricably linked. There is not one action of breathing in and another action of breathing out, but rather one integrated breathing action experienced in two phases. *Inhalation* and *exhalation* share a reciprocal and corresponding *giving* and *receiving* relationship. Ideally, it is impossible to *sense* one without the other.

Giving and receiving

This exercise is designed to put you in touch with your natural breathing rhythm.

Hook-lying position: Lie comfortably on your back. Bend your knees so that the soles of your feet make contact with the floor. Your feet should rest in an unstrained position near your buttocks. Direct your knees upward in line with your feet. Allow the weight of the floor to support you. (This exercise is called the hook-lying position because the folded legs form a hook-like shape.) Become aware of the rising and falling action of your breath. Receive a new breath—inhale. Give your breath away—exhale. Repeat the cycle. Observe the rhythm of your breath for several moments. Notice how each breath has a clearly defined beginning, middle, and end. Rest and repeat.

Observe the *giving* and *receiving* action of your breath from five different perspectives:

- *Energy: charge/release*. Sense the energy of your body increasing and decreasing as your breath enters and leaves your body.
- *Orientation: contact/withdraw*. Allow your awareness to travel outward on your outgoing breath and inward on your ingoing breath.
- *Size: expand/contract*. Sense how the size of your body increases and decreases to accommodate the incoming and outgoing breath.
- *Progression: center/periphery*. Allow the movement of your breath to begin in the center of your body (the middle of your belly and travel outward to the periphery in all directions (up into your chest and down toward your pelvis).
- *Free flow*. Allow the breath to come and go without physical or mental interruptions.

Breath progression: center/periphery

The *breathing center* is located in the middle of the belly. The natural progression of the breath flows freely from the middle of the belly outward to the *periphery* in all directions. Sensing the movement of the *diaphragm*, the large muscle of inspiration, which separates the chest and the abdomen, develops an awareness of the breathing center. The diaphragm descends during inhalation, causing a pronounced movement in the middle of the belly in corresponding outward and downward directions. The movement of the body during diaphragmatic breathing is similar to dropping a stone into a pool of water. The circular ripples of the water emanate most strongly from the *center* (the middle of the belly) and progress with less power and intensity as they move outward toward the *periphery* (upward into the chest and downward toward the pelvis). The progression is directly related to the intensity of the thought and feeling being expressed. Smaller thoughts and feeling travel a smaller distance from the center, while larger thoughts and feelings progress further outward to the periphery.

Peripheral breathing

Breathing that is not centered in the middle of the belly but in the upper chest is called *clavicle breathing*. In this type of breathing, the diaphragm is not initiating

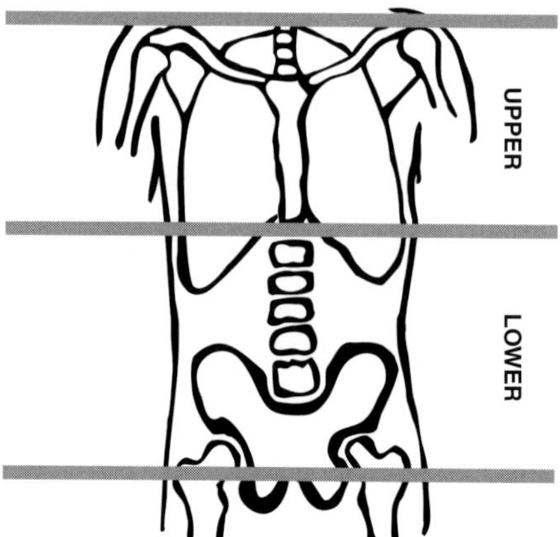

Figure 7.2 Breathing spaces.

and coordinating the breathing action, and the predominate movement in the body occurs in the upper chest near the collarbone. Breathing centered too high in the body poses numerous problems (Anderson 1977, 31–68):

- *Capacity*: The muscles of the upper chest and collarbone area are too high in the body to expand the lower lungs to full capacity. Since less breath is taken in, less breath is available to sustain the tone.
- *Efficiency*: The muscles of the upper chest and collarbone area do not have the power or strength of the diaphragm and the abdominal muscles to coordinate the breathing action.
- *Support*: The muscles that provide breath support are primarily located in the abdomen, not the upper chest. When breathing is centered too high in the body, the ability to control and stabilize the outgoing breath is compromised.
- *Location*: When muscles in the upper chest and throat are wrongly engaged to support the voice, the action of these muscles—largely because of their close proximity to the throat—interferes with the efficient functioning of the vocal folds. Because the abdominal muscles are further away from the vocal folds, they are able to support the voice efficiently without interfering with the action of the vocal folds.

Breathing center—panting

Panting—breathing in and out very rapidly—is a practical way to initiate and actively sense the action the breathing center. Though a larger and more expansive movement is ultimately the goal, this initial panning-action is foundational and paves the way for centered breathing. Because this action is quick and reflexive, it is virtually impossible to pant without engaging the diaphragm.

Begin in the *hook-lying position* as in the previous exercise.

Let the abdominal muscles soften. Allow your jaw to drop so that the breath flows freely in and out of your mouth. Initiate a quick and vibrant panting action from your breathing center. Escalate the intensity of the panting for several seconds. Then let it subside naturally. (Do not hyperventilate.) The panting sequence should have a clearly defined beginning, middle, and end. Sense the action of the diaphragm in the middle of your belly. Observe the progression of the breath from the center to the periphery. Repeat this process two or three more times, resting in between each panting-action.

Breath size: expand/contract

The journey of the breath from the *center* to the *periphery* creates obvious changes in the *size* of the body. The circumference of the chest and abdomen increases as the breath enters the body and decreases as the breath leaves the body. *Expansion* occurs during inhalation; *contraction* occurs during exhalation. The skillful expansion and contraction of the body involves the coordination of the *upper breathing space* and the *lower breathing space* (see Figure 7.2). The upper breathing space begins at the collarbone and extends downward to the bottom of the breastbone. The lower breathing space begins at the base of the breastbone and extends downward to the pubic bone. However, the breathing spaces extend around to the sides and the back of the body as well. Effective breathing involves the integrated action of the upper and lower breathing spaces.

In general, a greater degree of expansion should be sensed in the front of the body in the lower breathing space, because (see Figure 7.3):

1 During inhalation, the diaphragm descends downward toward the pelvis, creating a greater depth of movement in the lower breathing space.
2 The ribs in the lower breathing space do not extend all the way across the front of the body as they do in the upper breathing space. (The two lowest ribs are floating ribs and are not attached to the breastbone.) Consequently, a soft malleable space is created in the lower breathing space that is responsive to the inward and outward movement of the breath.
3 A portion of the front ribs in the lower breathing space are comprised of flexible cartilage and not solid bone like the ribs in the upper breathing space, allowing for a greater degree of movement in the lower breathing space.

Therefore, the most pronounced breathing action in the majority of skilled speakers and singers occurs in the front of the body in the lower breathing space.

This is not to suggest that there is no movement in the upper breathing space or on the sides and back of the body. Both the upper and lower breathing spaces must be free to move in response to the incoming and outgoing breath. Breathing is a full-bodied activity that with awareness and sensitivity can be felt from the

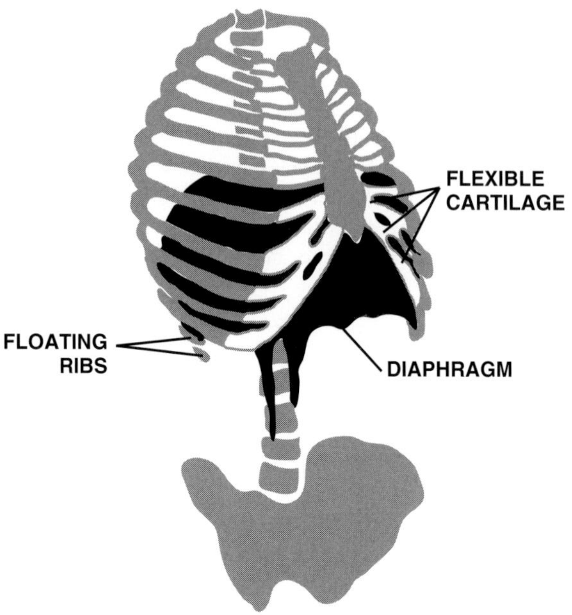

Figure 7.3 Breathing anatomy.

collarbone all the way down to the pubic bone. However, a disproportionate displacement in the upper breathing space interferes with the architectural design of the body and is most probably the result of misdirected muscular effort. But care must also be taken not to push or force the breath into the lower breathing space. Most often, the lower breathing space can be accessed indirectly by releasing unnecessary tensions in the belly that inhibit the breath from dropping deeply into the body. In practice, it is better to think of taking a *complete breath* rather than a *deep breath*. This directive invites a full and adequate inhalation that is never pressed or forced into the lower breathing space. Ultimately, the goal is a free and complete inhalation linked directly to the size of the thought and feeling being expressed.

Breathing spaces

Begin in the *hook-lying position* as described in the previous exercises. Place one hand on your chest (*upper breathing space*) and the other hand on your belly (*lower breathing space*). This will increase your awareness of the movement in the upper and lower breathing spaces. Pant quickly and vibrantly from your breathing center. Rest. Sense the relative degree of expansion and contraction in your upper and lower breathing spaces. Slow the panting sequence down, taking deeper and more complete breaths. Do not work too hard. Receive your breath naturally and give it away freely.

Allow your inhalation and the exhalation to be relatively equal in length. Sense the relative degree of *expansion* and *contraction* in your upper and lower breathing spaces. Rest. Repeat this action again, this time taking even slower and deeper breaths. Once again, sense the relative degree of *expansion* and *contraction* in your upper and lower breathing spaces. Rest. Always take care not to hyperventilate.

Breath orientation: contact/withdraw

The breath travels inside the body and outside into the environment. This *inner-to-outer* and *back-again* action plays a pivotal role in guiding and directing the *orientation* of the speaker. The sensations associated with *withdraw* are linked directly to inhalation; the sensations associated with *contact* are linked directly to exhalation. Inhalation reflects a period of inspiration—both physical and mental. The speaker is "inspired" by internal thoughts and feelings that have not yet been externally expressed. The contact phase occurs when the speaker shares this inspiration with the outside world.

When the natural process of contact and withdrawal is interrupted, breathing problems invariably develop. Individuals experiencing unwanted inner emotional turmoil often breathe shallowly and incompletely. By not breathing in, they hope to avoid the unpleasant feelings churning around inside them, thereby, interrupting the *withdraw phase* of the breath cycle. Similarly, individuals whose outer world is stressful are often afraid to breathe out. By not breathing out, they hope to avoid the conflict and negativity that surrounds them, thereby interrupting the *contact phase* of the breath cycle. Efficient breathing is linked directly to developing the courage and personal maturity needed to accept and deal responsibly with the host of internal and external stimuli that accompany living.

The inward and outward breath

Begin in the *hook-lying position* as described in the previous panting exploration. Sense the rise and fall of your breath for several moments. Rest. Become aware of the rising and falling action of your breath once again. Each time you receive a new breath, close your eyes and turn your attention inward—*withdraw*. Each time you breathe out, open your eyes and focus on something in the room—*contact*. Rest and repeat. Enjoy the contrasting sensations of *contact* and *withdrawal* associated with the outgoing and ingoing breath.

Breath flow: free/bound

Free breathing is fluid, flexible, adaptable, and unlabored. Bound breathing is rigid, shallow, pressed, and labored. The easiest way to free the breath is by releasing unnecessary tensions that interrupt the natural action of the breath. Common spots of tension often include the jaw, lips, tongue, and throat as well as the shoulders, rib cage, and belly. When releasing the tensions that are interrupting the freedom of the breath, take care not to over-relax the whole body. The directive to *relax* can often result in the unwanted experience of *collapse*. A drop in physical energy is invariably accompanied by a drop in mental and emotional energy. Freedom in the breathing musculature does not have to come at the expense of energy and vitality in the rest of the body. In a deeply relaxed state, the possibility for vital, active, energetic expression is severely limited. Ultimately, the actor must breathe freely when the body is alert, energized, and expressive as well as when it is released, relaxed, and restful. Remember that *tension* is a troublesome enemy, *energy* a trusted friend. Physical tensions in the body rarely need to be relaxed, only redirected into more useful physical actions that help us express our thoughts and feelings.

Breathing and feeling

When the breath is free, feeling is also free. The *feeling center* of the body and the *breathing center* of the body are both situated, more or less, in the middle of the belly. The ancient Greeks held that the diaphragm was the center of joy, laughter, grief, weeping, pride, and self-reliance. Our most powerful thoughts and feelings invariably manifest themselves in our breath. Consequently, anytime we are holding onto our feelings, we are inevitably holding our breath.

Breath energy: charge/release

Successful breath management involves regulating *energy* in the body by structuring and organizing the rate and flow of the exhalation. This involves cultivating two distinct physical sensations while exhaling:

- Release (the breath falls from the body).
- Charge (the body carries the breath).

Release (the breath falls from the body)

Allowing the *breath to fall from the body* is a simple and straightforward method of breath management. This type of exhalation occurs when the breath *passively* leaves the body. When we breathe in this manner, no effort is made to regulate or manage the outgoing breath. We simply receive a new breath in, then let the breath go. A practical way to practice this type of passive breath management is by *sighing*. [My understanding of the concept of the sigh is deeply indebted to my initial voice training with Kristin Linklater (1976, 25–34).] When we sigh, the breath falls from the body freely and without interruption. The body experiences this decrease in physical energy as a *release*: it is like blowing up a balloon and letting it go. Most important, this passive type of exhalation occurs without any assistance from the muscles of expiration. Learning to allow the breath to "fall from the body" involves cultivating the sensation of deep release not only in the breathing musculature but also in the whole body. This sighing-action is foundational and paves the way for more complex breath management. A breathing structure that cannot freely release the breath invariably has trouble managing larger and more sophisticated breathing actions. Consequently, the sigh is an essential first step in the breath management training process.

Charge (the body carries the breath)

Allowing the *body to carry the breath* is more complex. In this type of exhalation, the breath *actively* leaves the body: the rate and flow of the outgoing breath is stabilized and lengthened. A practical way to practice active exhalation is by *hissing*—sustaining an interrupted, continuous "sss" sound while exhaling. When breathing in this manner, the breath does not rush out passively but is actively sustained in the body. Ideally, the breath leaves the body in a coordinated and organized manner, not in erratic fits and starts. The body experiences this regulated emission of breath as a *charge*. Hissing, like sighing, paves the way for integrated breath management.

Essential to this active type of exhalation is cultivating the sensation of the whole "body carrying the breath." Ideally, the rate at which the breath is stabilized is determined by a variety of factors linked directly to the size and intensity of the thought or feeling being expressed.

All speech acts exists somewhere between *charge* and *release*. Efficient breathing requires striking the perfect balance of energy. Sometimes our speech is highly charged, sometimes it is more released, and sometimes it falls in the middle. As the body learns the varying degrees of charge and release required for various types of expression, the breathing musculature reflexively supports the voice of the speaker. When the body and the breath work together, the flow of the outgoing breath instinctively harmonizes with the movement of the body. The speaker does not have to think about releasing, regulating, or controlling the outgoing breath. The action of the body provides a structure and framework, which is transferred or telegraphed to the action of the breath. When this occurs, the breath is released, sustained, and replaced in harmony with the movement of the body without unnecessary stress or strain.

Pant, sigh, and hiss

Pant

Stand upright with your legs about shoulder-width apart. Allow your arms to rest comfortably at your sides. Let your abdominal muscles soften. Allow your jaw to drop so that the breath flows freely in and out of your mouth. Initiate a quick and vibrant panting action. Sense the action of the diaphragm in the breathing center.

Sigh

With an awareness of the breathing center, bend and unbend your knees in a comfortable plié-like action several times. As you bend your knees, allow the *breath to fall from your body*. Each time you straighten your knees, receive a new breath. The falling breath should be similar to a *sigh*—an unvoiced "huh" sound. Allow the release of physical energy in your whole body to coordinate the release of the outgoing breath. Rest and repeat.

Hiss

Take three steps forward. As you move forward, allow your *body to carry the breath* as you sustain a simple "sss" sound over the three-step phrase. Feel the buildup of physical energy in your whole body that lengthens and stabilizes the "sss" sound. Rest and repeat.

Pant + sigh + hiss

Initiate a new panting action. Rest. Allow your *breath to fall from your body* during four knee bends. Rest. Allow your *body to carry your breath* during four steps forward. Rest. Initiate another panting action and try five knee-bends and five steps forward, followed by another panting action and six, seven, eight knee-bends and corresponding forward steps, perhaps more, as many as feel comfortable. Do not push or strain by going beyond what you are able to manage. Enjoy the contrasting sensation of the *breath falling from* and *being carried by* your body—*charge* and *release*.

Pant, sigh, and hiss

The previous exploration presented a logical and sequential progression of physical energy that was intended to lead to a flexible and efficient breathing action. It is useful at this point to review the previous panting, sighing, and hissing actions in three sequential steps. The first step—the *pant* is designed to place you in touch with your *breathing center*. During this panting action, you should sense a very rapid and small expanding and contracting action in the middle of your belly. The second step—the *sigh* is an indirect and more comprehensive method of stimulating the global breathing musculature. It encourages you to take a more complete inhalation that leads to a more significant expansion in the *breathing space*. Finally, the *hiss* is designed to indirectly stimulate the muscular support system that reflexively stabilizes the release of the out-going breath. Take a few moments and review this three-step process: Pant for a few moments, receive a new breath and sigh, receive a new breath and hiss. This sequential panting, sighing, and hissing exercise is designed to put you in touch with a natural and integrated breath management experience in three successive stages.

STEP 3: TECHNIQUE

We can now put the principles of breathing into practice by exploring the *lying and breathing exercises* located in Chapter 12. At this second stage of the stacking process, you will explore how your breath unites with movement in integrated physical action. In each of the lying and breathing exercises, this (●) icon indicates the breathing component intended for exploration. It will be useful to repeat the entire stacking process—starting with movement (■) and then adding or stacking the breath (●). After completing the breathing component, return to the next section: *Step 4: Improvisation*.

STEP 4: IMPROVISATION

Breath and movement work

The b*reath* and m*ovement work* that comprises the stacking process begins with an exploration of energy.

The b*reath and movement work* that comprises the stacking process explores how the body and breath unite in integrated expressive action. The goal is to allow the outgoing breath to harmonize and intermingle with the movement of the body. The most important directive when exploring the *breath and movement work* is cultivating the ability to sense the physical properties inherent in the action of the body revealing themselves in the *sighing* and *hissing* actions of the breath. This occurs when the physical properties—*charge*, *fast*, *sharp*, *unstable*, etc.—experienced in the body are imprinted and transferred to the action of the breath. In this rich and dynamic sensory experience, the breath becomes fully integrated and embodied.

Release—breath falls from the body

Matt has taken a prompt and organized it into a playable expressive action. The expressive action looks something like this: Matt, in a full-bodied physical gesture takes a step forward and lifts up both arms and slowly releases them downward to their resting place. The lifting of the arms occurs very quickly, and the lowering of the arms occurs very slowly.

Matt plays his expressive action several times. I ask, "Are you expressing yourself on the *charge* or the *release*? Do you feel that your thoughts and feelings *fall from your body*, or are they *being carried by your body*?"

He says, "They fall. As I lower my arms thought and feeling seems to just dribble away."

We begin to work with the breath while exploring the physical phrase. He repeats the expressive action. "Where does your body release?" I ask.

"As I take a step forward and slowly lower my arms."

"Very good. Now when your body releases, can you explore allowing the breath to fall from your body as well?"

As the energy in his body releases, his breath releases on a simple sigh, a voiceless "huh" sound. The release of the breath and the release of the body are seemingly inseparable. The *weight shift* results in a corresponding *breath-shift*. The breath has become embodied. He repeats this several times. The expressive action becomes deeper and more committed. "What is different?" I ask.

"I feel like when I release my breath I get more in touch with my feelings. It is more vulnerable and committed."

"Yes, but every expressive action organizes the breath energy differently. Sometimes the organization of the breath energy makes us feel more aggressive, introspective or energized. It is always very different. The wonderful thing about the breath is that it often puts us directly in touch with our feelings."

Charge—body carries the breath

Julie has received a prompt and organized it into a playable expressive action that looks something like this: she takes a full-bodied weight shift and lifts both arms out in front of her body and takes several steps backward. Her action is methodical and measured. Her eyes are intense and beaming. She is clearly expressing a thought and feeling. I ask, "What are you doing?"

Julie responds, "I'm not sure."

"What does it feel like?"

"I just move backwards in a *slow, stable* way with *sharp* focus. Like I'm backing down . . . sorta . . . no, it's more like I am washing my hands of all this mess." She repeats the action several more times.

"Do you feel that the expressive action *falls from your body* or is being *carried by your body?*" I ask.

"It is carried. My body is charged the whole time that I step backward."

"Very good. Now as your body charges, can you explore allowing the body to carry the breath on a simple hiss—a voiceless "sss" sound?" Julie carries a simple "sss" sound over the entire physical phrase. The physical sensations in her body mix and mingle and ride on the out-going breath. You can hear the *slow, stable, sharp* quality in the action of her breath. Once again, the *weight shift* results in a corresponding *breath-shift.* The breath has become embodied. I ask her to repeat the expressive action several times. She does.

When she finishes, Julie says: "Each time I repeated the expressive action, I took a different number of steps backward. I just took how many steps I felt were right for the expressive action, and each time my body seemed to know how much breath I needed. I always had enough breath, and I never had to think about it."

"This is exactly the kind of integration of moving and breathing that we are looking for," I say.

Barre breathing

Continuing to develop your barre, you can now begin to explore the integrated action of your body and breath.

For each of the 20 actions that comprise your barre, explore one of the following while playing your action:

- *Release*: the breath falls from the body on a simple *sigh*—a voiceless "huh" sound.
- *Charge*: the body carries the breath on a simple *hiss*—a voiceless "sss" sound.

Chapter 8

Sounding

STEP 1: PRELIMINARIES

The investigation of the sounding center begins with some preliminary improvisations located in *Chapter 11: Preliminaries*. At this next step in the stacking process, you will explore how your sound unites with breath and movement in integrated expressive action. In each of the improvisations, this (◆) icon indicates the sounding component intended for exploration. It will be useful to repeat the entire stacking process—starting with movement (■), then adding or stacking the breath (●), then adding or stacking the sound (◆). After completing the sounding component of the preliminary improvisations, return to *Step 2: Principles* located below.

STEP 2: PRINCIPLES

This experiential approach to the principles of sound is a practical investigation of the *action of the voice*. It is rooted in an exploration of the physical sensations that make sounding possible. Its primary focus centers on how the voice *charges* and *releases*, *contacts* and *withdraws*, *expands* and *contracts* in a *free flowing* manner from the *center* outward to the *periphery*.

Sound vibrations begin in the *larynx* or voice box, a muscle-and cartilage structure at the top of the windpipe that houses the vocal folds. The pitch of the voice is determined by the action of the vocal folds. When the breath stream moves across the vocal folds, they begin to vibrate, creating the initial sound that makes speech possible—a sound similar to the vibrating sound a guitar string makes when plucked. As the vocal folds are stretched, they become thinner and vibrate more times per second, producing a higher pitch. As the vocal folds are released, they become thicker and vibrate fewer times per second, producing a lower pitch.

The function of the vocal folds is often best improved indirectly, through well-balanced posture, efficient breathing, optimum resonance, and economy in the body. Focusing directly on the action of the vocal folds can create tensions that disturb their natural function. Consequently, our practical work with the voice here is to learn to *feel sound in the whole body*. The goal is to view the voice as a full-bodied experience, not merely a localized phenomenon occurring from the neck up. This sensitivity to the embodiment of sound helps the speaker make a myriad of subtle, intuitive, semiconscious bodily changes that indirectly shape and focus the tone.

Sound energy: charge/release

Successful sound production depends on *energy*—structuring and organizing the contrasting sensations of *charge* and *release*. When the breath and body are charging and releasing efficiently, the way is paved for the fluid production of sound. Experientially, the management of breath and the management of sound are somewhat similar. When working with the breath, we determined that managing the exhalation involved cultivating two distinct physical sensations:

- Release (the breath falls from the body)
- Charge (the body carries the breath).

Moving from breath to sound is relatively straightforward: we simply allow sound vibration to ride or to be carried on the outgoing breath:

- Release (the sound falls from the body). [My concept of the sound falling from the body is deeply indebted to my initial training with master teacher Kristin Linklater and her work revealing the *touch of sound* (1976, 35–40).]
- Charge (the body carries the sound).

In this manner, the physical sensations of charge and release—the building up and letting go of energy—in the body and breath make sound production possible. The emphasis shifts from an isolated action of the vocal folds in the throat to a larger integrated action occurring in the whole body.

Fall, catch, carry, and shape

Fall

Stand upright with your legs about shoulder-width apart. Allow your arms to rest comfortably at your sides. Bend and unbend your knees in a comfortable plié-like action several times. Rest. Repeat this action. Each time your knees bend; allow a very simple, voiced "huh" sound to *fall* from your body. Each time your knees straighten, receive a new breath. As the breath falls from your body, allow sound vibrations to mix and mingle with the releasing breath. Encourage a clear, non-breathy release of your voice. Sense the release of physical energy in your whole body. Rest and repeat.

(*Continued*)

(Continued)

Fall, catch, and carry

As you take three steps forward, allow a very simple, voiced "huh" sound to *fall* from your body. As soon as the "huh" sound arrives in your mouth *catch* the sound by closing your lips. Then allow the body to *carry* the sound on a simple *hum*—an interrupted "mmm" sound as you continue moving forward. Let the sound vibrations mix and mingle with your breath. Sense the buildup of physical energy in the whole body. Rest and repeat.

Fall* + *catch* + *carry* + *shape

As you take three steps forward, allow a very simple, voiced "huh" sound to *fall* from your body. As soon as the "huh" sound arrives in your mouth *catch* the sound by closing your lips. Then allow the body to *carry* the sound on a simple *hum*—an interrupted "mmm" sound as you continue moving forward. When you feel the sound vibrations solidly on your lips, *shape* the sound by forming any selected vowel sound such as: "ee" as in "me," "ah" as in "mah" or "oo" as in "moo." Let the sound vibrations mix and mingle with your breath. Sense the buildup of physical energy in the whole body. Rest and repeat.

Now let the sound *fall* from your body during four knee bends and then *catch*, *carry* and *shape* the sound while taking four steps forward. Then try five knee bends and five steps forward, followed by six, seven, eight, perhaps more, as many as feel comfortable. Do not push or strain by going beyond what you are able to support. Enjoy the contrasting sensations of sound being *carried by* and *falling from* the body— *charge* and *release*.

Fall, catch, carry, and shape

The previous exploration presented a logical and sequential progression of energy that was intended to lead to a flexible and efficient sounding action. It is useful at this point to review this four-step process. The first step is to allow the sound to *fall* from the body on a simple voiced sighing action. The falling action is intended to assist the natural release of the breath and the forward placement of the sound. You should sense the sound arriving solidly in the middle of your mouth. The second step is to *catch* the sound on the lips, which creates a humming action. The humming action that *carries* the sound is intended to increase your awareness of vibration re-sounding in your body. Luxuriate in the sound vibrations bouncing around in your body. When the sound has fallen solidly into the mouth and the feeling of vibration has increased because of the humming action, you are ready to *shape* the vowel sound. Take a few moments and review this four-step process: Allow the simple directives to fall, catch, carry, and shape to assist you in the sounding process. This sequential exploration is designed to put you in touch with an integrated sound management experience in four successive stages.

Sound size: expand/contract

Resonance

Resonance is the vehicle for increasing the *size* and power of the voice. The sound produced by the vocal folds would be weak and difficult to hear without reinforcement and amplification. A *resonator* is simply a hollow space in which sound waves are in a sense "resounded" as they bounce around like an echo, which increases the power and intensity of the tone. The human voice has three resonators: the *oral cavity*, the *pharynx*, and the *nasal cavity*—the hollow spaces in the mouth, throat, and nose respectively (see Figure 8.1).

The impulse to speak is accompanied by a natural expansion of the resonators. The greater the mental and emotional need, the greater the degree of *expansion*. After the desire to communicate is exhausted, the expanded resonator naturally and reflexively recoils or *contracts*, marking a return to ease and equilibrium until a new impulse to communicate sets the resonators in motion again. This expanding and contracting action of the resonators determine the voice's quality and color. Labels such as warm, strident, heavy, shrill, shallow, hollow, bright, nasal, light, trapped, pleasant (and a host of others, both complimentary and derogatory) usually refer to qualities of resonance created by the size and shape of the resonating spaces.

A change in a resonators *size* is simultaneously a change in its *shape*. When you open and close your mouth, for example, you not only increase and decrease the size of the oral cavity, you modify its shape as well. These adjustments in size and shape occur primarily in the mouth and the throat, not in the nose. The mouth

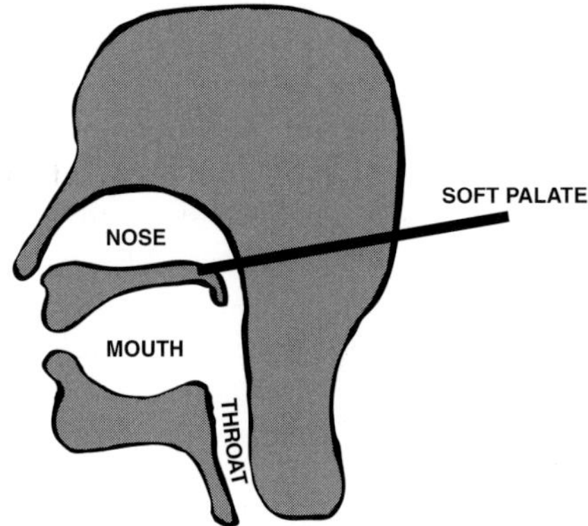

Figure 8.1 Resonating spaces.

Nasal resonance

The degree of nasal resonance present in the voice is determined largely by the action of the *soft palate*—the flexible, fleshy rear portion of the roof of the mouth—which functions somewhat like a floodgate. When lowered it diverts sound vibrations into the nasal resonator; when elevated it diverts sound vibrations into the mouth. When we hum, we naturally lower the soft palate and can feel the sound vibrations buzzing around in the nasal cavity.

and throat are quite flexible—the lips, jaw, tongue, soft palate, throat, even the cheeks are constantly expanding and contracting to serve the expressive needs of the speaker. Although the nasal cavity makes an important contribution to vocal resonance, you can't adjust its size or shape directly, because its walls are made primarily of bone and cartilage and are essentially inflexible. Consequently, our practical work on resonance focuses exclusively on making adjustments in the size and shape of the mouth and throat.

The resonance created in the mouth and throat is not unlike the treble and bass speakers of a stereo system. The pocket of resonant energy created in the mouth (*upper resonating space*) is the *tweeter*, the pocket of resonant energy created in the throat (*lower resonating space*) is the *woofer*. The upper resonating space (the mouth) provides the voice with light, bright, brilliant, ringing vocal resonance. The lower resonating space (the throat) provides the voice with heavy, dark, rich, deep vocal resonance.

Vocal resonance is balanced when more or less equal emphasis is given to both the upper and lower resonating spaces. It is as if the stereo speaker dial is centered midway between treble and bass: the upper resonating space (the mouth) gives the sound clarity and brilliance, while the lower resonating space (the throat) gives the sound weight, depth, and carrying power. A voice with too much mouth resonance is thin, light, and shrill. A voice with too much throat resonance can be heavy, muffled, and unintelligible. A balanced tone, however, simultaneously produces a brilliant and warm sound that is easily understood and has sufficient carrying power.

This doesn't mean that all acts of expression require balanced resonance. Nevertheless, a balanced tone provides the most opportunity for varied and flexible expression. Unbalanced voices tend to be arrested and fixed and are capable of little variation or modification in quality and color. A speaker with a balanced tone can shift easily between light, bright tones and dark, heavy tones and all the many variations in between. It's like mixing water and earth. The result is a type of clay or mud with varying consistencies and textures. The more water, the thinner the clay (the brighter and lighter the sound). The more earth, the thicker the clay (the darker and heavier the sound). The combinations are infinite, from a slippery soup to squishy mud to thick, rich mortar. The possibilities are as diverse and as variable as the thoughts and feelings of the speaker (Alderson 1979, 103).

Tuning the vowel space

Practical work on balancing the resonance of the voice involves adjusting the size and shape of the upper and lower resonating spaces. A useful and indirect way to adjust the size and shape of the resonating spaces is with *vowel sounds*. Vowel sounds form the natural resonance of the human voice. Vowel sounds are often thought of as a series of movements made by the lips, jaw, and tongue. While this is correct as far as it goes, a vowel sound is not created so much by the movement of the articulators but by the hollow space that their movements creates in the mouth and throat. A vowel sound is actually a by-product of a pocket of resonant energy created in the mouth (upper resonating space), and a pocket of resonant energy created in the throat (lower resonating space). When the right *vowel space* is created, the right vowel sound emerges. A vowel sound is an acoustical phenomenon. In sum, a vowel is essentially a hollow space—a resonator—in which sounds vibrations reverberate. Change the size and shape of the vowel space, and you change the vowel sound created. Consequently, working with vowels is work with resonance.

Additionally, vowel sounds provide an integrated method of exploring the entire vocal tract. All of the various "parts" of the vocal tract unite to form vowel sounds. The lips, tongue, mouth, jaw, soft palate, and throat move together to create the space that makes the vowel sound. Consequently in the process of working with vowel sounds each of the individual "parts" of the vocal tract are indirectly and simultaneously strengthened and liberated. An individual with rich and resonant vowel sounds invariably has flexible lips, jaw, tongue, and throat.

This process of adjusting the size and shape of the vowel space for improved resonance is called *tuning the vowel*. Acoustically, the process of adjusting the vowel space for improved resonance is a complex science involving *harmonics*, *overtones*, *frequencies*, *partials*, and *formats* that is beyond the scope of this book. However, practical work on tuning the vowel space is relatively simple to explain: some previously dormant muscles must be activated to enhance resonance, while other tense muscles inhibiting resonance must be released. It is both an active and a passive process.

When you tune a vowel, all the moveable parts of the mouth and throat are "wiggled" into proper alignment until you find a "sweet spot"—the point at which maximum vibration is produced with minimal effort. It's like tuning in a radio: you keep moving the dial around until you find the spot where you receive the best reception. This tuning involves the readjustment of the size and shape of the entire vocal tract: not so much pronounced muscular movements, but subtle shifts in the moveable parts of the mouth and throat that affect the manner in which the vowel sound vibrates in the body. In fact, the vowel is often tuned so imperceptibly that it can be difficult to know precisely how the mouth and throat were adjusted for increased power and purer quality. In the majority of cases, tuning the vowel space involves expanding the *size* of the resonator, providing room for a fuller, more vibrant tone. Just as a concert grand piano has more power than a baby grand, the larger the resonating spaces, the more powerful and full the voice. Vowel tuning is enhanced by:

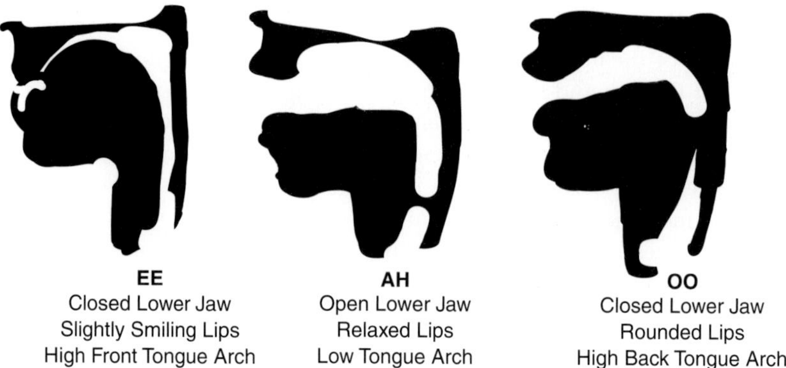

Figure 8.2 Vowel space.

- an increased awareness of vibration—the feeling of the vowel sound resonating in the body;
- flexibility and fluidity in the moveable parts of the mouth and throat;
- a sense of ease and expansiveness in the upper and lower resonating spaces.

Forward/open/full vowels

A practical method of tuning the vowel space involves training the resonator to *expand* and *contract* in all directions by vocalizing on the "ee," "ah," "oo" vowels (as in the words "me," "ma," "moo," respectively). When progressing through this three-vowel sequence—a type of *articulatory triangle*—all the moveable parts of the mouth receive a complete articulatory workout (see Figure 8.2). All other vowel sounds fall somewhere in between the "extreme" tongue, jaw, and lip positions needed to make these three vowel sounds. The tongue arch moves from its most forward position, on "ee," to its most back position, on "oo." The jaw moves from its most narrow opening, on "ee," to its widest opening, on "ah." The lips move from their most rounded position, on "oo," to their most relaxed position, on "ah," and to a slightly smiling position, on "ee." A fluid and seamless transition from "ee" to "ah" to "oo" requires a flexible, stable, well-tuned resonator. Most important, the resonance of a vowel is said to be balanced when it has the qualities characteristic of the *forward* "ee" vowel, the *open* "ah" vowel, and the *full* "oo" vowel:

1 A *forward tone* falls freely into the front of the mouth. Its vibration can be sensed directly on the lips, teeth, and hard palate. A forward tone has a bright, light, ringing quality that gives the voice clarity and vibrancy. It occurs when the upper resonating space (the mouth) is making an optimum contribution to the tone. A forward tone can be sensed most fully on the "ee "vowel. The forward tongue position and narrow jaw opening of the "ee" vowel directs the sound into the very front of the mouth and produces a solid vibration in the upper resonating space. Optimum resonance in the upper resonating space is

accompanied by the feeling of vibration in the head and face, or mask. It occurs when sympathetic sound vibrations resounding in the mouth travel upward through the bones of the head and face.

2 An *open tone* is characterized by expansiveness, freedom, and fluidity in both the upper and lower resonating spaces. An open tone travels freely through the throat and mouth without constriction or interference. This feeling of openness integrates the upper and lower resonating spaces and is essential to balanced resonance. An open tone can be sensed most fully on the "ah" vowel. The wide jaw position and relatively low tongue position of the "ah" vowel ensure the vocal vibrations are traveling freely through both the upper and lower resonating spaces.

3 A *full tone* is characterized by depth, weight, and solidity. It has a dark, warm, sonorous quality that provides power and substance. It occurs when the lower resonating space makes an optimal contribution to the tone. A full tone can be sensed most completely on the "oo" vowel. The high back tongue position and rounded lips of the "oo" vowel allow optimal vibration in the lower resonating space. Optimum resonance in the lower resonating space is accompanied by the feeling of vibrations resounding in the chest. This occurs when sympathetic sound vibrations in the throat travel downward through the bones of the chest.

When the actor is working for balanced resonance, a *forward, open, full tone* should be cultivated on all vowel sounds. Every vowel should have the resonant properties characteristic of the forward "ee," the open "ah," and the full "oo" sounds. When these three vowels are well-tuned, all others tend to fall into place.

Vowel tuning

Select any comfortable pitch in the middle of your vocal range, not too high and not too low. Sustain an "ee" vowel for several seconds but not longer than you are able to comfortably support the sound. Direct the vibration forward into the front of your mouth. Make any necessary adjustments in the vowel space to produce a vibrant forward tone. Sense the vibrations directly on your lips, teeth, and hard palate. Let the vibrations play freely in your head and face. Rest and repeat.

Next, sustain an "ah" vowel on the same pitch for several seconds but not longer than you are able to comfortably support the sound. Encourage a sense of openness and expansiveness in your mouth and throat. The "ah" vowel should travel freely and fluidly through the resonating spaces. Make any necessary adjustments in the vowel space to produce a free and open tone. Rest and repeat.

Now sustain an "oo" vowel for several seconds but not longer than you are able to comfortably support the sound. Enjoy the warmth, weight, depth, and richness of this vowel sound. Make any necessary adjustments in the vowel space to produce a rich and full tone. Let the vibrations play freely in your chest cavity. Rest and repeat.

(Continued)

(Continued)

Now progress through this three-vowel sequence, from the forward "ee" to the open "ah" to the full "oo," on one sustained tone. As you move from vowel to vowel, encourage a great deal of expanse and freedom in the upper and lower resonating spaces. Notice the point at which each vowel sound takes on its richest resonance. When the upper and lower resonating spaces are adequately expanded, it is possible to sequence from vowel to vowel without any abrupt shift or deterioration in tone. All three vowels possess an equally rich and stable resonance that is best described as *forward*, *open*, and *full*. Repeat this three-vowel sequence several times using a variety of comfortable pitches.

Repeat the above exploration while closing off your nostrils with your thumb and index finger. When you produce the "ee," "ah," and "oo" vowels, you should not experience any ringing or buzzing in your nose. (In English, the nasal resonator is only used directly when making the "m," "n," and "ng" consonants.) If sound vibrations are ringing in your nose, the *soft palate* is not adequately expanded and sound vibrations are being inappropriately shifted into the nasal resonator. If this occurs, encourage a great sense of openness and expansiveness in the back of the mouth and throat. Wiggle all the moveable parts of your mouth around until you feel the sound vibrations leave your nose and fall forward into your mouth.

Sound progression: center/periphery

Progression refers to the degree of fluidity and ease with which the speaker can progress or travel up and down the vocal range. The middle voice, the largest area, comprises those pitches in and around the *center* of the vocal range. The vocal center falls midway between the highest and lowest notes of the speakers range. It is the very center of the *middle voice*. The bulk of the actors work, like daily conversation, falls in and around the vocal center, but one should always sense the notes above and below and the possibilities they offer. The pitches of the upper and lower voice lie on the *periphery*, above and below the middle voice. The average vocal range is approximately two octaves (15 white keys on the piano keyboard). While some voices may extend further, a two-octave range is more than adequate for fluid expression.

The upper, middle, and lower voice comprise a series of consecutive pitches that share a similar and consistent quality and color. Like the notes on the piano keyboard, the higher vocal pitches have a light and bright quality, the lower vocal pitches have a warm and dark quality. The middle vocal pitches reflect a balance of light and dark, bright and warm qualities, and are the most dynamic and flexible. Most speech occurs in the middle voice, with the upper and lower voice used to express the most extreme and powerful thoughts and feelings. As the ability to progress up and down the musical scale is improved, the whole voice is developed and strengthened. Improved range leads to improved resonance, breath management, and tonal quality.

Vocal center

Some speakers pitch their vocal center above or below what is normal and healthy for their voices. Voices pitched too high have limited room to travel upward. Voices pitched too low have limited room to travel downward. Only when the vocal center is clearly established can the full range be accessed with ease and spontaneity. The vocal center is not a position to be maintained but a place the voice consistently moves through and returns to as it progresses up and down the musical scale. The journey of a free and flexible voice begins in the center, travels to the periphery, and returns again to the center before taking another voyage to the periphery. The vocal center is a balanced point of efficient departure.

It is common for the vocal center to shift in the course of developing and strengthening the range. As new pitches are gained in the upper and lower voice, the vocal center readjusts to accommodate the increased range. Additionally, some days we experience our vocal center a little higher, other days a little lower. The vocal center is more flexible than commonly thought and reflects the varying degrees of tenseness and laxness in the whole body. Tired and lethargic bodies center lower, just as active and alert bodies center higher. Allowing the vocal center to shift when necessary reflects a profound kind of sensory awareness of the changing and flexible nature of the human person. It is essential to being yourself.

Periphery

Progression through the upper and lower voice is aided by a series of shifting physical sensations that occur naturally in the body. Certain physical sensations are particularly suited to exploring the upper voice, and certain physical sensations are particularly suited to exploring the lower voice. These contrasting physical sensations help us express our thoughts and feelings. For reasons not completely understood, certain thoughts and feelings find their expressive life in the upper voice, while others find their expressive life in the lower voice. Just as the high notes on the piano keyboard have a light, bright, energetic emotive quality and the lower notes on the piano keyboard have a heavy, dark, languid emotive quality, the human voice has a similar organization and structure. Consequently, cultivating specific physical sensations corresponding to these emotive qualities makes expanding one's vocal range not merely a technical exercise but an organic and psychological exploration as well. In the fluid and integrated expression of thought and feeling, shifts in the vocal range are ideally accompanied by corresponding shifts in sensations in the whole body (see Figure 8.3).

Energy: charge/release

To access the upper and lower voice, we need to regulate our physical energy. As we move up the musical scale, more energy is required; as we move down the musical scale, less energy is required. Ideally, this increase of energy is experienced not simply in the voice but in the entire body. A limp and lifeless body does not have the necessary energy to access the upper voice. Similarly, a radiant and racing body does not have the necessary release to access the lower voice. Focusing

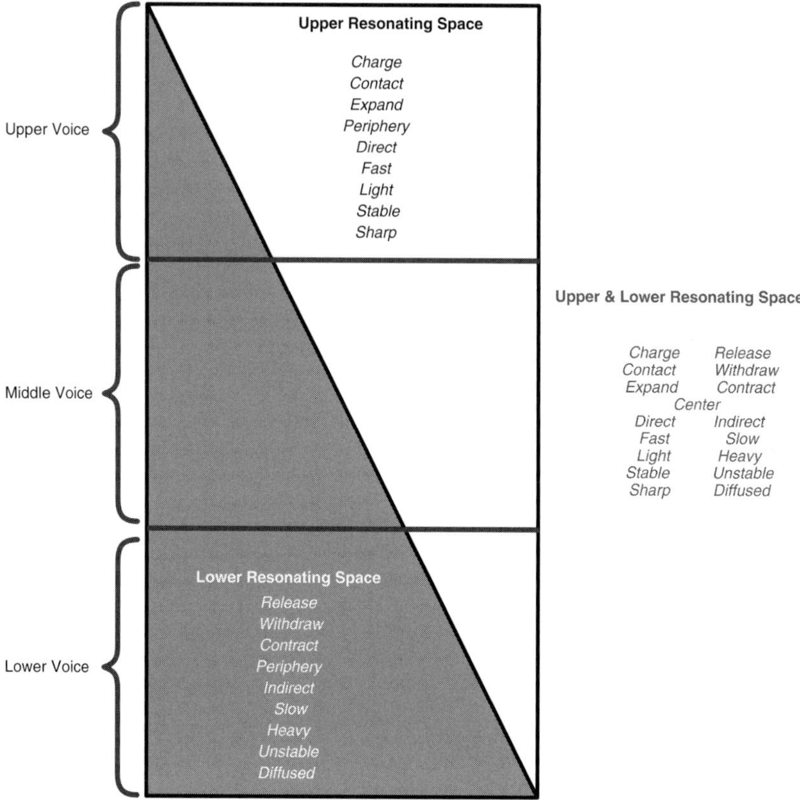

Figure 8.3 Resonance and range.

on reorganizing the energy of the body is more useful than reaching for high notes and pressing for low notes.

Size: *expand/contract*

Ideally, movement in the upper and lower voice is accompanied by gradual increases in the size of the resonators. As the pitch moves progressively up or down the musical scale away from the vocal center, the size of the resonators gradually increase in unique and different ways. This increased expansion frees the tone and prohibits the tightening, pressing, and squeezing that occur when an individual reaches for high notes or presses for low notes. Generally, we sense a greater degree of expansion in the *upper resonating space* (mouth) as we move up the scale; and a greater degree of expansion in the *lower resonating space* (throat) as we move down the scale. However, both the upper and lower resonating spaces are always working together as a team, and these simple directives fail to take into account the many complex and nuanced adjustments that can be made in the resonating spaces when speaking.

Speed: fast/slow

To access the upper and lower voice, we need to regulate the speed with which our vocal folds vibrate—faster when moving up the musical scale and slower when moving down the musical scale. While the benefits of focusing on this seemingly autonomous action of the vocal folds is questionable, thoughts and feelings associated with the upper voice are most often sensed in the body as fast, while thoughts and feelings associated with the lower voice are most often sensed in the body as slow. Substituting fast and slow for the traditional descriptions of high and low tends to prevent reaching up for high notes and pressing down for low notes.

Weight: heavy/light

To access the upper and lower voice, we need to regulate the weight of the sound. Allowing the body to become lighter when moving up the scale and heavier when moving down the scale facilitates an integrated exploration of range. Encourage the free and active interplay of vibrations in the face and head, which are commonly associated with the upper resonating space as you move up the scale. Encourage the free and active interplay of vibrations in the chest, which are commonly associated with the lower resonating space as you move down the scale. This facilitates a fluid and free transition into the upper and lower voice.

A sensory exploration of other physical properties may also be useful when extending the vocal range:

- upper voice: *contact, direct, stable, sharp*;
- lower voice: *withdraw, indirect, unstable, diffused.*

Vocal stereotypes

Developing the full vocal range often requires battling biases and stereotypes. These conditioned responses develop for any number of reasons. Many reflect traditional ideas with respect to appropriate masculine and feminine behaviors. *"That sounds girly." "Those sounds are improper for a lady."* Still others are specific and individual, some conscious and others unconscious: *"I don't want to sound like my mother." "My voice must match my body size."* Sometimes a limited range is the result of being afraid to express oneself. For many actors, work on range is more than strengthening and extending the technical instrument: it means extending and redefining who they are. Extending the range is ultimately an extension of the whole person. As new pitches in the voice are discovered, new methods of emotional and physical expression are discovered as well. The best approach is to be patient and diligent, simultaneously encouraging both the mind and the body to find new methods of expression.

Range

Take a moment and find a comfortable starting pitch, somewhere in the middle of your vocal range. Rest. Now send a light and bright "ee" sound (as in "me") up into your head. This light, bright sound buzzing in your head is your upper voice. Now, drop a deep "oo" sound (as in "moo") down into your chest. The deep place where this "oo" is rumbling is your lower voice.

Once again, find a comfortable pitch in your lower voice. While sustaining the selected pitch, progress through the three-vowel sequence "oo," "oh," "ah" (as in "moo," "mow," "ma"). Rest. Repeat several times. As you repeat the three-vowel sequence, take several steps forward in a *released, contracted, slow,* and *heavy* manner. Let this released, contracted, slow, heavy movement influence the color and quality of your voice. Repeat this three-vowel sequence several times on a number of comfortable pitches in your lower voice. Rest.

Now select a comfortable pitch in your upper voice. While sustaining the selected pitch, progress through the three-vowel sequence "ee," "ay," "ai" (as in "me," "may," "my"). Repeat several times. As you repeat the three-vowel sequence, take several steps forward in a *charged, expansive, fast,* and *light* manner. Let this charged, expansive, fast, light movement influence the quality and color of your voice. Repeat this three-vowel sequence several times on a number of comfortable pitches in your upper voice.

Sound orientation: contact/withdraw

The speech act begins with a period of *withdraw*, characterized by an inward and retreating movement, during which the internal thoughts and feelings of the speaker are gathered and assembled. This brief internal period is usually followed by a longer and more sustained period of *contact*, characterized by a forward and advancing movement, during which these internal thoughts and feelings receive physical form in words, phrases, and sentences and are shared with others. A clear understanding of the content and quality of one's thoughts and feelings and a heartfelt desire to share those thoughts and feelings is essential

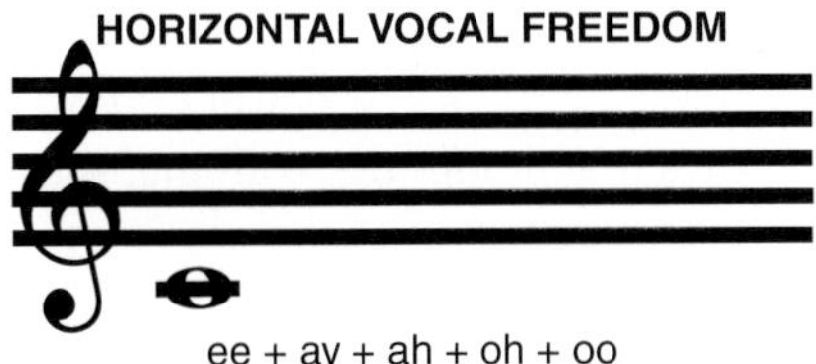

Figure 8.4 Horizontal and vertical vocal freedom.

to effective contact and withdraw. Either mental or emotional uncertainty or physical timidity can interrupt the fluid and free flowing inward and outward orientation of the speaker. Efficient and coordinated vocal production is linked directly to the successful sequencing of contact and withdraw.

Sound flow: free/bound

A bound voice is locked or arrested in one place. A free voice is fluid, dynamic, and capable of an infinite variety of adjustments in resonance and range. A free voice is essential to successful expression. Most important, a free voice is able to flow in any direction the thoughts and feelings of the speaker take it.

There are two types of vocal freedom (see Figure 8.4):

1 *Horizontal vocal freedom* is developed by progressing through a full collection of vowel sounds ("ee," "ay," "ah," "oh," "oo," as in "me," "may," "ma," "mow," "moo," for example) on any single pitch in the vocal range. If the speaker can clearly and fluidly move "horizontally" from one vowel to the next without any distortion or interruption in tone, the vowel is said to have been freed "horizontally." Horizontal vocal freedom involves the exploration of multiple vowels on a single note.

2 *Vertical vocal freedom* is developed by progressing through a sequence of musical notes on a single vowel sound. Triads, arpeggios, five-note scales or other melodic musical progressions are used in developing vertical vocal freedom. If the speaker can clearly and fluidly move "vertically" from one note to the next without any distortion or interruption in tone, the selected vowel is said to have been freed "vertically." Vertical vocal freedom involves the exploration of multiple pitches on a single vowel.

The best vocal exercises involve the most possibilities for all the vowel sounds to interact with all the pitches of the vocal range. In this way the voice is strengthened and developed systematically, vowel by vowel and note by note. There are an infinite number of ways to conduct this training, some of which are presented in *Chapter 12: Voice and body exercises.*

STEP 3: TECHNIQUE

We can now put the principles of sounding into practice by exploring the *Sitting and sounding exercises* located in Chapter 12. At this next step in the stacking process, you will explore how your sound unites with breath and movement in integrated physical action. In each of the sitting and sounding exercises, this (◆) icon indicates the sounding component intended for exploration. It will be useful to repeat the entire stacking process—starting with movement (■), then adding or stacking the breath (●), then adding or stacking the sound (◆). After completing the sounding component, return to the next section: *Step 4: Improvisation.*

STEP 4: IMPROVISATION

The *sound and movement work* that comprises the stacking process explores how the body, breath, and sound unite in integrated expressive action. Remember, breath is the framework and foundation for sound. When the action of the breath is fully integrated with the action of the body, the groundwork is laid for the successful transition into integrated vocal action. The goal is to allow the voice to ride on the action of the breath, which is in turn riding on the action of the body. The most important directive when exploring sound and movement work is to feel the *action of the body* in the *action of the sound.* When we are moving and sounding in an integrated manner, even the most subtle and nuanced shifts in the body manifest themselves in the sound of the voice. The goal is to allow the physical action to "place" the voice in the body. When this occurs, we hear the voice through the body. The thoughts and feelings in the body are imprinted on the voice and travel outward on resonant sound waves to reveal the emotional and mental state of the speaker. The voice is best viewed as the oral extension of the body—it is through the voice that the body speaks. In this rich and dynamic sensory experience, the sound becomes fully integrated and embodied.

Sound and movement work

The *sound* and *movement work* that comprises the stacking process begins with an exploration of energy:

- Release—sound falls from the body.
- Charge—body carries the sound.

Jon has taken the prompt "to plod" and arrived at a repeatable and playable expressive action: he plods around the room in a *released*, *slow*, and *heavy* manner. I have him play the expressive action several times while making sound. Jon works on an "ee" vowel as in the word "me." There seems to be a disconnect between his body and his voice. The sound is disembodied. The "ee" sound has a very *charged*, *light*, and *fast* quality that appears to be a war with his *released*, *slow* and *heavy* plodding action.

"The expressive action seems to be fully expressed in your body," I suggest, "but I'm having trouble with the sound. We seem to have missed a step. Could you try to settle more fully into the sensation? How does this *slow*, *released*, *heavy* plodding action in your body affect your voice?"

He repeats the expressive action several times. Clearly, Jon is more deeply connected to the physical sensations of the plodding action. I suggest that we return to the *breath and movement work*. On a "seemingly" sustained sighing-action, the breath appears to fall from Jon's body rather slowly over the entire plodding action. With time and repetition, it is possible to see the breath integrate with the action of the body. The breath is *heavy*, *slow*, and *released*. I can hear it and sense its physical properties as Jon plods around the room.

"How does that feel?" I ask.

Jon smiles. "Much better, I feel my body and breath are one."

"Great." I reply. "Now all you have to do is allow sound vibrations to ride on the out-going breath. We select an "*oo*" vowel for exploration. (If one vowel is not working, it is useful to try another or sometimes one or two vowels strung together). John begins to explore the integrated relationship between the *weight shift* and the *sound-shift*. Each time there is a weight shift in his body, there is a corresponding shift in the sound of his voice. "Does the sound *fall from your body* or is the sound *carried by your body*?" I ask.

"I'm not exactly sure. I feel like the sound falls *from my body* each time I take a step, but I also feel like my body *carries the sound* over the entire plodding action."

"I think you're right," I say. "While some expressive actions clearly *fall from the body* and others are clearly *carried by the body*, with others it can be difficult to tell. What we have here is a very complex organization of energy. First, explore the expressive action by allowing an "*oo*" sound to fall from your body, then carry the "*oo*" sound and see what you discover." Jon does so. Both appear to be working equally well, and it is difficult to distinguish between the two. I ask, "Now, do you have any idea whether your expressive action is more *charged* or more *released*?"

"Yes," said Jon. "It's difficult to tell, but I feel that it's more released than charged, because I sense my body falling as I release the text."

"Trust your sensation." I suggest. "We usually have a preference. We can tell when something is "more" sweet or less sweet, more sourer or less sour. What feels right usually is right. Sometimes sensation can be tricky. We can both be looking at the same color and you might say that this color is orange, and I might say that this color is red. What is important is that you recognize your experience of the sensation in your body. If you say it's red, it's red. If you say this action is released, it's released. These are the sensations in your body, and they are yours to name as you wish.

Sounding barre

Continuing to develop your barre, you can now begin to explore the integrated action of your body, breath, and voice.

For each of the 20 actions that comprise your barre, explore one of the following while playing your action:

- *Release*: the sound falls from the body on any selected vowel(s) sound.
- *Charge*: the body carries the sound on any selected vowel(s) sounds.

Chapter 9

Speaking

STEP 1: PRELIMINARIES

The investigation of the speaking center begins with the preliminary improvisations located in *Chapter 11: Preliminaries*. At this next step in the stacking process, you will explore how your speech unites with movement, breath, and sound in integrated expressive action. In each of the improvisations, this (▲) icon indicates the speaking component intended for exploration. It will be useful to repeat the entire stacking process—starting with movement (■), then adding or stacking the breath (●), then adding or stacking the sound (◆), then adding or stacking speech (▲). After completing the speaking component of the preliminary improvisations, return to *Step 2: Principles* located below.

STEP 2: PRINCIPLES

An actor's study of speech is a broad topic that incorporates a great variety of subjects: anatomy, physiology, articulation, pronunciation, etymology, linguistics, phonetics, poetry, rhetoric, and yet still other subjects that remain unlisted. When I reference, "speaking" or "speech" in the context of acting, I mean to include the totality of the experience—all the various components of this multifaceted, interdisciplinary study. Suffice it to say that the study of speech could easily fill up multiple volumes. The perspective presented here is foundational and by no means comprehensive and almost exclusively physical.

Speaking is the final step in the stacking process. The expectation is that at this last step the body will "speak the words" effortlessly. The premise is that if the physical foundations of meaning are fully embodied in the moving, breathing, and sounding centers that the words will effortlessly and naturally find their authentic and appropriate expression. Central to this supposition is the belief that the foundations of meaning begin in and spring from physical experience.

It is commonly recognized that words are the building blocks of thought and the wrapper in which our thoughts or delivered. The link between thinking and speaking is so significant that they are often assumed to be one and the same. We are said to "speak our minds" and "voice our opinions." To state that someone is "articulate" is an acknowledgement of intelligence. People who speak well are automatically assumed to be smart. Often, the relationship between thinking and speaking is extended to listening and learning. To have "heard something" is synonymous with "knowing something." Perhaps, this is why it is said that a wise man is a good listener.

This traditional coupling of *speaking* and *thinking*, *words* and *thoughts*, *language* and *mind* fails to reveal the complete picture of where meaning and understanding, knowledge and comprehension originate. Mark Johnson states, "if we reduce meaning to words and sentences (or concepts or propositions) we miss or leave out where meaning really comes from" (2007: 11). Johnson asserts that we often suffer from a "disembodied view of meaning." Which is to assume that only words, phrases and sentences have meaning and that the body is incapable of contributing to the thinking process. Johnson insists that "meaning is more than words and deeper than concepts:"

> It is our organic flesh and blood, our structural bones, the ancient rhythms of our internal organs, and the pulsing flow of our emotions that give us whatever meaning we can find and that shape our very thinking.
>
> (2007, 3)

Fundamentally, the architecture of our thinking is built upon the scaffolding of the body. In daily living, our thoughts, and the words we use to deliver them to others, begin with a series of sensations and movements that form patterns and structures in our bodies. These patterns and structures are the physical foundations of meaning and understanding. Often this physical process occurs at a preconscious or semiconscious level. The stacking process—the process of beginning with the physical and progressing to the verbal—increases the actor's awareness of this semiconscious or preconscious meaning-making process. In this unique type of improvisation meaning emerges before and sometimes without the need for words.

An expressive action is essentially a physical action that is the embodiment of the thinking process. Consequently, "thinking is action" and words are in essence our thoughts in motion. When language is embodied via expressive action, it evokes specific physical properties. Language, just as our thinking processes, can actually *charge* and *release*, *contact* and *withdraw*, *expand*, and *contract*. It can be *free* or *bound*, *direct* or *indirect*, or *sharp* or *diffused*. Some thoughts race, soar, and expand; others slip away, dwindle, and subside; still others plod along in "fits and starts"—the physical possibilities are endless. In a good play, skillfully structured language suggests specific physical sensations that lead and direct the actor toward the appropriate expressive action. This subtle and indirect, understated and under celebrated, communication between talented playwright and gifted actor is one of the most magical and mysterious aspects of theatrical collaboration.

When Henry V commands:

"Once more unto the breach, dear friends, once more"

(*Henry* V III.i.1)

Henry's thinking and speaking is *charged* and *expansive* as the text suggests. When Lewis laments:

> Life is as tedious as a twice-told tale
> Vexing the *d*ull ear of a *d*rowsy man

(*King John* III.iv.108–9)

The "t's" and "d's" themselves suggest a tedious, dull drowsiness that directs the actor towards a slow and plodding expressive action.

When Juliet exclaims:

> Gallop apace, you fiery-footed steeds,
> Toward Phoebus' lodging. Such a wagoner
> As Phaeton would whip you to the west
> And bring in cloudy night immediately.

(*Romeo and Juliet* III.ii 1–3)

The words "gallop" and "whip" along, prompting an appropriate fast and charged expressive action.

In the theater, the words that the actor speaks most often do not begin in the body of the actor, but spring from the pen of a playwright. Consequently, it is the actor's job to give those words a physical life. This requires a specialized type of collaboration between body, breath, sound, and speech in a heightened awareness of the physical. The most important questions for the actor are not: *What am I saying?* and *How do I say it?*; but rather, *What do the thoughts on the page want to do?* and *What physical properties do they need to do this?*

There is an old theater joke in which two actors argue over how a character is to say a line. One insists it is "*Hark*, I hear the cannons roar"; the other insists it is "Hark, *I* hear the cannons roar." Neither line reading leads to satisfactory results, and both actors are equally the butt of the joke (Hornby 1997, 43). Unfortunately, sitting down with a script and a pencil and making rational decisions about which words are important and should be given special vocal emphasis can lead to stilted and mechanical line readings. I call this misguided process *playing the text.* The problem is, this *how-will-I-say-this-line approach* can lead to a superficial exploration of the obvious and literal meaning of the words at the expense of the experiential, sensorial, and emotional power of the body. The result is often all head and little heart. The actor's job is not merely to grasp the meaning of the language with the mind, but most importantly to find the meaning of the language through the body.

When an actor merely plays the text, the line delivery is often pedantic, shallow, declamatory, and devoid of genuine feeling. The results are less than satisfying. "I *need* a vacation." "I hate *her*." "Is *today* Wednesday?" The actor states, tells, emphasizes, stresses, and underscores the basic meaning of the text but expresses little else. Everything is rattled off as an intense statement of fact. A possible subtext for mechanical line deliveries like these could be "I really mean it" or "*listen to what I'm saying.*"

Without question, the intellectual meaning of the text can be understood by analyzing the structure of language. For example, it might be very helpful to recognize that the words "winter" and "summer" and "discontent" and "glorious" are used in opposition to create meaning in the opening soliloquy in Richard III:

> Now is the *winter* of our discontent
> Made glorious *summer* by this sun of York
>
> (I.i.1)

However, understanding the rhetorical structure of the text does not always ensure that the actor has embodied the thought. It is fitting that we call the actor "an actor" and not "an orator" or "a reciter." The job of the actor is not to set down clever and predetermined ways of turning a phrase, but rather to find a series of expressive actions that embody the thought. As Hamlet's eloquent advice to the players suggests, "suit the action to the word and the word to the action. . . ." Most importantly, all expressive actions have specific physical properties—a *speed, weight, direction, flow, progression*—a physical architecture that forms the very blood, bone, and muscle of the thinking process.

Ideally, the appropriate expressive action always emphasizes the appropriate words. Words and actions meet differently in every context. Almost any part of speech can be stressed: verbs, nouns, even pronouns, prepositions, and articles. The complexity of emphasis is linked directly to the expressive action and cannot be solely determined mechanically or intellectually. The subtleties and nuances of complex stress sometimes confound the intellect, transcend the literal, and run contrary to common sense. The *body has its reasons.* The "*sense*" *of things in the mind* is linked directly to *what is "sensed" in the body*. This is why we instinctively know that *what we feel about something* and *what we think about something* are inextricably intertwined.

STEP 3: TECHNIQUE

We can now put the principles of speaking into practice by exploring the *sitting and sounding exercises* located in *Chapter 12: Voice and body exercises*. At this next step in the stacking process, you will explore how speech unites with sound, breath, and movement in integrated expressive action. It will be useful to repeat the entire stacking process—starting with movement (■), then stacking or adding the breath (●), then stacking or adding the sound (◆); and finally, stacking or adding speech (▲). There is no formally prescribed speech (▲) exploration in the sitting and sounding exercises, and you will not find this icon (▲) printed in any of the sitting and sounding exercises. When you arrive at the final, speaking stage in the stacking process, select any simple piece of text for exploration. Any piece of text will work. You can spontaneously compose a phrase or a simple sentence. You might explore a nursery rhyme or the words to the song "Happy Birthday" or counting from 132,256 to 132,261. In other instances, take lines from actual playscripts. It is helpful to include a great variety of playwrights and writing styles—the more the better. After completing the speaking component, return to the next section: *Step 4: Improvisation.*

STEP 4: IMPROVISATION

The *speech and movement work* is the final step in the stacking process. The goal is to allow for the sensuous interplay between the action of the body, breath, voice, and the words being spoken. If the integration of the moving, breathing, and sounding action has been fully realized, the process of speaking should be, as a result, embodied.

Sound and movement vs. noise and activity

It is important to make a technical distinction between *sound and movement* and *noise and activity*. For example, an actor making the "sound of a clock ticking" is said to be making a *noise*. While an actor "shrieking in ecstasy" is said to be making a *sound*. Similarly, an actor "swaying from side to side" like the pendulum of a clock is said to be involved in an *activity*, while an actor "cowering backward" with trepidation is said to be performing a *movement*. Essentially, *sound and movement* is defined as a specific experience that reflects the physical embodiment of emotional and mental content. *Noise and activity*, on the other hand, refers to mechanical, arbitrary, random, and insignificant physical and vocal activity that is void of emotional and mental content. Typically sound and movement occurs when the actor improvising is playing an expressive action. Noise and activity occur when the actor improvising is not playing an expressive action. Before adding words and phrases, it is useful to ask yourself, "Am I making a *sound* or a *noise?*" and "Is this a *movement* or an *activity?*"

Speech and movement work

Martin has been exploring the expressive action "to catapult," and he has composed a piece of text: "*So why is everybody always picking on me.*" Each time Martin repeats the expressive action, he mechanically emphasizes different words. *"Why* is everybody always picking on me?" "Why is *everybody* always picking on me?" "Why is everybody always picking on *me*?" The result is pedantic and stilted. He is simply "playing the text." All head and no heart. The words are not yet fully embodied.

I ask Martin to return to an exploration of the physical phrase. He does so and instantaneously his body catapults into action. "There are the physical materials we are looking for," I say. I ask Martin to do some *switching work*.

Switching work

Switching work is a method of improvisation in which the actor alternates back and forth between any two steps in the stacking process. For example, an actor might "switch" back and forth between:

- *movement work* and *breath and movement work*;
- *breath and movement work* and *sound and movement work*;
- *sound and movement work* and *speech and movement work.*

The purpose of the switching work is to ensure that at each step in the stacking process that the embodiment of the expressive action has not been compromised along the way. When progressing through the stacking process, if at any point along the way the actor loses the essential physical connection to the expressive action, it is useful to "switch back" to the previous step in the stacking process and re-connect.

Martin switches between *sound and movement work* and *speech and movement work.* Martin "switches" between playing the expressive action on an "ah" sound and playing it while speaking the text. As he switches, I encourage him to allow the physical and vocal sensations to mix and mingle with the words he is speaking. He does so and achieves a fine level of integration. "*Why is everybody always picking on me?*" seems to catapult from his body in a *fast*, *charged*, *direct*, and fatal shot. A *weight shift* has resulted in a corresponding *breath-shift* and *sound-shift*; and as a result, the text has become embodied.

I ask what Martin has discovered.

"I was thinking about the words so much that all the extra mental effort was disconnecting me from my body. When it was really working, I felt like the text and sound were coming out of my whole body and not just my brain."

Martin sits down.

"Tell me more about your expressive action." I say.

"It was definitely charged. I could feel my body was carrying my breath, voice and speech."

"Do you know who you were speaking to?" I ask.

"No," he says, "It kept changing. Sometimes I thought I was talking to my sisters, sometimes it was as if I was talking to you. Other times, it seemed to be a group of people, I did not even know. It kept changing."

"Do you know anything else about why you felt picked on?" I ask.

"It wasn't just one thing. When I was repeating the expressive action, all kinds of things came to my mind. Like I was a small child or that people were teasing me for being in love with a girl—crazy stuff—some of my thoughts made sense, some of them didn't. Sometimes, I was just so focused on how I was catapulting that I didn't have time to think about *why* or *who* I was catapulting at."

"So you simply played the expressive action *in and of itself and for its own sake*?"

"Yes, and whatever came up, came up. Sometimes I was furious and other times really vulnerable and hurt. It was often very different. It kept shifting and changing."

"We have been focusing on the *expressive action in its first function*; consequently, clear intellectual answers about why we are playing the expressive action are secondary and less important than discovering things about the physical life of the expressive action in the body."

Speaking barre

Continuing to develop your barre, you can now begin to explore the integrated action of body, breath, voice, and speech.

For each of the 20 actions that comprise your barre, explore one of the following while playing your action:

- *Release*: the text falls from the body on a simple sentence.
- *Charge*: the body carries the text on a simple sentence.

Any piece of text will work. You can spontaneously compose a phrase or a simple sentence. You might explore a nursery rhyme or the words to the song "Happy Birthday" or counting from 132,256 to 132,261. In other instances, take lines from actual playscripts. It is helpful to include a great variety of playwrights and writing styles—the more the better.

Chapter 10

Extending the barre

Now that you have completed building your barre, you can now use the following additional exercises to extend your study. These exercises can be performed successfully only when the barre is fully memorized and can be repeated without interruption or prompting.

Segues and sets

Working with *segues* and *sets* is an advanced method of exploring the phrasing of a series of actions that comprise your *barre*. During the initial exploration and the development of your barre, you most probably took a brief rest or pause in between each expressive action. For example:

to bark (*rest*) to fumble (*rest*) to meddle (*rest*) to cower (*rest*) to surrender (*rest*).

However, it is possible to phrase your barre somewhat differently. *Segue* is a musical term meaning to continue without interruption or pause. A segue occurs in the barre exploration when two or more expressive actions are played one right after the other without a pause or rest in between. For example:

to bark ➔ to fumble ➔ to meddle (*rest*) to cower ➔ to surrender (*rest*)

A *set* refers to the group or series of actions that are strung together without interruption. In the example above, the method of phrasing created two sets:

1st set: to bark ➔ to fumble ➔ to meddle (*rest*)
2nd set: to cower ➔ to surrender (*rest*)

Explore the phrasing of your barre by *segueing* from one action to the next in any manner that you choose, creating multiple and varied *sets* of connected actions.

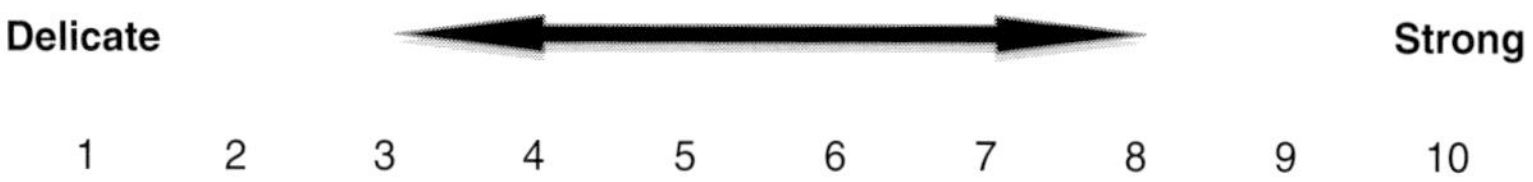

Figure 10.1 Dynamics.

Dynamic (delicate ↔ strong)

The *dynamic* is the degree of intensity with which an expressive action is played. Certain expressive actions have a high dynamic—"to explode" or "to scream bloody murder." Other expressive actions have a low dynamic—"to tiptoe" or "to whisper." Expressive actions with a high dynamic are referred to as *strong*. Expressive actions with a low dynamic are referred to as *delicate*. Many expressive actions ("to plead," "to warn," or "to beg," for example) can be played with many dynamic variations. Therefore, it is useful to place *strong* and *delicate* on a scale from one to ten, *one* being the most delicate dynamic and *ten* being the strongest (See Figure 10.1).

Explore each of the 20 expressive actions in your barre with dynamic variations. Play them all at a very low dynamic. Play them all at a very high dynamic. Play them all at a medium dynamic. Give each one a different dynamic. You may find it helpful to assign each expressive action a number reflecting their specific dynamic as illustrated in Figure 10.1.

Switching

Select one physical property for extended exploration while you play your barre. (Certain expressive actions will change significantly in this exercise and in many ways express new and different thoughts and feelings.)

Let's say that you select *unstable* for extended exploration. Every action in your barre must now be played in an unstable manner. Your first expressive action must now be both *unstable* and *charged*, your second expressive action *unstable* and *released*, your third expressive action *unstable* and *expansive*, your fourth *unstable* and *contracted*, and so on. (With respect to *control*, a stable expressive action is already *stable* and can't be played as *unstable*, so it is omitted.) Here's a detailed breakdown:

- *energy*: charge + unstable/release + unstable;
- *orientation*: contact + unstable/withdraw + unstable;
- *size*: expand + unstable/contract + unstable;
- *progression*: center + unstable/periphery + unstable;
- *flow*: free + unstable/bound + unstable;
- *direction*: direct + unstable/indirect + unstable;

- *speed*: fast + unstable/slow + unstable;
- *weight*: heavy + unstable/light + unstable;
- *focus*: sharp + unstable/diffused + unstable.

Repeat, "switching" each of the other physical properties into your barre.

Head/heart/pelvis

Head/heart/pelvis is an exploration of the impulse origin of an expressive action. When the impulse of motivation for an expressive action begins with an intellectual idea, its impulse origin is in the *head*. When the impulse or motivation for an expressive action begins with an emotional need or longing, its impulse origin is the *heart*. When the impulse or motivation for an expressive action begins with a need for survival, its impulse origin is in the *pelvis*.

The concept of head/heart/pelvis is based on Paul D. Maclean's "triune brain theory" (Cory et al. 2002). Maclean suggests that the human brain is actually three brains in one. In a diluted and adapted version of his theory, the three brains are the *reptilian brain*, *mammalian brain*, and *human brain*.

The *reptilian brain* regulates the "fight or flight" response to stress and relates most directly to the survival instincts. It is strongly associated with establishing home territory, reproduction, and social dominance. The reptilian brain operates automatically, has a ritualistic quality, and is resistant to change. In the improvisations, we will explore the *pelvis* as the center for the *reptilian brain*.

The *mammalian brain* is the center of emotion and feeling. It comes into play to arouse sentiments such as fear, pity, anger, joy, loss, love, longing, and celebration. In the improvisations, we will explore the *heart* as the center for the *mammalian brain*.

The *human brain* is the neocortex. It is the logical, rational, reasoning, and critical thinking center of the body. In the improvisations, we will explore the *head* as the center for the *human brain*.

The purpose here is not to become overly scientific, but rather to use this seemingly complex, but simple concept to make experiential changes in your embodiment of an expressive action. When it feels right, it probably is right! Play each expressive action in your barre from your *pelvis*. Play each expressive action in your barre from your *heart*. Play each expressive action in your barre from your *head*. Some expressive actions naturally will find an impulse in the head, heart, or pelvis. Others may have resisted a particular impulse origin. Nevertheless, many expressive actions can be played with multiple impulse origins.

Expression/explosion/repression/exaggeration

A prerequisite for expression is a surge in mental, emotional, and physical *energy*. Big thoughts and feelings generate high levels of energy in the body, and smaller thoughts and feelings generate lower levels of energy in the body. Sometimes the body mismanages or is unable to shape and organize the energy required for rewarding and meaningful expression. When this occurs, expression is circumvented or short-circuited and the increased energy—or lack of it—is diverted into three types of regulatory actions—*repression*, *explosion*, and/or *exaggeration*.

In the context of this exercise, the term *expression* is technically reserved for the skillful management of emotional, mental, and physical energy. It occurs only when the movement of our body, the sound of our voice and the words we choose to speak adequately reveal the content of our thoughts and feelings. Expression is typically a satisfying and rewarding human experience that leads to growth and positive change. Repression, explosion, and exaggeration, on the other hand, reflect a mismanagement of emotional, mental, and physical energy that in the context of this specialized exploration are not technically labeled as "expression." Expression in this context refers to genuine expression.

Repression

Repression is the most common way in which the body mismanages seemingly unwanted emotional, mental, and physical energy. The easiest way to define repression is to distinguish it from expression. While expression is the process of releasing, revealing, and clarifying thought and feeling, repression is, by contrast, the process of binding and concealing thought and feeling. Repression occurs when an individual experiences unwanted or seemingly negative thoughts and feelings that for whatever reason—conscious or unconscious—they will not or cannot express.

On a physical level, repression manifests itself in patterns of muscular holding. Typically, the mostly voluntary muscles located on the periphery of the body are engaged in an attempt to stifle the deeper involuntary muscles located in the center of the body. The purpose is to interrupt or circumvent the spontaneous expression of unwanted thoughts and feelings. Repression reflects an individual in a state of inner and outer distress. On one hand, a subconscious impulse to express the unwanted thought and feeling prompts the body to move in an outward direction; while, on the other hand, a need to conceal and regulate the thought and feeling pulls the body in an inward direction. The result is an individual literally divided against itself.

Explosion

Explosion is another method with which the body attempts to cope with seemingly unwanted mental, emotional, and physical energy. Explosion occurs when an individual experiences large and seemingly uncontrollable thoughts and feelings that cannot, because of lack of personal maturity or technical skill, be shaped and organized into meaningful forms of expression. In this instance, the energy is discharged in a violent and uncontrollable manner. An explosion typically occurs after a period of great frustration and is the result of the uncontrolled release of physical and psychological tensions that have been building up for some time. During an explosion the individual momentarily loses control of his or her mental, emotional and physical faculties. Though an explosion typically involves anger, it is possible to explode with laughter, tears, fear, physical pain, or any other uncontrollable thought and feeling.

Exaggeration

If an explosion is the result of being overwhelmed by large thoughts and feelings, exaggeration is the result of being underwhelmed. Exaggeration occurs when an individual artificially manufactures the energy that would in ideal situations arise involuntarily and spontaneously. Exaggeration occurs most frequently in social situations—a belabored apology, an overly enthusiastic thank you, a forced laughter, and patronizing praise are all types of exaggeration. Often the easiest way to survive is to exaggerate the depth and intensity of our thoughts and feelings: "Dinner was really delicious." "What a great haircut." "We would love to see you again." "Your children are angels." However, any thought or feeling can be exaggerated—sadness, joy, seriousness, light-heartedness, anger, or remorse. Artificially fabricating the energy needed for expression leads to a manufactured and disingenuous muscular effort. It is this excessive effort that often reveals the falseness and artificiality associated with exaggeration and the humor in irony and in comedy.

Explode each action in your barre. Repress each action in your barre. Exaggerate each action in your barre. Finally, clearly, efficiently, and appropriately express each action in your barre. It is possible that some expressive actions naturally leant themselves to expression, explosion, repression, or exaggeration. Others may have resisted one or more these directives. Nevertheless, many expressive actions can be experienced from one or more of these differing perspectives.

Part V

Technique

Chapter 11

Preliminaries

Rocking exercise

The rocking exercises are a simple method of deepening the connection between the movement center of the body (pelvis) and the periphery (legs, arms, hands, feet, and head). They also coordinate the integrated action of the moving, breathing, sounding, and speaking centers.

■ *Movement work*

Hook-lying position

Lie on your back. Allow your knees to bend so that the soles of your feet are making solid contact with the floor. Your feet should be about shoulder-width apart and as close to your pelvis as possible without causing strain or discomfort. Direct you knees in line with your feet. Allow your whole back to lengthen and widen into the floor. (This position is called a h*ook-lying position* because the legs are bent at the knees forming a hook-like shape.)

■ *Rocking action*

In a continuous and uninterrupted manner slowly, fluidly, and simultaneously crease and decrease in both of your thigh sockets. This creasing and decreasing action will simultaneously tilt both halves of the pelvis upward and downward as the lumbar spine arches and rounds. This upward and downward rocking action is similar to the action of a rocking chair. Encourage freedom and flexibility in your thigh sockets and lumbar spine. Allow this centered movement to radiate through your whole body. Release any unnecessary muscular tension that is keeping the energy in your body from flowing freely from the center to the periphery. Rest. Repeat this gentle rocking action until your lumbar spine and thigh sockets feel loose and limber, and your whole body is rocking on the floor in response to the action of your pelvis.

■ *Variations—physical properties*

As you rock, explore each of the physical properties in the expressive continuum. Take a brief rest in between the exploration of each physical property.

Expressive continuum

Each of the preliminary exercises involves an exploration of the *expressive continuum*. A copy of the expressive continuum is located in Appendix I.

Intermission

Charge/release and fall/carry

Typically, the breath, sound, and speech components of the improvisations begin with an exploration of *energy: charge/release*. It is not that energy is the only physical sensation that influences the breath, voice, and speech of the actor. To the contrary, each of the physical properties have a direct affect on each of the respective body centers. However, energy often plays a pivotal role in the process of integration. When the energy is skillfully orchestrated, many other factors tend to fall into place. The energy that we experience in the body manifests itself, in one degree or another, in all of the other physical properties. The degree and intensity of any physical property—*fast, sharp, indirect*, or *stable*—is related directly to the degree of energy experienced in the whole body. When we work with energy, the other physical properties simultaneously come along for the ride.

The directive to allow the body to *carry* or to *fall* are metaphorical descriptions of the physical sensations associated with a charging or a releasing action in the breathing, sounding, and speaking centers. When the *body carries* there is a buildup of energy that supports the breath, sound, and speech of the actor. When the *body falls* there is a letting go of energy that releases the breath, voice, sound, and speech of the actor. We experience *carry (charge)* and *fall* (*release*) in a corresponding wave-like action. The *rising action* of the wave reflects a *carry (charge)*, and the *falling action* of the wave reflects a *fall* (*release*). This principle reinforces the central premise that in integrated physical action the body plays a primary role in directing, guiding, and shaping the breathing sounding and speaking actions of the actor.

As an introduction to this principle, let's explore, this falling and carrying action in an isolated and peripheral action of the arm. After this principle has been experienced and clarified in this simple action, continue the rocking exercise below, applying the principle in a larger and more complex, centered, full-bodied movements of the pelvis.

- Raise your lower arm upward toward your shoulder by bending at the elbow. This upward action, a way from the earth, is a *charge*.
- Reverse the action and lower the arm. This downward action, towards the earth is a *release*.
- Raise your arm again. Allow your breath to accompany this movement on a simple *hiss*—a voiceless "sss" sound. This is the experience of the *body carrying the breath* (*charge*).
- Lower your arm. Allow your breath to fall from your body on a simple *sigh* a voiceless "huh" sound as the arm falls. This is the experience of the *breath falling from the body* (*release*).
- Raise your arm again. Allow your sound to accompany the movement on a simple "ee" sound as in the word "me." This is the experience of the *body carrying the sound* (*charge*).
- Lower your arm. Allow your sound to fall from the body on a simple *sigh* a voiced "ee" sound as the arm falls. This is the experience of the *sound falling from the body* (*release*).
- Raise your arm again. Allow a simple sentence to accompany the movement. This is the experience of the *body carrying the text* (*charge*).
- Lower your arm. Allow a simple sentence to fall from the body as the arm falls. This is the experience of the *text falling from the body* (*release*).

● *Breath and movement work*

As you rock, explore the following breathing actions:

- *Release*: the *breath falls from the body* on a simple *sigh*—a voiceless "huh" sound. Release the breath as the pelvis rounds in to the floor. Receive a new breath as the pelvis arches up and away from the floor. This relatively quick exchange of breath is similar to a pant. Rest and repeat.
- *Charge*: the *body carries the breath* on a simple *hiss*—a voiceless "sss" sound. This "sss" sound is sustained over several successive sets or segments of rocking. Rest and repeat.

● *Variations—physical properties*

As you rock, explore each of the physical properties in the expressive continuum. Take a brief rest in between the exploration of each physical property.

Integration and isolation

When improvising with the physical properties, you will experience the *integrated action* of the moving, breathing, sounding, and speaking centers. For example, this would occur when a *charge* in the body is simultaneously experienced in the moving, breathing, sounding, and speaking centers. Integration is the experience of all the body centers participating in a shared physical experience. When improvising with the physical properties, you may also experience certain *isolated actions* in the moving, breathing, sounding, and speaking centers. For example, this would occur when the body *releases* and the voice *charges*, or when a *fast* movement of the body is accompanied by a *slow* movement of the breath. Though the possibilities are seemingly innumerable. Isolation is the experience of one or more of the body centers participating in a physical experience that is in opposition to the physical experience occurring in other centers of the body. Developing an awareness of integrated and isolated physical action is an important component of this method of acting training. (See *Chapter 4: Integration*.)

◆ *Sound and movement work*

As you rock, explore the following:

- *Release*: the *sound falls from the body* on a selected vowel sound. Receive a new breath in between each individual rocking action. This relatively quick exchange of sound is similar to a "voiced" pant. Rest and repeat.
- *Charge*: the *body carries the sound* on a selected vowel sound. The vowel sound is sustained over several successive sets or segments of rocking. Rest and repeat.

◆ *Variations—vowel sounds*

Repeat the exercises described above on the following vowel sounds "ee" (as in "me"), "ay" (as in "may"), "ah" (as in "ma'), "oh" (as in "mow"), "oo" (as in "moo"). Allow the physical sensations in your body to shape and influence the quality and color of the vowel sounds. Repeat with other vowel sounds of your choosing.

◆ *Variations—physical properties*

As you rock, explore each of the physical properties in the expressive continuum. Take a brief rest in between the exploration of each physical property.

▲ *Speech and movement work*

As you rock, explore the following:

- *Release*: the *text falls from the body* on a simple sentence. This simple sentence releases from the body over several successive sets or segments of rocking. Rest and repeat.
- *Charge*: the *body carries the text* on a simple sentence. This simple sentence is sustained over several successive sets or segments of rocking. Rest and repeat.

You may compose a simple sentence of your own or use a sentence from a play-script of your choice.

▲ *Variations—physical properties*

As you rock, explore each of the physical properties in the expressive continuum. Take a brief rest in between the exploration of each physical property.

Swarming

■ *Movement work*

Move from the middle of the room outward to any point along any one of the four sides of the room. After arriving at this outermost point, change direction and return to the center of the room. Once back at the center, repeat this "swarming action" to and from other outermost points for a minute or so. (The name of this exercise is derived from the way in which bees swarm around their hive.)

■ *Variations—physical properties*

Continue swarming, exploring each of the physical properties in the expressive continuum. Take a rest in between each physical property being explored.

● *Breath and movement work*

As you swarm, explore the following:

- *Release*: the *breath falls from the body* on a simple *sigh*—a voiceless "huh" sound. This sighing-action occurs each time you change directions. Receive a new breath as necessary in between each sighing-action.
- *Charge*: the *body carries the breath* on a simple *hiss*—a voiceless "sss" sound. This hissing-action is sustained during the swarming action. Receive a new breath each time you change directions.

● *Variations—physical properties*

Continue swarming, exploring each of the physical properties in the expressive continuum. Take a rest in between each physical property being explored.

◆ *Sound and movement work*

As you swarm, explore the following:

- *Release*: the *sound falls from the body* on a selected vowel sound. This brief sounding-action occurs each time you change directions. Receive a new breath as necessary in between each sounding-action.
- *Charge*: the *body carries the sound* on a selected vowel sound. This sounding-action is sustained during the swarming action. Receive a new breath each time you change directions.

◆ *Variations—vowel sounds*

Repeat with other vowel sounds of your choosing.

◆ *Variations—physical properties*

As you swarm, explore each of the physical properties in the expressive continuum. Take a brief rest in between the exploration of each physical property.

▲ *Speech and movement work*

As you swarm, explore the following:

- *Release*: the *text falls from the body* on a simple sentence. This simple sentence releases from the body as you swarm around the room. Rest and repeat.
- *Charge*: the *body carries the text* on a simple sentence. This simple sentence is sustained in the body as you swarm around the room. Rest and repeat.

You may compose a simple sentence of your own or use a sentence from a playscript of your choice.

▲ *Variations—physical properties*

As you swarm, explore each of the physical properties in the expressive continuum. Take a brief rest in between the exploration of each physical property.

Lying—sitting—standing—walking

■ *Movement work*

Begin by lying on the floor. Rest. Move to sitting on the floor. Rest. Move to standing. Rest. Move to sitting in a nearby chair. Rest. Begin walking around the room. Rest. Return to standing near the chair. Rest. Return to sitting in the chair. Rest. Return to sitting on the floor. Rest. Return to lying on the floor. Rest.

Explore the movement sequence physically. Allow it to develop into a repeatable physical pattern that your body can remember.

■ *Variations—physical properties*

Repeat the movement sequence while exploring the physical properties in the expressive continuum: For example, begin by lying on the floor in a *charged* manner. Rest. Move to sitting on the floor in a *fast* manner. Rest. Move to standing in a *sharp* manner … and so on.

● *Breath and movement work*

During the movement sequence, explore the following:

- *Release*: the *breath falls from the body* on a simple *sigh*—a voiceless "huh" sound. This sighing-action will occur one time during each individual action of the movement sequence. Receive a new breath in between each action in the movement sequence.
- *Charge*: the *body carries the breath* on a simple *hiss*—a voiceless "sss" sound. This hissing-action occurs during each individual actions of the movement sequence. Receive a new breath in between each action in the movement sequence.

● *Variations—physical properties*

Repeat the movement sequence while exploring the physical properties in the expressive continuum.

◆ *Sound and movement work*

During the movement sequence, explore the following:

- *Release*: the *sound falls from the body* on a selected vowel sound. This sounding-action will occur one time during each individual action of the movement sequence. Receive a new breath in between each action in the movement sequence.
- *Charge*: the *body carries the sound* on a selected vowel sound. This sounding-action occurs during each individual actions of the movement sequence. Receive a new breath in between each action in the movement sequence.

◆ *Variations—physical properties*

Repeat the movement sequence while exploring the physical properties in the expressive continuum.

◆ *Variations—vowel sounds*

Repeat with other vowel sounds of your choosing.

▲ *Speech and movement work*

During the movement sequence, explore the following:

- *Release*: the *text falls from the body* on a simple sentence. This simple sentence releases from the body one time during each individual action of the movement sequence. Receive a new breath in between each individual action of the movement sequence.
- *Charge*: the *body carries the text* on a simple sentence. This simple sentence is sustained in the body during each individual action of the movement sequence. Receive a new breath in between each individual action of the movement sequence.

You may compose a simple sentence of your own or use a sentence from a playscript of your choice.

▲ *Variations—physical properties*

Repeat the movement sequence while exploring the physical properties in the expressive continuum.

Rudolf Laban I

This exercise is adapted from an exercise developed by Rudolf Laban (1971: 77).

■ *Movement work*

Select an action from the following list: punch, slash, dab, flick, press, wring, glide, or float.

Explore the action physically. Allow it to develop into a repeatable phrase that has a clearly defined beginning, middle, and end.

■ *Variations—physical properties*

Repeat the action while exploring each of the physical properties in the expressive continuum. Take a rest in between each physical property being explored.

■ *Variations—repetition*

Repeat with the other actions listed above or with other actions listed in Appendix II.

● *Breath and movement work*

As you play your action, explore the following:

- *Release*: the *breath falls from the body* on a simple *sigh*—a voiceless "huh" sound. This sighing-action will occur each time you play your action. Receive a new breath after you play your action as necessary. Repeat.
- *Charge*: the *body carries the breath* on a simple *hiss*—a voiceless "sss" sound. This hissing-action is sustained while playing your action. Receive a new breath after you play your action as necessary. Repeat.

● *Variations—physical properties*

Repeat the action while exploring each of the physical properties in the expressive continuum. Take a rest in between each physical property being explored.

● *Variations—repetition*

Repeat with the other actions listed above or with other actions listed in Appendix II.

◆ *Sound and movement work*

As you play your action, explore the following:

- *Release*: the *sound falls from the body* on a selected vowel sound. This sounding-action will occur each time you play your action. Receive a new breath after you play your action as necessary. Repeat.
- *Charge*: the *body carries the sound* on a selected vowel sound. This sounding-action is sustained while playing your action. Receive a new breath after you play your action as necessary. Repeat.

◆ *Variations—physical properties*

Repeat the action while exploring each of the physical properties in the expressive continuum. Take a rest in between each physical property being explored.

◆ *Variations—vowel sounds*

Repeat with other vowel sounds of your choosing.

◆ *Variations—repetition*

Repeat with the other actions listed above or with other actions listed in Appendix II.

▲ *Speech and movement work*

As you play your action, explore the following:

- *Release*: the *text falls from the body* on a simple sentence. This simple sentence releases from the body each time you play your action. Receive a new breath after you play your action as necessary. Repeat.
- *Charge*: the *body carries the text* on a simple sentence. This simple sentence is sustained in the body while playing your action. Receive a new breath after you play your action as necessary. Repeat.

You may compose a simple sentence of your own or use a sentence from a playscript of your choice.

◆ *Variations—physical properties*

As you play your action, explore each of the physical properties in the expressive continuum. Take a brief rest in between the exploration of each physical property.

Rudolf Laban II

This exercise is adapted from an exercise developed by Rudolf Laban (1971, 27).

■ *Movement work*

Select a movement sequence from the list below:

1 running—tossing—crouching—whirling
2 bowing—lifting—closing—opening
3 swaying—circling—spreading—hovering
4 trembling—shrinking—dropping—sprawling
5 waving—perching—pouncing—creeping
6 racing—turning—jumping—sagging

Explore the movement sequence physically. Allow it to develop into a repeatable physical phrase that your body can remember. Rest briefly in between each individual action in the movement sequence.

■ *Variations—physical properties*

Repeat the movement sequence while exploring each of the physical properties in the expressive continuum.

■ *Variations—repetition*

Repeat with other movement sequences listed above or create a new movement sequence with the actions listed in Appendix II.

● *Breath and movement work*

During the movement sequence, explore the following:

- *Release*: the *breath falls from the body* on a simple *sigh*—a voiceless "huh" sound. This sighing-action will occur one time during each individual action of the movement sequence. Receive a new breath in between each individual action of the movement sequence.
- *Charge*: the *body carries the breath* on a simple *hiss*—a voiceless "sss" sound. This hissing-action is sustained while playing each of the four actions of the movement sequence. Receive a new breath in between each individual action of the movement sequence.

● *Variations—physical properties*

During the movement sequence, explore each of the physical properties in the expressive continuum.

● *Variations—repetition*

Repeat with other suggested movement sequences or create a new movement sequence using actions listed in Appendix II.

◆ *Sound and movement work*

During the movement sequence, explore the following:

- *Release*: the *sound falls from the body* on a selected vowel sound. This sounding-action will occur one time during each individual action of the movement sequence. Receive a new breath in between each individual action of the movement sequence.
- *Charge*: the *body carries the sound* on a selected vowel sound. This sounding-action is sustained while playing each of the four actions of the movement sequence. Receive a new breath in between each individual action of the movement sequence.

◆ *Variations—physical properties*

During the movement sequence, explore each of the physical properties in the expressive continuum.

◆ *Variations—vowel sounds*

Repeat with other vowel sounds of your choosing.

◆ *Variations—repetition*

Repeat with other suggested movement sequences or create a new movement sequence using actions listed in Appendix I.

▲ *Speech and movement work*

During the movement sequence, explore the following:

- *Release*: the *text falls from the body* on a simple sentence. This simple sentence releases from the body one time during each individual action of the movement sequence. Receive a new breath in between each individual action of the movement sequence.
- *Charge*: the *body carries the text* on a simple sentence. This simple sentence is sustained in the body during each individual action of the movement sequence. Receive a new breath in between each individual action of the movement sequence.

You may compose a simple sentence of your own or use a sentence from a playscript of your choice.

▲ *Variations—physical properties*

As you swarm, explore each of the physical properties in the expressive continuum. Take a brief rest in between the exploration of each physical property.

Chapter 12

Voice and body exercises

12.1 LYING AND BREATHING EXERCISES

These lying and breathing exercises are integrated explorations of the breath and the body and are modeled on the *architecture of an expressive action*. During the lying and breathing exercises, your pelvis and legs are tossed and swung and raised and lowered in a variety of positions and patterns. The purpose of these exercises is to develop the ability to integrate the action of your pelvis, legs, and feet with the action of your breath. When this skill is mastered, it is possible to stand upright and make bold and momentous physical movements without disrupting the flow of the breath.

Phrasing

As you explore the exercises, observe the structured rhythm of the physical phrase. Allow each physical phrase to have a clearly defined beginning, middle, and end. In this manner, the breath is not simply released or sustained, but rather initiates, develops, and resolves in much the same way that a sentence has a clearly defined beginning, middle, and end. A well-coordinated physical phrase promotes fluid and integrated breathing. Ideally, this structured exploration of the breath and body prepares the way for the well-supported phrasing of language.

When writing, it is difficult to communicate precisely *when to inhale* and *when to exhale*. Breathing is always somewhat personal. The exercises simply provide general directives with respect to when to receive a breath and when to give that breath away. With time and experience, the breath is released, sustained, and replaced organically and ineffably in concert with the movement of the body. Integrated breathing and moving is a natural and normal human activity. When it feels right, it probably is right! Additionally, all of the exercises can be done at a variety of speeds. In the beginning, the best advice is to go as fast or as slowly as necessary.

Applying the principles

Successful practice is linked directly to applying the principles presented in previous chapters. The written descriptions of the exercises simply articulate the basic structure or form of the exercise. They do not rearticulate the principles. When learning the exercises, begin by developing an overall understanding of their basic structure and then proceed with the important work of applying the principles. Once the basic structure of the exercise is understood—"roll onto the left side," "toss the arm to the right," "carry an 'sss' sound"—the principles can be applied—"I *contact* the environment as my body *expands* and *withdraw* as my body *contracts*." "The energy in my body *charges* before it *releases*," "I begin with a *centrally initiated weight shift* in the pelvis," "My arms are *tasseling* and *boomeranging* with the pelvic center."

A superficial understanding of the basic structure of the exercise is relatively easy to obtain. However, a sophisticated re-education of the body structure requires a diligent and conscientious application of the principles. All the exercises are designed to reflect the physical structure of the *Major properties of an expressive action*. All the exercises, in one form or another, *charge* and *release*, *contact* and *withdraw*, *expand* and *contract* as the whole body moves from the *center* to the *periphery* in a *free flowing* manner. An awareness of this structure is essential to integrated and successful practice.

Additionally, the application of the following principles will assist you in your exploration:

- integrated weight shifts;
- pelvic center;
- upper body sequence (pelvis + ribcage + head);
- lower body sequence (pelvis + knee + ankle + foot);
- creasing and decreasing in the thigh socket;
- tasseling and boomeranging arms and legs;
- up the front (charge)/down the back (release);
- undercurve and overcurve movement pathways;
- breathing center—the diaphragm;
- upper and lower breathing spaces;
- falling or carrying breath—sighing and hissing;
- giving and receiving the breath.

Movement center—simple weight shifts

The simple weight shifts below reflect a fundamental exploration of the pelvic center. These rocking, swing and circling actions each engage the pelvic center by a creasing and decreasing action in the thigh socket, the forward and backward tilt of the pelvis and the arching and rounding of the lumbar spine. In integrated full-bodied physical action, all movement begins with a variation and a combination of these simple rocking, swinging, and/or circling actions.

■ *Basic exercise—pelvis rocking*

Long lying position: Lie on your back with your legs and arms lengthened. Your feet should be comfortably close together, with your arms resting away from your body at approximately a 45 degree angle. The legs and feet will rotate naturally and fall outward.

In a continuous and uninterrupted manner slowly, fluidly, and simultaneously crease and decrease in both of your thigh sockets. This creasing and decreasing action will simultaneously tilt both halves of the pelvis upward and downward as the lumbar spine arches and rounds. This upward and downward rocking action is similar to the action of a rocking chair. Repeat this action for several moments. As you rock your pelvis, sense the *tasseling action* of your legs and feet. Relieve any muscular tension that is preventing your legs from responding to the movement of your pelvis. Allow your whole body to respond to this centered rocking action. Repeat this rocking action for several moments. Luxuriate in this centered weight shift. Rest. Repeat as necessary.

● *Panting*

Allow a very quick and reflexive panting-action to integrate with the action of your pelvis.

■ *Basic exercise—pelvis swing*

Begin in the long-lying position as in the previous exercise. In a continuous and uninterrupted manner, slowly and fluidly shift one side of your pelvis upward as the other side of your pelvis shifts downward. (This movement is created by creasing in one thigh socket as you decrease in the other thigh socket.) Rest. Repeat this swinging action several times. The swinging action of the pelvis is similar to a pendulum swinging back and forth. As you swing your pelvis, sense the *tasseling action* of your legs and feet. Relieve any muscular tension that is preventing your legs from responding to the movement of your pelvis. Allow your whole body to respond to this centered swinging action. Repeat this swinging action for several moments. Luxuriate in this centered weight shift. Rest. Repeat as necessary.

● *Panting*

Allow a very quick and reflexive panting-action to integrate with the action of your pelvis.

■ *Basic exercise—pelvis circling*

Begin in a long-lying position as in the previous exercise. In a continuous and uninterrupted manner, slowly and fluidly make a circle with your pelvis. This circling action is a combination of the rocking and swinging actions explored previously. The circling action of the pelvis is similar to the hands of the clock moving around the dial. As you circle your pelvis, sense the *tasseling action* of your legs and feet. Relieve any muscular tension that is preventing your legs from responding to the movement of your pelvis. Allow your whole body to respond to this centered circling action. Repeat this circling action for several moments. Luxuriate in this centered weight shift. Rest. Repeat as necessary.

● *Panting*

Allow a very quick and reflexive panting-action to integrate with the action of your pelvis.

Pelvic tilt

(See Figures 12.1 and 12.2.)

■ *Basic exercise*

1 *Hook-lying position*: Lie comfortably on your back. Bend your knees so that the soles of your feet make contact with the floor. Your feet should rest in an unstrained position near your buttocks. Direct your knees upward in line with your feet. Allow the weight of the floor to support you. (This exercise is called the hook-lying position because the folded legs form a hook-like shape.)
2 In an easy and fluid movement, slowly tilt your pelvis in an upward direction approximately two inches off the floor.
3 Reverse the tilting action so that your pelvis returns downward to the floor. Sense the creasing and decreasing action in your thigh sockets, which tilts your pelvis in an upward and downward direction. Repeat four times. Rest.

■ *Phrasing*

Repeat the basic exercise four times, while counting aloud this **4**-*2 count phrase*: **1**–2, **2**–2, **3**–2, **4**–2. Tilt your pelvis up on the first count and down on the second count of each phrase. Rest and repeat.

● *Release—breath falls from the body*

Repeat the basic exercise. Receive a new breath each time your pelvis tilts upward. Allow your breath to *fall from your body* on a simple *sigh*—a voiceless "huh" sound—each time your pelvis tilts downward and returns to the floor. The sensation of your body yielding to gravity should accompany the passive release of your outgoing breath.

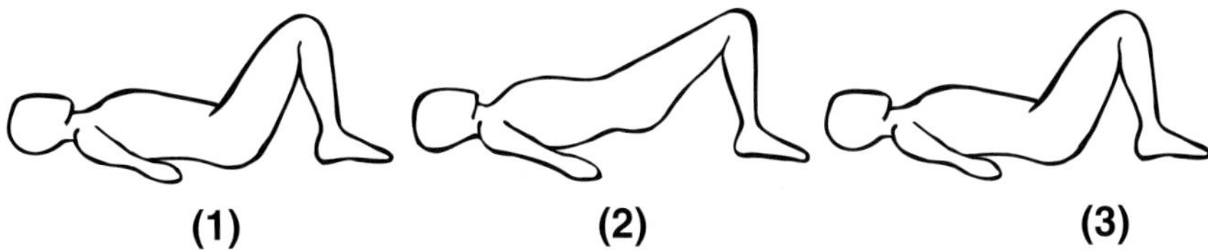

Figure 12.1 Pelvic tilt.

	1ST PHRASE		2ND PHRASE		3RD PHRASE		4TH PHRASE		REST
■	TILT UP	TILT DOWN	TILT UP	TILT DOWN	TILT UP	TILT DOWN	TILT UP	TILT DOWN	
■	**1** - 2		**2** - 2		**3** - 2		**4** - 2		
●	*	SIGH	*	SIGH	*	SIGH	*	SIGH	
●	*ssssssssssssssssssssssssssssssssssssssssssssssssssssssssssssssssssss								

* = receive a new breath
ssss = a sustained "s" sound

Figure 12.2 Pelvic tilt table.

● *Charge—body carries the breath*

Repeat the basic exercise. Receive a new breath at the top of the first phrase just as your pelvis tilts upward. Immediately after receiving the breath, allow your *body to carry the breath* on a simple *hiss*—an uninterrupted voiceless "sss" sound—over the entire ***4**–2 count phrase*. The sensation of your body carrying your breath should accompany the actively sustained "sss" sound.

Partial bridge

(See Figures 12.3 and 12.4.)

■ *Basic exercise*

1 Begin in a hook-lying position as in the previous exercise.
2 In an easy and fluid movement, slowly roll your pelvis in an upward direction away from the floor (This is the same tilting action performed in the previous exercise.) Then continue rolling your pelvis upward until the weight of your body is balanced evenly over your shoulders and your feet. Allow

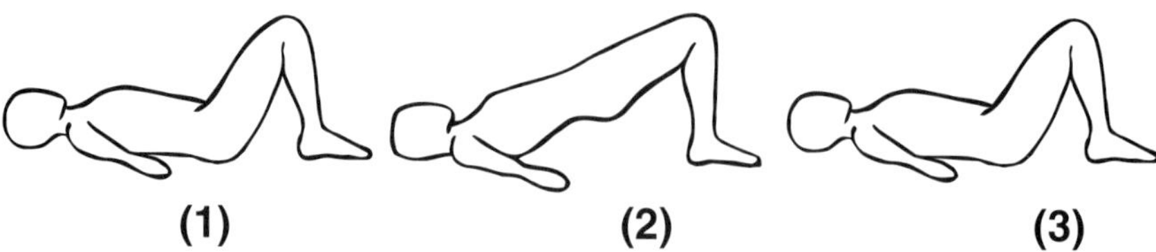

Figure 12.3 Partial bridge.

	1ST PHRASE			2ND PHRASE			3RD PHRASE	
■	ROLLING UP	ROLLING DOWN	R	ROLLING UP	ROLLING DOWN	R	ROLLING UP	ROLLING DOWN
■	1 - 2 - 3 - 4 - 5 - 6 - 7 - 8		E S T	2 - 2 - 3 - 4	5 - 6 - 7 - 8	E S T	2 - 2 - 3 - 4	5 - 6 - 7 - 8
●	*	SIGH		*	SIGH		*	SIGH
●	*sssssssssssssssssssss			*sssssssssssssssssssss			*sssssssssssssssssssss	

* = receive a new breath
ssss = a sustained "s" sound

Figure 12.4 Partial bridge table.

your spine and legs to follow your rising pelvis. This will cause your belly to float upward toward the ceiling. Your shoulder girdle and head remain in contact with the floor. The muscles of your legs and buttocks remain soft and free throughout the movement. Your legs remain stable and aligned. The soles of your feet are well grounded, lengthening and widening into the floor. Avoid muscling your body upward by lifting in your chest or pushing in your legs and feet.

3 Reverse the rolling action, lowering your pelvis and spine toward the floor one vertebra at a time. Your pelvis returns to the floor last.

4 Sense the decreasing action in the thigh sockets, which lifts your pelvis up and away from the floor, and the creasing action in the thigh sockets, which lowers your pelvis down toward the floor. Repeat three times, resting briefly in between each phrase.

■ *Phrasing*

Repeat the basic exercise three times, while counting aloud this **3**–*8 count phrase*: **1**–2–3–4–5–6–7–8, **2**–2–3–4–5–6–7–8, **3**–2–3–4–5–6–7–8. Roll your pelvis up on counts one through four and down on counts five through eight. Take a brief rest in between each of the eight-count phrases.

● *Release—breath falls from the body*

Repeat the basic exercise. Receive a new breath each time your pelvis rolls up and away from the floor. Allow your breath to *fall from your body* on a simple *sigh*—a voiceless "huh" sound—each time your pelvis returns to the floor. The sensation of your body yielding to gravity should accompany the passive release of your outgoing breath.

● *Charge—body carries the breath*

Repeat the basic exercise. Receive a new breath at the top of each eight-count phrase just as your pelvis tilts upward. Immediately after receiving your breath, allow your *body to carry your breath* on a simple *hiss*—an uninterrupted voiceless "sss" sound—for the remainder of the eight-count phrase. The sensation of your body carrying the breath should accompany the actively sustained "sss" sound.

Side roll

(See Figures 12.5 and 12.6.)

■ *Basic exercise*

1 Begin in a long-lying position as in the previous exercise.
2 Draw your left knee upward to your chest.
3 Roll your pelvis over so that you are lying on your right side. As you roll onto your right side, allow your right knee to gently cascade into the floor. Your knee will continue to slide across the floor until your pelvis, torso, and the right side of your head are resting on the floor. Your right arm remains extended out and away from your torso. Allow your left arm to passively follow the movement of your upper body, gently resting across your back at about waist level. (The rolling action should take place in this sequence: pelvis, ribcage, head, and arm.)
4 After a brief pause, reverse the rolling action, so that your body returns to its starting position.

Sense the creasing action in your thigh socket, which draws your leg upward toward your chest, and the decreasing action in your thigh socket, which assists in rolling over onto your side. Rest. Repeat the side roll on the opposite side.

■ *Phrasing*

Repeat the basic exercise. Count the exercise aloud in a ***4**–8 count phrase*: **1**–2–3–4–5–6–7–8, **2**–2–3–4–5–6–7–8, **3**–2–3–4–5–6–7–8, **4**–2–3–4–5–6–7–8. Roll over onto your right side on the first eight-count phrase and back on the second eight-count phrase. Roll over onto your left side on the third eight-count phrase and back on the fourth eight-count phrase. Take a brief rest between each of the four eight-count phrases.

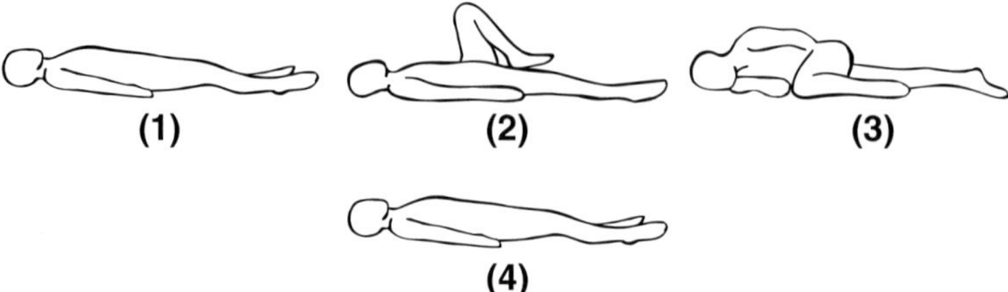

Figure 12.5 Side roll.

Right Side-Roll

	1ST PHRASE			2ND PHRASE		
■	ROLL OVER ONTO THE RIGHT SIDE		R	ROLL BACK INTO THE LONG-LYING POSITION		R
■	**1** – 2 – 3 – 4 – 5 – 6 – 7 – 8		E	**2** – 2 – 3 – 4 – 5 – 6 – 7 – 8		E
●	*	SIGH	S	*	SIGH	S
●	*sssssssssssssssssssssssssssssssss		T	*sssssssssssssssssssssssssssssssssss		T

Left Side-Roll

	3RD PHRASE			4TH PHRASE		
■	ROLL OVER ONTO THE LEFT SIDE		R	ROLL BACK INTO THE LONG-LYING POSITION		R
■	**3** – 2 – 3 – 4 – 5 – 6 – 7 – 8		E	**4** – 2 – 3 – 4 – 5 – 6 – 7 – 8		E
●	*	SIGH	S	*	SIGH	S
●	*sssssssssssssssssssssssssssssssss		T	*sssssssssssssssssssssssssssssssss		T

* = receive a new breath
ssss = a sustained "s" sound

Figure 12.6 Side roll table.

● *Release—breath falls from the body*

Repeat the basic exercise. Receive a new breath during the first half of each phrase, counts one through four. Allow your breath to *fall from your body* on a simple *sigh*—a voiceless "huh" sound—during the second half of each phrase, counts five through eight. The sensation of your body yielding to gravity should accompany the passive release of your outgoing breath.

● *Charge—body carries the breath*

Repeat the basic exercise. Receive a new breath at the top of each eight-count phrase. Immediately after receiving your breath, allow your *body to carry your breath* on a simple a *hiss*—an uninterrupted voiceless "sss" sound—for the remainder of the eight-count phrase.

Eight swings

(See Figures 12.7 and 12.8.)

■ *Basic exercise*

1 *Egg-lying position*: Lie on your back. Allow your knees to bend making a deep crease in your thigh sockets. This will fold your legs in and upward toward your chest. Allow your whole back to lengthen and widen into the floor. Extend both arms out and away from the sides of your body at approximately a forty-five degree angle. You should not feel as if you are holding your legs up in the air, but rather, that they are stabilized and supported from your pelvis. Encourage the sensation of your legs floating or hovering above your center. (This position is called an *egg-lying position* because the body is in an oval shape like that of an egg.)
2 With your folded legs centered over your pelvis, initiate a circular swinging action from your pelvis, which tosses your folded legs over to the right side
3 And then back to center.
4 Without interruption, continue the circular swinging action tossing your folded legs over to the left side
5 And then back to center.

These two circles, on the right and left side, unite to form a figure-eight pattern. This swinging action is created by an alternating creasing and decreasing action in your thigh sockets. Allow the momentum created by the swinging action to assist with the movement of your legs. Little or no discernible muscular effort should be sensed in your swinging legs and feet as they are released and supported from your pelvis during the swinging action. Repeat four times. Rest.

● *Phrasing*

Repeat the basic exercise. Count the exercise aloud in a ***4****–6 count phrase*: **1**–2–3–4–5–6, **2**–2–3–4–5–6, **3**–2–3–4–5–6, **4**–2–3–4–5–6. Complete the first eight swing on the first six-count phrase, the second eight swing on the second six-count phrase, and so on. Take a brief rest after completing the fourth six-count phrase.

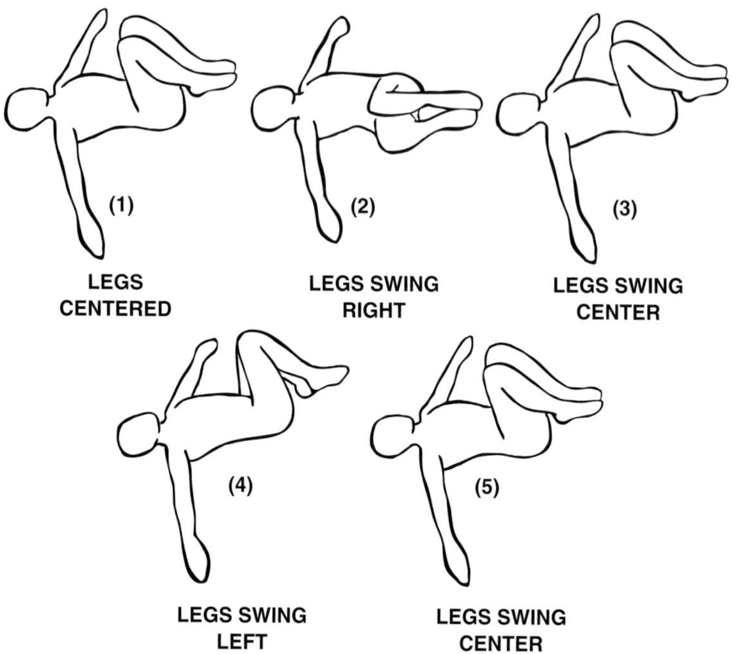

Figure 12.7 Eight swings.

	1ST PHRASE				2ND PHRASE			
■	1 – 2 – 3 – 4 – 5 – 6				2 – 2 – 3 – 4 – 5 – 6			R E S T
■	SWING RIGHT	SWING CENTER	SWING LEFT	SWING CENTER	SWING RIGHT	SWING CENTER	SWING LEFT	
●	* SIGH	*	SIGH	*	SIGH	*	SIGH	
●	*SSSSSSSSSSSSSSSSSSSSSSSSSSSSSSSSSSSSSSSSSSSSSSSSSSSSSSSSSSSSSSSSSSSSSSSS							

	3RD PHRASE				4TH PHRASE			
■	3 – 2 – 3 – 4 – 5 – 6				4 – 2 – 3 – 4 – 5 – 6			R E S T
■	SWING RIGHT	SWING CENTER	SWING LEFT	SWING CENTER	SWING RIGHT	SWING CENTER	SWING LEFT	
●	* SIGH	*	SIGH	*	SIGH	*	SIGH	
●	*SSSSSSSSSSSSSSSSSSSSSSSSSSSSSSSSSSSSSSSSSSSSSSSSSSSSSSSSSSSSSSSSSSSSSSSS							

* = receive a new breath
ssss = a sustained "s" sound

Figure 12.8 Eight swings table.

● *Release—breath falls from the body*

Repeat the basic exercise. Receive a new breath immediately before beginning the first eight swing. Allow your *breath to fall from your body* on a simple *sigh*—a voiceless "huh" sound—as your legs swing out to the right side. Receive a new breath as your legs swing back through the center of the body. Allow your breath to fall from your body on a simple *sigh*—a voiceless "huh" sound—as your legs swing out to your left side. Continue for the remaining three phrases. The sensation of your body yielding to gravity should accompany the passive release of your outgoing breath.

● *Charge—body carries the breath*

Repeat the basic exercise. Receive a new breath at the top of each six-count phrase. Immediately after receiving the breath, allow your *body to carry your breath* on a simple *hiss*—an uninterrupted voice-less "sss" sound—for the remainder of the six-count phrase. The sensation of your body carrying the breath should accompany the actively sustained "sss" sound.

Thigh socket creases

(See Figures 12.9–12.11.)

■ *Basic exercise*

1 Begin in an egg-lying position as in the previous exercise.
2 Shifting your pelvis, move your right and then your left leg and foot in an alternating downward and upward directions toward and away from the floor. During the first alternating sequence, your right and then your left toe tip lightly touch the floor. Repeat twice.
3 During the second alternating sequence, your entire right and left foot touch the floor fluidly—toe, ball, heel—and leave the floor fluidly—heal, ball, toe. Repeat twice.
4 During the third alternating sequence, your right and then your left foot slide gently across the floor so that each leg is partially lengthened. Repeat twice.
5 During the fourth sequence, your right and then your left foot slide gently across the floor so that each leg is completely lengthened. Repeat twice.

Your legs and feet should remain approximately shoulder-width apart throughout this exercise. Don't let your feet thud and pound into the floor—stabilize their release from your pelvis. Sense the alternating creasing and decreasing action in your thigh sockets, which raises and lowers your legs and feet toward and away from the floor.

■ *Phrasing*

Repeat the basic exercise. Count the exercise aloud in a ***4**–4 count phrase*: **1**–2–3–4, **2**–2–3–4, **3**–2–3–4, **4**–2–3–4. In alternation, allow each toe to touch the floor

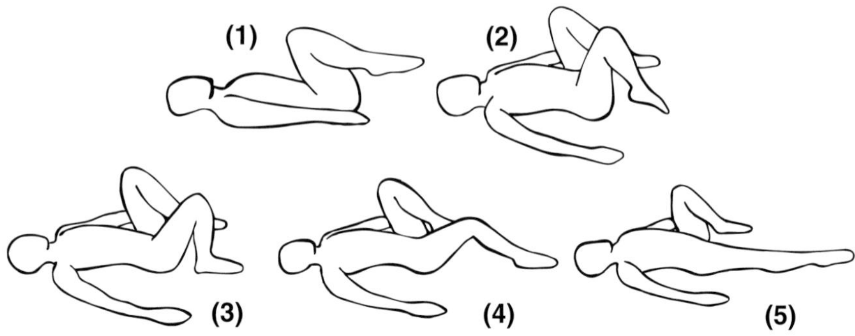

Figure 12.9 Thigh socket creases.

	1ST PHRASE				2ND PHRASE			
■	TOE TIP \ / RIGHT+ LEFT		TOE TIP \ / RIGHT+ LEFT		WHOLE FOOT \ / RIGHT + LEFT		WHOLE FOOT \ / RIGHT + LEFT	
■	1 - 2 - 3 - 4				2 - 2 - 3 - 4			
●	SIGH	SIGH	SIGH	SIGH	SIGH	SIGH	SIGH	SIGH
●	*ssssssssssssssssssssssssssssssssssssss				*ssssssssssssssssssssssssssssssssssss			

	3RD PHRASE				4TH PHRASE				
■	PARTIAL LEG LENGTEHNED \ / RIGHT+ LEFT		PARTIAL LEG LENGTEHNED \ / RIGHT+ LEFT		COMPLETE LEG LEGTHENED \ / RIGHT+ LEFT		COMPLETE LEG LEGTHENED \ / RIGHT+ LEFT		R E S T
■	3 - 2 - 3 - 4				4 - 2 - 3 - 4				
●	SIGH	SIGH	SIGH	SIGH	SIGH	SIGH	SIGH	SIGH	
●	*ssssssssssssssssssssssssssssssssssssss				*ssssssssssssssssssssssssssssssssssss				

* = receive a new breath
ssss = a sustained "s" sound

Figure 12.10 Thigh socket creases table.

twice during the first four-count phrase. In alternation, allow each foot to touch the floor twice during the second four-count phrase. In alternation, allow each leg to partially lengthen twice during the third four-count phrase. In alternation, allow each leg to completely lengthen twice during the fourth four-count phrase. Rest.

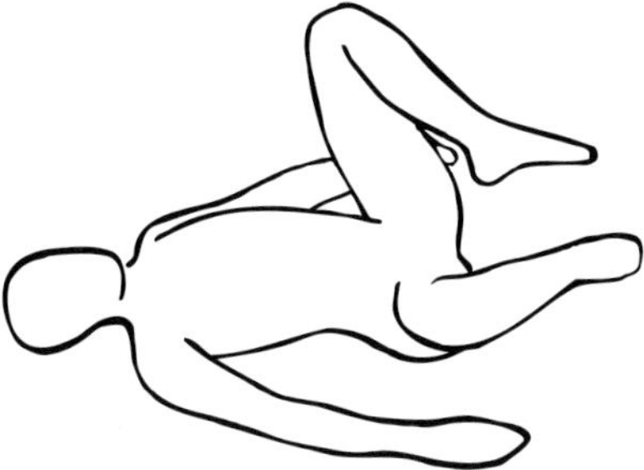

Figure 12.11 Thigh socket creases (rotation).

● *Release—breath falls from the body*

Repeat the basic exercise. Allow your *breath to fall from your body* on a simple *sigh*—a voiceless "huh" sound—each time one of your legs releases toward the floor. Your breath replaces immediately after exhaling. Take a very quick catch breath between each alternating action of your legs and feet. (This breathing action is relatively quick and similar to a pant.) The sensation of your body yielding to gravity should accompany the passive release of your outgoing breath.

● *Charge—body carries the breath*

Repeat the basic exercise. Receive a new breath at the top of each four-count phrase. Immediately after receiving your breath, allow your *body to carry your breath* on a simple *hiss*—an uninterrupted voiceless "sss" sound—over the remainder of the four-count phrase. The sensation of your body carrying your breath should accompany the actively sustained "sss" sound.

Variation

(See Figure 12.11.)
You can easily modify this exercise by reconfiguring the relationship of your legs and feet: rotate them outward at the thigh socket at approximately a forty-five degree angle.

Leg swings—parallel(advanced)

(See Figures 12.12 and 12.13.)

■ *Basic exercise*

1 Begin in a long-lying position as in previous exercises.
2 Allow your pelvis to toss or swing your left leg up off the floor. This forward and upward movement of your leg is similar to the action of kicking a

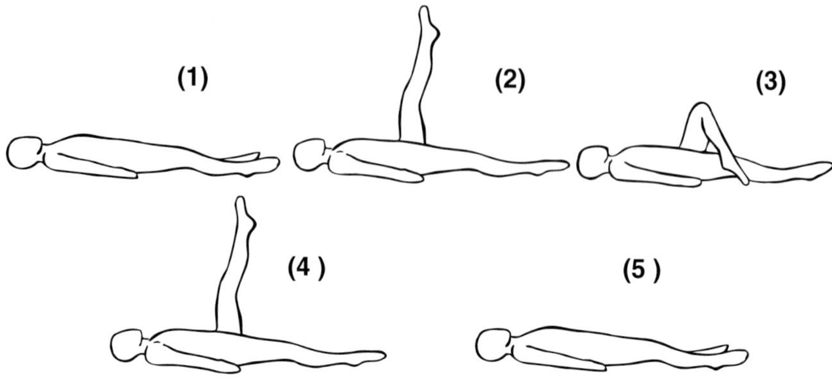

Figure 12.12 Leg swings (parallel).

	1st Phrase				2nd Phrase			
■	Swinging Right Leg Up & Over		Swinging Right Leg Back		Swinging Left Leg Up & Over		Swinging Left Leg Back	
■	1 – 2		– 3 – 4		2 – 2		– 3 – 4	
●	*	Sigh	*	Sigh	*	Sigh	*	Sigh
●	*ssssssssssssssssssssssssssssssssssssss				*sssssssssssssssssssssssssssssssssss			

	3rd Phrase				4th Phrase				
■	Swinging Right Leg Up & Over		Swinging Right Leg Back		Swinging Left Leg Up & Over		Swinging Left Leg Back		R E S T
■	3 – 2		– 3 – 4		4 – 2		– 3 – 4		
●	*	Sigh	*	Sigh	*	Sigh	*	Sigh	
●	*sssssssssssssssssssssssssssssssssss				*sssssssssssssssssssssssssssssssssss				

* = receive a new breath
ssss = a sustained "s" sound

Figure 12.13 Leg swings (parallel) table.

football when standing. Let your leg swing as high as is comfortable without bending or locking your knee.

3 When your swinging leg reaches its vertical apex, allow your pelvis to toss it across your right leg in a downward direction. During this swinging action, your knee will bend gently until your left foot lightly touches the floor near the outside of your right knee.
4 After your left foot has touched the floor, initiate a new swinging or tossing action in your pelvis, reversing the process.
5 Your swinging leg returns to its initial long-lying position.

The swinging and tossing of your leg and the bending of your knee should be viewed as one continuous and uninterrupted fluid movement. Sense the creasing action in your thigh socket, which raises your leg up and away from the floor, and the decreasing action in your thigh socket, which lowers your leg downward toward the floor. Repeat on the opposite side. Repeat twice. Rest.

■ *Phrasing*

Repeat the basic exercise. Count the exercise aloud in a ***4**–4 count phrase*: **1**–2–3–4, **2**–2–3–4, **3**–2–3–4, **4**–2–3–4. Swing your left leg up, over and back on the first four-count phrase. Swing your right leg up, over and back on the second four-count phrase. Repeat on counts three and four. Take a brief rest after completing the fourth four-count phrase.

● *Release—breath falls from the body*

Repeat the basic exercise. Receive a new breath each time your leg swings upward. Allow your *breath to fall from your body* on a simple *sigh*—a voiceless "huh" sound—each time your swinging leg releases toward the floor. The sensation of your body yielding to gravity should accompany the passive release of your outgoing breath.

● *Charge—body carries the breath*

Repeat the basic exercise. Receive a new breath at the top of each of the four-count phrases just as your leg begins to swing upward. Immediately after receiving your breath, allow your *body to carry your breath* on a simple *hiss*—an uninterrupted voiceless "sss" sound—over the remainder of the four-count phrase. The sensation of your body carrying the breath should accompany the actively sustained "sss" sound.

Leg swings—rotation (advanced)

(See Figures 12.14 and 12.15.)

■ *Basic exercise*

1 Begin in a long-lying position as in previous exercises.
2 Allow your pelvis to toss or swing your left leg off the floor away from the center at approximately a forty-five degree angle. Let your leg swing as high as is comfortable without bending or locking your knee.
3 As your swinging leg reaches its vertical apex, gently allow your knee to bend. Your bent leg is then swung in a downward direction so that the toes of your left foot gently touch the inside of your right knee.
4 After the toes of your left foot have touched your knee, initiate a new tossing or swinging action from your pelvis, reversing the process.
5 Your swinging leg returns to its initial long-lying position.

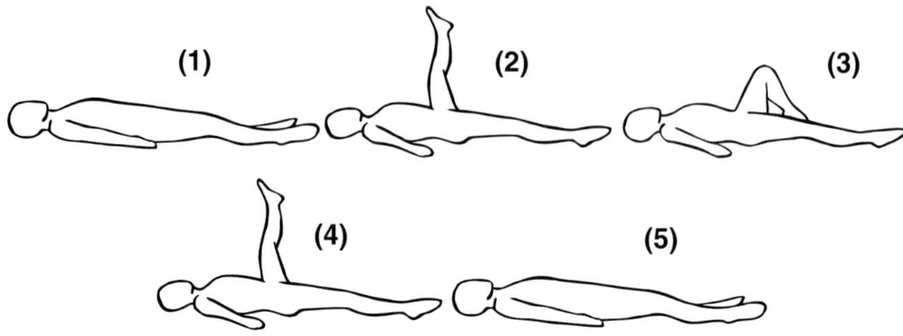

Figure 12.14 Leg swing (rotation).

	1st Phrase				2nd Phrase			
■	Swinging Right Leg Up & Down		Swinging Right Leg Back		Swinging Left Leg Up & Down		Swinging Left Leg Back	
■	**1** – 2 – 3 – 4				**2** – 2 – 3 – 4			
●	*	Sigh	*	Sigh	*	Sigh	*	Sigh
●	*ssssssssssssssssssssssssssssssssssssss				*ssssssssssssssssssssssssssssssssssss			

	3rd Phrase				4th Phrase				
■	Swinging Right Leg Up & down		Swinging Right Leg Back		Swinging Left Leg Up & down		Swinging Left Leg Back		REST
■	**3** – 2 – 3 – 4				**4** – 2 – 3 – 4				
●	*	Sigh	*	Sigh	*	Sigh	*	Sigh	
●	*ssssssssssssssssssssssssssssssssssssss				*ssssssssssssssssssssssssssssssssssss				

* = receive a new breath
ssss = a sustained "s" sound

Figure 12.15 Leg swing (rotation) table.

The swinging and tossing of your leg and the bending of your knee should be viewed as one continuous and uninterrupted fluid movement. Sense the creasing action in your thigh socket, which raises your leg up and away from the floor, and the decreasing action in your thigh socket, which lowers your leg downward toward the floor. Repeat on your right side. Repeat twice. Rest.

■ *Phrasing*

Repeat the basic exercise. Count the exercise aloud in a ***4**–4 count phrase*: **1**–2–3–4, **2**–2–3–4, **3**–2–3–4, **4**–2–3–4. Swing your right leg up, down and back on the first four-count phrase. Swing your left leg up, down, and back on the second four-count phrase. Repeat on counts three and four. Take a brief rest after completing the fourth four-count phrase.

● *Release—breath falls from the body*

Repeat the basic exercise. Receive a new breath each time your leg swings upward. Allow your *breath to fall from your body* on a simple *sigh*—a voiceless "huh" sound—each time your swinging leg releases toward the floor. The sensation of your body yielding to gravity should accompany the passive release of your outgoing breath.

● *Charge—body carries the breath*

Repeat the basic exercise. Receive a new breath at the top of each of the four-count phrases just as your leg begins to swing upward. Immediately after receiving your breath, allow your *body to carry your breath* on a simple *hiss*—an uninterrupted voiceless "sss" sound—over the remainder of the four-count phrase. The sensation of your body carrying your breath should accompany the actively sustained "sss" sound.

Roll-up (advanced)

(See Figures 12.16 and 12.17.)

■ *Basic exercise*

1 Begin in a long-lying position as in previous exercises.
2 Tilt your pelvis in a backward and downward direction. This will cause your lumbar spine to release into the floor. From this preparatory position, quickly roll your pelvis in a forward and upward direction. This will create a rounding action in your lumbar spine, which moves in sequence through your torso, shoulders, and head.
3 Continue rolling your entire spine forward and up until you arrive in a seated position. In this seated position, your spine is rounded, allowing your torso, head, and shoulders to hover over your legs and feet. The rolling action of your spine is integrated with corresponding movements in your arms and legs. As your spine rolls upward, your arms and legs are naturally drawn in toward the center of your body. When in the rounded, seated position, your hands rest comfortably near the floor on each foot, and your knees are bent comfortably, with the soles of your feet resting on the floor.
4 Once upright, the rolling action is reversed. Your pelvis tilts in a backward and downward direction and your body unrolls.
5 Your body returns to its initial position.

Observe the creasing and decreasing action in your thigh sockets, which coordinates the rolling and unrolling action of your spine. Repeat three times. Rest.

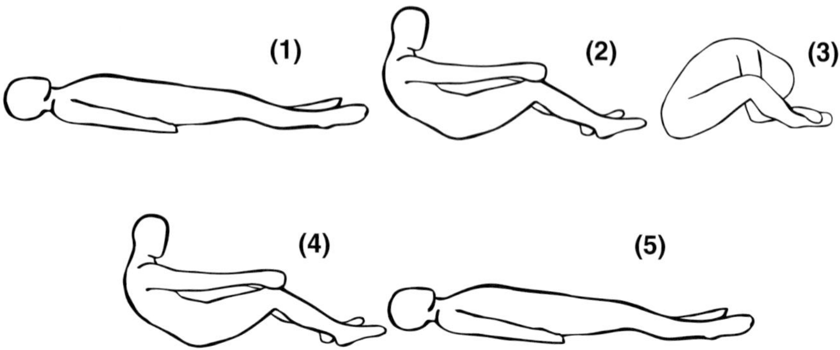

Figure 12.16 Roll-up.

	1st Phrase		2nd Phrase		3rd Phrase		R E S T
■	ROLLING UP	ROLLING DOWN	ROLLING UP	ROLLING DOWN	ROLLING UP	ROLLING DOWN	
■	**1** – 2 – 3 – 4 – 5 – 6 – 7 - 8		**2** – 2 – 3 – 4 – 5 – 6 – 7 – 8		**3** – 2 – 3 – 4 – 5 – 6 – 7 - 8		
●	*	SIGH	*	SIGH	*	SIGH	
●	*ssssssssssssssssssssssss		*sssssssssssssssssssssssss		*ssssssssssssssssssssssss		

* = receive a new breath
ssss = a sustained "s" sound

Figure 12.17 Roll-up table.

Roll-up vs. sit-up

It is common to look at the external shape of this exercise and assume that what is intended is a simple sit-up. However, when performed correctly, the roll-up is significantly different from the traditional sit-up, in which peripheral abdominal muscles are contracted and often crunched. Here, be sure to direct the rolling-up action from your thigh socket and not your belly muscles. This allows for the free and fluid movement of your breath while providing the stability and control necessary to support your lower back.

■ *Phrasing*

Repeat the basic exercise. Count the exercise aloud in a ***3**–8 count phrase*: **1**–2–3–4–5–6–7–8, **2**–2–3–4–5–6–7–8, **3**–2–3–4–5–6–7–8. Roll up and down on the first eight-count phrase. Roll up and down on the second eight-count phrase. Roll up and down on the third eight-count phrase. Take a brief rest after completing the third eight-count phrase.

● *Release—breath falls from the body*

Repeat the basic exercise. Receive a new breath at the start of each eight-count phrase just as your pelvis initiates the rolling action. Allow your *breath to fall from your body* on a simple *sigh*—a voiceless "huh" sound—as your upper body yields to gravity and falls over your legs and feet. Receive a new breath when your pelvis reverses its direction and initiates the backward rolling action. Allow your breath to fall from your body on a simple *sigh*—a voiceless "huh" sound—as your upper body releases back down into the floor. The sensation of your body yielding to gravity should accompany the passive release of your outgoing breath.

● *Charge—body carries the breath*

Repeat the basic exercise. Receive a new breath at the start of each eight-count phrase just as your pelvis initiates the rolling action. Immediately after receiving your breath, allow your *body to carry your breath* on a *hiss*—an uninterrupted voiceless "sss" sound—over the remainder of the eight-count phrase. The sensation of your body carrying the breath should accompany the actively sustained "sss" sound.

Spine rounding

(See Figures 12.18–12.20.)

All of the breathing exercises presented have been performed lying down. This is not to suggest that breathing exercises cannot be performed in sitting and standing positions. In fact, almost any sitting or standing exercise can easily be adapted into a breathing exercise. This exercise is one example.

■ *Basic exercise*

Long sit position: Sit on the floor with your body's weight equally distributed on your pelvis. Allow your lengthened legs to float easily and freely from your thigh sockets and rest comfortably on the floor. Your legs are comfortably close together. Your knees are straight, but not locked, and facing the ceiling. Your pelvis, rib cage, and head are vertical and

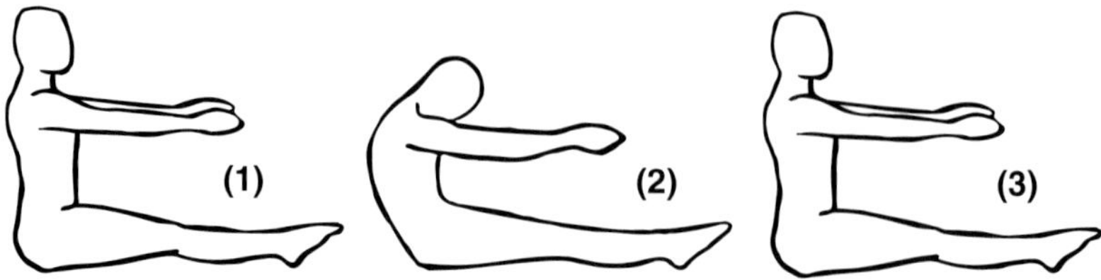

Figure 12.18 Spine rounding.

	1ST PHRASE		2ND PHRASE		3RD PHRASE		REST
■	ROUND	LENGTHEN	ROUND	LENGTHEN	ROUND	LENGTHEN	
■	1 – 2		2 – 2		3 – 2		
●	*	SIGH	*	SIGH	*	SIGH	
●	*ssssssssssssssssssssss		*ssssssssssssssssssssss		*ssssssssssssssssssssss		

* = receive a new breath
ssss = a sustained "s" sound

Figure 12.19 Spine rounding table.

Figure 12.20 Stride-sit position.

upright. Your rib cage and head balance evenly and comfortably over your pelvis. Encourage the sensation of your whole torso lengthening and widening.

1 Tilt your pelvis in a downward and backward direction until your whole spine rounds to form a "C" curve.
2 Once in this rounded position, reverse the action. Tilt your pelvis in a forward and upward direction, which lengthens your spine to its former upright and vertical position.

Sense the creasing and decreasing action in your thigh sockets, which coordinates the rounding and unrounding action of your spine. Repeat three times.

■ *Phrasing*

Repeat the basic exercise. Count the basic exercise aloud in a ***3*–*2 count phrase*:** **1**–2, **2**–2, **3**–2. Round your spine on the first count and lengthen your spine on the second count of each phrase. Take a brief rest after completing the third two-count phrase.

● *Release—breath falls from the body*

Repeat the basic exercise. Allow your *breath to fall from your body* on a simple *sigh*—a voiceless "huh" sound—each time your spine rounds. Receive a new breath each time your spine lengthens. The sensation of your body yielding to gravity should accompany the passive release of your outgoing breath.

● *Charge—body carries the breath*

Repeat the basic exercise. Receive a new breath at the top of each phrase just as your pelvis rounds downward. Immediately after receiving your breath, allow your *body to carry your breath* on a simple *hiss*—an uninterrupted voiceless "sss" sound—over the entire ***3*–*2 count phrase.*** The sensation of your body carrying the breath should accompany the actively sustained "sss" sound.

Variation

The spine rounding exercise can be modified by positioning your legs and feet in front of the body in a "V"—the stride sit position (see Figure 12.20).

12.2 SITTING AND SOUNDING EXERCISES

Overview

These sitting and sounding exercises provide the integrated exploration of the body, breath, and voice and are modeled on the architecture of an expressive action. During these exercises, the spine is looped over the legs and feet in a circular pattern (see Figure 12.21) in a variety of sitting positions, on a variety of vowel and consonant sounds, and on a variety of pitches in the vocal range. The purpose of these exercises is to learn to move the upper body in a substantial way without interfering with the action of the breath and voice. When this skill is mastered, it is possible to stand upright and make bold and momentous physical movements in the upper body without disrupting the sound of the voice.

Figure 12.21 Looping.

Looping

- Each looping action in the sitting and sounding exercises begins with a weight shift in the pelvis.
- The looping action is created by *creasing* and *decreasing* in the thigh socket, which simultaneously rounds and un-rounds the spine. Creasing the thigh sockets loops the pelvis, rib cage, and head in a downward direction over the legs and feet. Decreasing the thigh sockets loops the pelvis, rib cage, and head in an upward direction away from the legs and feet. Creasing and decreasing the thigh sockets several times in succession creates a continuous looping action in the upper body. The looping action is performed in a circular pattern and not as an isolated up-and-down movement in which the upper body is systematically raised and lowered over the legs and feet (see Figure 12.21).
- The looping movement occurs in the following sequence: pelvis + rib cage + arm + head.
- Encourage the sensation of the upper body being suspended from the pelvis and hovering outward over the legs and feet rather than collapsing downward toward the floor.
- During this looping action, the arms and legs passively respond to the movement of the body. (See *tasseling* and *boomeranging* on pp. 88–89.) They should be supple and responsive. The legs and feet are not tense and tight but are actively stabilizing and grounding the body.

Pitch

In these exercises, the vocal range is often navigated in half steps up and down the musical scale. In certain parts of your range, your voice may be unable to move up and down the scale in half steps. When this happens, simply use any comfortable approximate pitch. As your voice is strengthened and greater control achieved, the half steps will become easier to navigate.

First, the *middle voice* is explored on a variety of comfortable pitches. Then work proceeds systematically into the *lower voice* and finally the *upper voice*. If your voice feels pushed or strained, return to your middle voice and then begin the journey up or down the scale again.

Phrasing

As you explore these exercises, observe the structured rhythm of the physical and vocal phrases:

- Allow each vocal phrase to have a clearly defined beginning, middle, and end.
- Avoid excessive tension or wasted breath at either the top or the bottom of the vocal phrase.
- Allow the release of the breath and the onset of sound to occur simultaneously.

Tuning the vowel

The exercises involving *tuning the vowel space* (see pp. 131–132). This will be enhanced by:

- Encouraging vibration—the feeling of the sound resonating in the body.
- Encouraging flexibility and fluidity in the moveable parts of your mouth and throat.
- Encouraging a sense of ease and expansiveness in the resonating spaces.
- Encouraging a stable and steady tone that does not wobble or waiver.

Additionally, the application of the following principles will assist you in your integrated exploration:

- falling/carrying the sound;
- upper and lower resonating spaces;
- balanced resonance;
- forward, open and full tone;
- vocal center;
- upper, middle and lower voice;
- horizontal vocal freedom;
- vertical vocal freedom.

Diamond loop

(See Figures 12.22–12.25.)

This exercise consists of twelve looping actions, three to the center, three to the right side, three to the left side, and three more to the center.

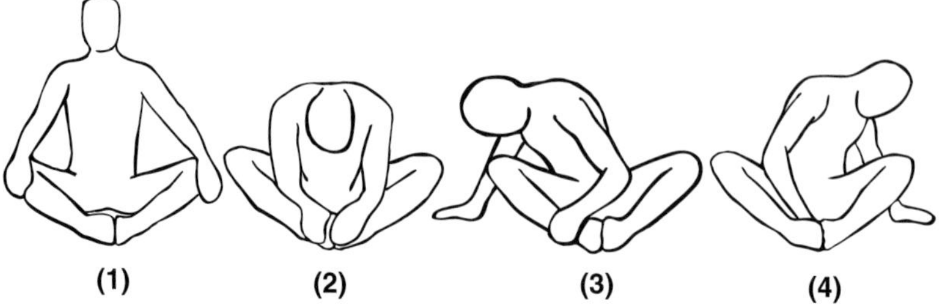

Figure 12.22 Diamond-sit loop.

		Loop Down	Loop Up	Loop Down	Loop Up	Loop Down	Loop Up
3 LOOPS	Center	* HUH	*	HUH	*	HUH	*
3 LOOPS	Right	* HUH	*	HUH	*	HUH	*
3 LOOPS	Left	* HUH	*	HUH	*	HUH	*
3 LOOPS	Center	* HUH	*	HUH	*	HUH	*

* = receive a new breath.

Figure 12.23 Falling onto sound.

		1st Loop	2nd Loop	3rd Loop
3 LOOPS	Center	* HUH + MMMMMMMMMMMMMMMMMMMMMMMMMMMMMM		
3 LOOPS	Right	* HUH + MMMMMMMMMMMMMMMMMMMMMMMMMMMMMM		
3 LOOPS	Left	* HUH + MMMMMMMMMMMMMMMMMMMMMMMMMMMMMM		
3 LOOPS	Center	* HUH + MMMMMMMMMMMMMMMMMMMMMMMMMMMMMM		

* = RECEIVE A NEW BREATH.

Figure 12.24 Carrying the sound.

■ *Basic exercise*

1 *Diamond-sit*: Begin in a seated position with your body's weight distributed evenly over your pelvis, with your knees bent and the soles of your feet touching. The outside edge of each foot rests comfortably on the floor. The space between your legs forms a diamond shape. Your legs rest easily in your thigh socket. The pelvis and spine are vertical and upright. Your rib cage and head balance evenly and comfortably over your pelvis. Encourage the sensation of your whole torso lengthening and widening.

2 Crease your thigh sockets, looping the pelvis, rib cage and head in a downward direction over your legs and feet. Then decrease your thigh sockets,

		Descending /Ascending Pitches	Ascending/Descending Pitches
3 LOOPS	Center	Starting Pitch	Starting Pitch
3 LOOPS	Right	Lower pitch 1/2 Step	Raise pitch 1/2 Step
3 LOOPS	Left	Lower pitch 1/2 Step	Raise pitch 1/2 Step
3 LOOPS	Center	Lower pitch 1/2 Step	Raise pitch 1/2 Step
3 LOOPS	Right	Raise Pitch 1/2 step	Lower Pitch 1/2 step
3 LOOPS	Left	Raise Pitch 1/2 step	Lower Pitch 1/2 step
3 LOOPS	Center	Raise Pitch 1/2 step (Starting Pitch)	Lower Pitch ½ Step (Starting Pitch)

Figure 12.25 Working with pitch.

looping the pelvis, rib cage and head in an upward direction away from your legs and feet. Repeat three times. When finished with the third loop, return to an upright and vertical position.

3 Rotate your pelvis, rib cage and head to the right. Loop three times over your right leg. Return to an upright and vertical position.
4 Rotate your pelvis, rib cage and head to the left. Loop three times over your left leg. Return to an upright and vertical position.
5 Rotate your pelvis, rib cage and head to the center. Loop three times. Rest.

◆ *Sound falls from the body*

Repeat the basic exercise. Receive a new breath at the top of the first phrase as the pelvis initiates the first looping action. Allow a simple *sigh*—a voiced "huh" sound to fall from your body each time you loop downward. Receive a new breath each time you loop upward (see Figure 12.23). The sound falling from your body should be in the center of the vocal range—comfortably in your middle voice. (You should sense the possibility of notes above and below your starting pitch.) Allow the looping action of your body to propel the "huh" sound directly into your mouth. The sensation of your body yielding to gravity should accompany the passive release of the voice. Integration has been achieved when the release of your body, breath, and voice seem inseparable.

◆ *Charge—body carries the sound*

Repeat the basic exercise. Receive a new breath at the top of the first phrase as the pelvis initiates the first looping action. Immediately after receiving the breath, allow a simple "huh" sound to fall from your body. As soon as the "huh" sound arrives in your mouth, *catch* the sound by closing your lips. The sound is then carried by the body on a simple *hum*—an uninterrupted "mmm" sound for the remainder of the three-loop phrase (see Figure 12.24). The sound should be in the center of the vocal range—comfortably in your middle voice. (You should sense the possibility of notes above and below the starting pitch.) The sensation of your body carrying the sound should accompany the actively sustained humming sound. Enjoy the physical sensations that accompany the interplay of movement and vibration. Integration has been achieved when the carrying-action of the body, breath, and voice seem inseparable.

◆ *Working with pitch*

Select a comfortable starting pitch in your middle voice. Using your selected starting pitch, allow a simple "huh" sound to fall from your body each time you loop to the center. Lower the pitch a half step. Allow a simple "huh" sound to fall from your body each time you loop to the right. Lower the pitch a half step. Allow a simple "huh" sound to fall from you body each time you loop to the left (see Figure 12.25). Lower the pitch a half step. Allow a simple "huh" sound to fall from your body each time you loop to the center. Repeat the looping sequence again, ascending the musical scale until you return to your starting pitch. Rest. Repeat the entire sequence again, this time ascending and then descending the musical scale. Avoid pushing when ascending the scale or pressing when descending the scale. Now explore the musical scale carrying a *simple hum* as outlined above.

Cross-legged loop

(See Figures 12.26–12.28.)

■ *Basic exercise*

Cross-legged sit: Sit on the floor. Your body's weight is distributed evenly over your pelvis. Your knees are bent and your ankles are crossed one on top of the other—right over left or left over right. Your legs rest easily in the thigh socket. Your pelvis and spine are vertical and upright. Your rib cage and your head balance evenly and comfortably over your pelvis. Encourage the sensation of your whole torso lengthening and widening. This exercise uses the same basic looping action explored in the previous exercise but in a cross-legged sit position.

◆ *Sound falls from the body*

Repeat the basic exercise. Allow a forward "ee" (as in "me"), an open "ah" (as in "ma") and a full "oo" (as in "moo") to fall from your body while looping, as illustrated in Figure 12.27. The pitch should be near the center of your vocal range—comfortably in your middle voice. (You should sense the possibility of notes above and below your starting pitch.)

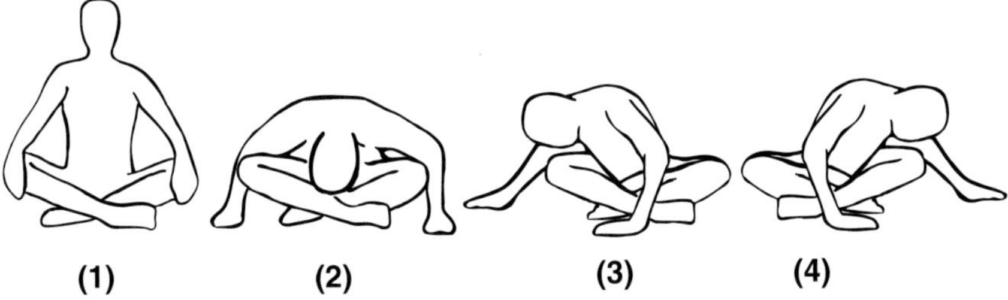

Figure 12.26 Cross-legged loop.

		Loop Down	Loop Up	Loop Down	Loop Up	Loop Down	Loop Up
3 LOOPS	Center	* EE	*	EE	*	EE	*
3 LOOPS	Right	* AH	*	AH	*	AH	*
3 LOOPS	Left	* OO	*	OO	*	OO	*
3 LOOPS	Center	* EE	*	AH	*	OO	*

* = RECEIVE A NEW BREATH.

Figure 12.27 Falling ee ah oo.

		Loop Down	Loop Up	Loop Down	Loop Up	Loop Down	Loop Up
3 LOOPS	Center	*EEEEEEEEEEEEEEEEEEEEEEEEEEEEEEEEEEEEEEEEEE					
3 LOOPS	Right	*AAAAAAAAAAAAAAAAAAAAHHHHHHHHHHHHHHHHHH					
3 LOOPS	Left	*OOOOOOOOOOOOOOOOOOOOOOOOOOOOOOOOOOOO					
3 LOOPS	Center	*EEEEEEEEEE+AAAAAAAAAAHHHHHHHHHH+OOOOOOOO					

* = RECEIVE A NEW BREATH.

Figure 12.28 Carrying ee ah oo.

◆ *Charge—body carries the sound*

Repeat the basic exercise. Allow a forward "ee" (as in "me"), an open "ah" (as in "ma") and a full "oo" (as in "moo") to be carried by your body while looping, as illustrated in Figure 12.28. The sensation of your body carrying the sound should accompany the actively sustained vowel sounds. When looping on the forward "ee," enjoy a free play of vibration in your head and face. Allow the sound to fall directly into the front of your mouth onto your hard palate, teeth, and lips. When looping on the open "ah," enjoy a sense of expanse in your mouth and throat. When looping on the full "oo," enjoy the depth and weight of the sound vibrating in your chest. Integration has been achieved when the carrying-action of the body, breath, and voice seem inseparable.

◆ *Working with pitch*

The progression of the musical scale is the same as in the previous exercise.

Cross-legged loop with arms

(See Figures 12.29–12.31.)

This is a variation of the previous exercises. Three looping actions with an undercurve toss of the arm are performed on the right side and then on the left side. (Sensing that the arm is being tossed by the looping action of the pelvis ensures its fluid integration with the pelvis, rib cage, and head.)

■ *Basic exercise*

1 Begin in the cross-legged sit as in the previous exercise. Rotate your pelvis, torso, and head to the right.
2 Crease your thigh socket, looping your pelvis, rib cage, and head downward over the right leg and foot. As your upper body loops downward, allow your left arm and hand to move in an undercurve scooping action along the floor on the right side of your body.
3 When the loop has completed its full outward trajectory, decrease your thigh socket so that your pelvis, rib cage and head loop upward. As your upper body loops upright, your extended left arm is tossed upward toward the ceiling.
4 The loop is complete when your left arm falls in toward the center of your body.

Repeat three times. Rotate your pelvis to the left. Repeat three times.

◆ *Release—sound falls from the body*

Repeat the basic exercise. Receive a new breath at the top of each phrase as your pelvis initiates the first looping action. Allow a forward "ee" to fall from your body on the first loop (see Figure 12.30), an open "ah" on the second loop, and a full "oo" on the third loop. Receive a new breath each time your body loops upward. The sound falling from your body should be in the center of your vocal range—comfortably in your middle voice. (You should sense the possibilities of notes above and below your starting pitch.) The sensation of your body yielding to gravity should accompany the passive release of your voice. Integration has been achieved when the release of the body, breath, and voice seem inseparable.

Figure 12.29 Cross-legged loop (arm).

		1ST LOOP		2ND LOOP		3RD LOOP	
3 LOOPS	RIGHT	*	EE	*	AH	*	OO
3 LOOPS	LEFT	*	EE	*	AH	*	OO

* = RECEIVE A NEW BREATH.

Figure 12.30 Falling ee ah oo (arm).

		1ST LOOP	2ND LOOP	3RD LOOP
3 LOOPS	RIGHT	* EEEEEEEE +	AAAAHHHH +	OOOOOOOO
3 LOOPS	LEFT	* EEEEEEEE +	AAAAHHHH +	OOOOOOOO

* = RECEIVE A NEW BREATH.

Figure 12.31 Carrying ee ah oo (arm).

◆ *Charge—body carries the sound*

Repeat the basic exercise. Allow your body to carry the forward "ee" into the open "ah" and finally into the full "oo" sound in uninterrupted and connected sequence while looping, as illustrated in Figure 12.31. The sensation of your body carrying the sound should accompany the actively sustained vowel sounds. When sequencing from "ee" to "ah" to "oo," encourage the efficient and fluid movement of all the moveable parts of your mouth and throat. Ideally, all three vowels should have a forward, open, and full resonance. Focus on moving from vowel sound to vowel sound without any significant deterioration or abrupt shift in tonal

		1ST LOOP	2ND LOOP	3RD LOOP
		LIP CONSONANTS		
3 LOOPS	RIGHT	*MEE	*MAH	*MOO
3 LOOPS	LEFT	*BEE	*BAH	*BOO
3 LOOPS	RIGHT	*PEE	*PAH	*POO
3 LOOPS	LEFT	*WEE	*WAH	*WOO
		TONGUE-TIP CONSONANTS		
3 LOOPS	RIGHT	*DEE	*DAH	*DOO
3 LOOPS	LEFT	*TEE	*TAH	*TOO
3 LOOPS	RIGHT	*SEE	*SAH	*SOO
3 LOOPS	LEFT	*ZEE	*ZAH	*ZOO
		PALATAL CONSONANTS		
3 LOOPS	RIGHT	*GEE	*GAH	*GOO
3 LOOPS	LEFT	*KEE	*KAH	*KOO
3 LOOPS	RIGHT	*ngEE	*ngAH	*ngOO
3 LOOPS	LEFT	*JEE	*JAH	*JOO

* = receive a new breath.

Figure 12.32 Consonants.

quality or color. Integration has been achieved when the carrying-action of the body, breath, and voice seem inseparable.

◆ ***Working with pitch***

The progression of the musical scale is the same as in previous exercises.

Looping with vowels and consonants

(See Figure 12.32.)

In celebrating the importance of vowel sounds, care must be taken not to neglect and shortchange consonant sounds. Clear and effective vowel and consonant sounds are equally essential to the expression of thought and feeling. It is often said that *feeling* is expressed through the open and expansive vowels and that *thought* is expressed through the dexterity and clarity provided by the consonants. Consonants reign in boundless vowels, giving language shape and definition. When focusing on vowel sounds, freedom and fluidity are needed throughout the resonator. Consonants, on the other hand, require flexibility and dexterity. The physical and robust nature of consonants is often feared because it is thought they may somehow distort or interrupt the free and fluid resonance of the vowels, when in fact the proper shaping of the vowel space is improved by robust consonant action.

Using the same basic looping action as in the previous exercise, explore the *lip consonants*, *tip-of-the-tongue consonants* and *palatal consonants* as follows:

◆ *Basic exercise*

1 Lip consonants are made when the lips come in contact with each other. Repeat the basic looping exercise, integrating the "ee," "ah," and "oo" sounds with the lip consonants "m," "b," "p," and "w," as illustrated in Figure 12.32.
2 Tip-of-the-tongue consonants are made when the tip of your tongue comes in contact with your gum ridge. Repeat the basic looping exercise, integrating the "ee," "ah," and "oo" sounds with the tip-of-the-tongue consonants "d," "t," "s," and "z" as illustrated in Figure 12.32.
3 Palatal consonants are made when the body of your tongue comes in contact with the roof of your mouth. Repeat the basic looping exercise, integrating the "ee," "ah," and "oo" sounds with the palatal consonants "g," "k," "ng," and "j" as illustrated in Figure 12.32.

◆ *Working with pitch*

The progression of the musical scale is the same as in previous exercises.

◆ *Variations*

Consonants may be explored after the vowel ("eem," "ahm," "oom") or on both sides of the vowel ("meem,' "mahm," "moom").

Arched and rounded yawn/sigh

(See Figure 12.33.)

Before beginning an advanced workout on your upper and lower voice, it is useful to stretch your vocal tract through a simple yawing/sighing action while arching and rounding the spine.

■ *Basic exercise*

1 Begin in the cross-legged sit as in the previous exercise. Tilt your pelvis backward and downward, allowing your whole spine to round.
2 Once in the rounded position, reverse the action; tilt your pelvis forward and upward, lengthening your spine and returning it to its upright and vertical position.
3 From this upright and vertical position, tilt your pelvis slightly forward and downward, arching your spine.

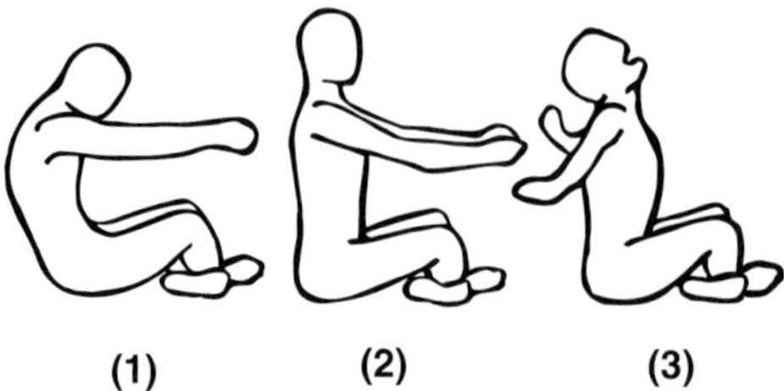

Figure 12.33 Yawn/sigh.

Repeat this arching and rounding action three times. Rest.

During the arching and rounding actions, allow your jaw to tassel freely from your head and spine. In the arched position, your lower jaw will drop down away from your upper jaw, creating a wide opening in your mouth and throat. In the rounded position, your lower jaw will swing upward near your upper jaw, creating a narrower opening in your mouth and throat.

Corresponding movement in your arms accompanies the arching and rounding action of your spine. As your spine rounds backward, your arms are naturally drawn in toward the center of your body. Your arms bend slightly at the elbows and float upward in front of your body. The palms of your hands face inward toward your chest. As the spine arches, your arms extend outward and away from the sides of your body at approximately a 90-degree angle.

● *Adding a yawn/sigh*

Repeat the basic exercise. When your spine reaches its most arched position and your jaw falls into its most open position, allow your breath to release on a voiceless "hah" sound. Think of it as a yawning/sighing action. Yawning encourages expansiveness and openness in your mouth and throat. Sighing encourages the free and fluid release of your outgoing breath. Receive a new breath as your spine rounds. Repeat this arching and rounding action three times. Rest.

Side loop with arm toss (lower voice) (advanced)

(See Figures 12.34–12.36.)

This exercise consists of three side-looping actions to the right and left side, performed with an overcurve arm toss.

■ *Basic exercise*

1 Begin in the cross-legged sit as in the previous exercise. Allow your right arm to float upward above your head. Your elbow should be loose, not locked.

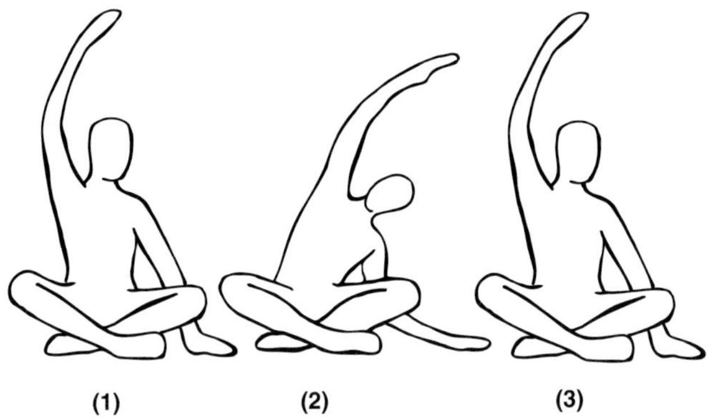

Figure 12.34 Side loop.

		1st Loop	2nd Loop	3rd Loop
3 LOOPS	Right	*OH	*OO	*AH
3 LOOPS	Left	*OH	*OO	*AH

* = RECEIVE A NEW BREATH.

Figure 12.35 Falling—lower voice.

		1st Loop	2nd Loop	3rd Loop
3 LOOPS	Right	*OOOOHHHHHH+OOOOOOOOOOOO+AAAAAAAHHHHHHH		
3 LOOPS	Left	*OOOOHHHHHH+OOOOOOOOOOOO+AAAAAAAHHHHHHH		

* = RECEIVE A NEW BREATH.

Figure 12.36 Carrying—lower voice.

Release the shoulders onto your rib cage. Your elevated arm should be placed slightly forward and in the front of your body.

2 In a side-looping action, allow your pelvis to toss your rib cage, head, and arm over to the left.
3 After looping a comfortable distance over to the left, allow your pelvis to toss your rib cage, head, and arm back to their initial upright and vertical position.

Repeat three times on the left side. Repeat three times on the right side. Rest.

The weight of your upper body should not collapse or drop when lowered to the side. Encourage a sense of expansiveness and openness in your rib cage. Your pelvis remains anchored to the floor to provide a stable base of support.

◆ *Release—sound falls from the body*

Repeat the basic exercise. Select a comfortable starting pitch in your lower voice. (The specific pitch doesn't matter as long as it does not produce strain.) Allow an "oh," "oo," and "ah' sound (as in "mow," "moo," and "ma") to fall from your body each time you loop to the side, as illustrated in Figure 12.35. The sensation of your body yielding to gravity should accompany the passive release of the vowel sounds.

◆ *Charge—body carries the sound*

Once again, select a comfortable starting pitch in your lower voice. Repeat the basic exercise, allowing your body to carry the "oh," "oo," and "ah" sounds in uninterrupted and connected sequence, as illustrated in Figure 12.36. Focus on moving from vowel sound to vowel sound without any significant deterioration or abrupt shift in tonal quality or color. The sensation of your body carrying the sound should accompany the actively sustained vowel sounds.

◆ *Working with pitch*

Beginning on a comfortable pitch in your lower voice, move down the musical scale in half steps each time you repeat the "oh," "oo," and "ah" vowel sequence. When you explore the pitches of your lower voice, the sound may either fall from your body or be carried by your body. It is possible to extend your lower voice to an almost inaudible, rumbling sound without damage or strain. Only go as low as you can without pushing or pressing. Legitimate increases in range are always a by-product of economy and ease. In time and with repetition, your lower voice will be freed and strengthened.

As the pitch moves lower:

- Encourage a sense of expansion in your mouth and throat.
- Encourage a sense of release in the energy in your body.
- Allow your body to move more slowly. Thought and feeling are typically revealed at a slower pace in your lower voice than they are in your upper voice.
- Sense the weight of your body becoming heavier to encourage greater solidity and depth in tonal quality and color.

Forward loop with arm toss (upper voice) (advanced)

(See Figures 12.37–12.39.)

This exercise consists of three forward looping actions performed with an over-curve arm toss.

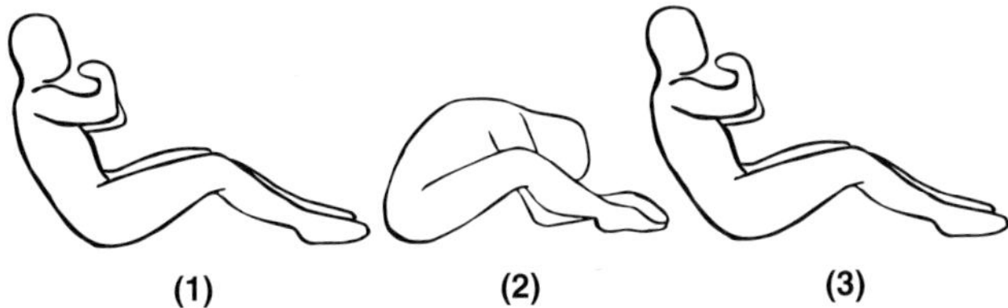

Figure 12.37 Forward loop.

		1ST LOOP	2ND LOOP	3RD LOOP
3 LOOPS	FORWARD	* MEE	* MAY	* MY
3 LOOPS	FORWARD	* MEE	* MAY	* MY
3 LOOPS	FORWARD	* MEE	* MAY	* MY

* = RECEIVE A NEW BREATH.

Figure 12.38 Falling—upper voice.

		1ST LOOP	2ND LOOP	3RD LOOP
3 LOOPS	FORWARD	*MMMEEE +	MMAAYY +	MMMYYY
3 LOOPS	FORWARD	*MMMEEE +	MMAAYY +	MMMYYY
3 LOOPS	FORWARD	*MMMEEE +	MMAAYY +	MMMYYY

* = RECEIVE A NEW BREATH.

Figure 12.39 Carrying—upper voice.

■ *Basic exercise*

1 Begin in a seated position with your pelvis tilted downward and backward. Allow your whole spine to round. Bend your arms at your elbows and let them float upward in front of your body. The palms of your hands face your chest. Your knees are bent slightly, and the soles of your feet rest comfortably on the floor.

2 Crease your thigh sockets, looping your pelvis, rib cage, head, and arms forward, up and over your legs and feet.

3 When the loop has completed its full forward trajectory, decrease your thigh sockets so that your pelvis, rib cage, head, and arms loop upward. Repeat this looping action three times.

◆ *Release—sound falls from the body*

Repeat the basic exercise. Select a comfortable starting pitch in your upper voice. The specific pitch doesn't matter as long as it doesn't produce strain. Close your lips and hum the selected note up into your head. Allow the "me," "may," and "my" sounds to fall from your body each time you loop forward, as illustrated in Figure 12.38. The sensation of your body yielding to gravity should accompany the passive release of the vowel sounds.

◆ *Charge—body carries the sound*

Once again, select a comfortable starting pitch in your upper voice. Repeat the basic exercise. Carry the "me," "may," and "my" sounds in an uninterrupted and connected sequence, as illustrated in Figure 12.39. Focus on moving from vowel sound to vowel sound without any significant deterioration or abrupt shift in tonal quality or color. The sensation of your body carrying the sound should accompany the actively sustained vowel sounds.

◆ *Working with pitch*

Beginning on a comfortable pitch in the upper voice, move up the musical scale in half steps, raising the pitch each time the "me," may," and "my" vowel sequence is repeated. When you explore the pitches of your upper voice, the sound may either fall from your body or be carried by your body. Allow the momentum created by the looping action in your body to help you access your upper voice. Don't reach or strain for the higher notes. At the first sign of tightening or constricting in the throat, return to a comfortable starting pitch and begin again.

As the pitch moves higher:

- Encourage a sense of expansion in your mouth and throat.
- Encourage a sense of charge in the energy in your body.
- Allow your body to move more quickly. Thought and emotion are typically revealed at a faster pace in your upper voice than they are in your lower voice.
- Sense the weight of your body becoming lighter to encourage greater brilliance and radiance in tonal quality and color.

Loop-sit loop (horizontal vocal freedom) (advanced)

(See Figures 12.40–12.41.)

This exercise consists of five forward looping actions performed with an undercurve arm toss. It develops your ability to move from vowel sound to vowel sound on any single note in your vocal range without any significant changes in tonal quality and color.

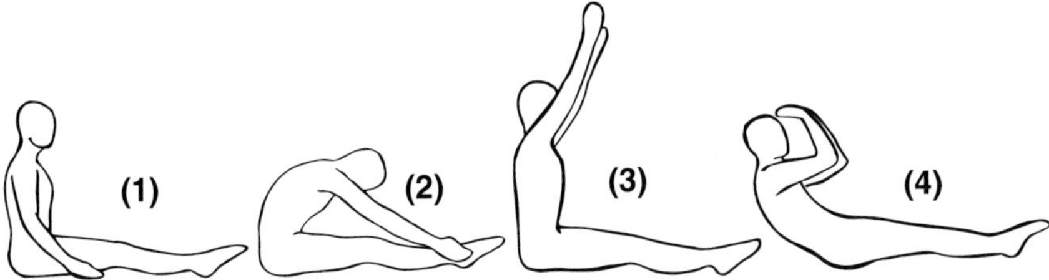

Figure 12.40 Long-sit loop.

UNDERCURVE LOOP	*EEEE + AAAAYYY + AAAAHHH +OOOOHHH + OOOO	PITCH CHANGE
UNDERCURVE LOOP	*EEEE + AAAAYYY + AAAAHHH +OOOOHHH + OOOO	PITCH CHANGE

* = RECEIVE A NEW BREATH.

Figure 12.41 Horizontal freedom.

■ *Basic exercise*

1 *Long-Sit*: Sit on the floor with your body's weight equally distributed over your pelvis. Allow your legs to rest comfortably on the floor. Your knees are straight but not locked and face the ceiling. Your rib cage and head balance evenly and comfortably over your pelvis. Encourage the sensation of your whole torso lengthening and widening.

2 Crease your thigh sockets, looping your pelvis, rib cage, and head downward over your legs and feet. As your upper body loops forward and downward, allow your arms and hands to slide out across the floor along the outside of each leg.

3 When the loop has completed its full forward trajectory, decrease your thigh sockets so that your pelvis, rib cage and head loop upward and your extended arms are tossed up toward the ceiling.

4 Complete the loop by rounding your spine and letting your arms fall in toward the center of your body.

Repeat five times.

◆ *Working with pitch*

Repeat the basic exercise. During the first loop, begin on a comfortable starting pitch in your middle voice. Allow your body to carry your voice on an "ee" sound (as in "me") changing to an "ay" sound (as in "may") changing to an "ah" sound (as in "ma") changing to an "oh" sound (as in "mow") changing to an oo" sound (as in "moo") in an uninterrupted and connected sequence as illustrated in Figure 12.41. Lower the pitch one half step and repeat the process. Continue down the scale into your lower voice as far as is comfortable. Rest. Reverse the process and work back up the scale to your starting pitch. Rest. Repeat the entire five-vowel sequence again; raising the pitch in half steps as far as is comfortable. Reverse the process and move back down the scale to your starting pitch. Focus on moving from vowel sound to vowel sound without any significant deterioration or abrupt shift in tonal quality or color. The sensation of your body carrying the sound should accompany the actively sustained vowel sounds.

Under/over loop (vertical vocal freedom) (advanced)

(See Figures 12.42–12.45.)

This exercise consists of two forward looping actions, the first loop performed with an undercurve arm toss, the second with an overcurve arm toss. It develops your ability to move through a series of connected notes in your vocal range on a single vowel sound without any significant or abrupt changes in tonal quality or color.

■ *Basic exercise*

1 Begin in long-sit as in the previous exercise.
2 Crease your thigh sockets, looping your pelvis, rib cage, and head downward over your legs and feet. As your upper body loops forward, allow your arms, and hands to slide out across the floor along the outside of each leg.
3 When the loop has completed its full forward trajectory, decrease your thigh sockets, looping your pelvis, rib cage, and head upward. As your upper body loops upright, your extended arms are tossed upward toward the ceiling.
4 Complete the loop by rounding your spine and letting your arms fall in toward the center of your body.
5 Begin the overcurve arm toss where the undercurve arm toss ended.
6 Crease your thigh sockets, looping your pelvis, rib cage, head, and arms upward. As your upper body loops upward, your extended arms are tossed upward toward the ceiling.
7 As your upper body continues to loop up and over your extended legs and feet, allow your arms to fall forward along the outside of each leg near the floor.
8 When the loop has completed its full forward trajectory, decrease your thigh sockets, returning your pelvis, rib cage, and head to their initial starting position.

Repeat the entire looping sequence five times.

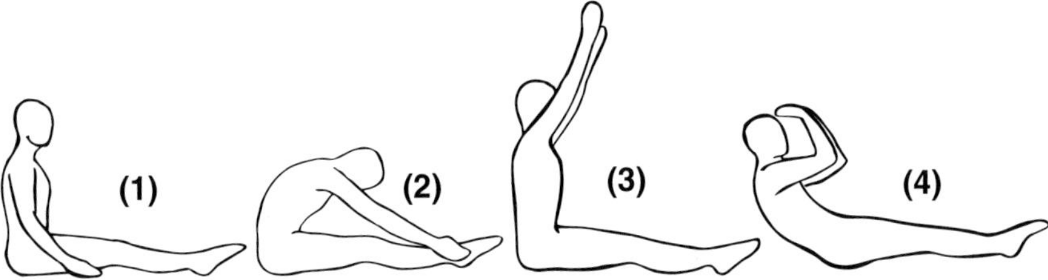

Figure 12.42 Under/over loop 1.

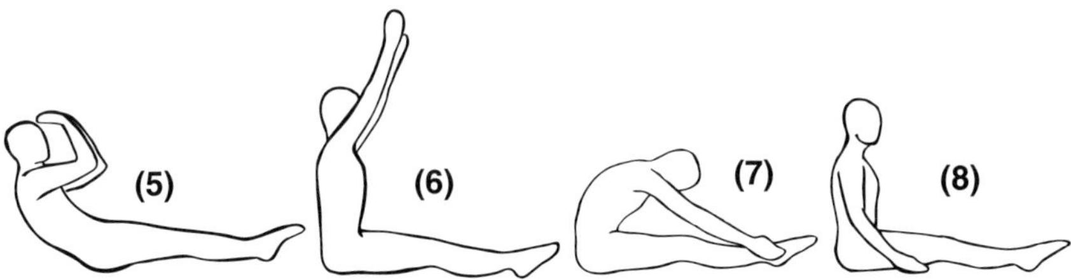

Figure 12.43 Under/over loop 2.

Figure 12.44 Arpeggio scale.

◆ *Working with pitch (arpeggio)*

Repeat the exercise using an arpeggio scale (see Figure 12.44). Begin on a comfortable pitch in your middle voice. Allow your body to carry an "ee" sound (as in "me") on an arpeggio scale during the first under and overcurve loops. Lower the pitch one half step. Repeat on "ay," "ah," "oh," and "oo" sounds (as in "may," "ma," "mow," "moo"), lowering the pitch one half step each time the

<table>
<tr><td>1st Loop</td><td colspan="2">* EEEEEEEEEEEEEEEEEEEEEEEEEEEEEEEEEEEEEEEEEEEEEEEEE</td><td>1st Arpeggio</td></tr>
<tr><td>2nd Loop</td><td colspan="2">* AAAAAAAAAAAAAAAAAAAAAAYYYYYYYYYYYYYYYYYYYYYYYY</td><td>2nd Arpeggio</td></tr>
<tr><td>3rd Loop</td><td colspan="2">* AAAAAAAAAAAAAAAAAAAAAAAIIIIIIIIIIIIIIIIIIIIIIIIIIIIIIIIIIIIIIIIIIIIIIIIIIIIIIIIIIIIIIIIII</td><td>3ed Arpeggio</td></tr>
<tr><td>4th Loop</td><td colspan="2">* OOOOOOOOOOOOOOOOOOOOHHHHHHHHHHHHHHHHHHHHHHHH</td><td>4th Arpeggio</td></tr>
<tr><td>5th Loop</td><td colspan="2">* OOOOOOOOOOOOOOOOOOOOOOOOOOOOOOOOOOOOOOOOOO</td><td>5th Arpeggio</td></tr>
<tr><td></td><td>Undercurve Toss of the Arm</td><td>Overcurve Toss of the Arm</td><td></td></tr>
</table>

* = RECEIVE A NEW BREATH.

Figure 12.45 Arpeggio vowels.

vowel sound is changed (see Figure 12.45). Reverse the sequence by returning up the scale in half steps to your starting pitch. Rest. Repeat, moving up the scale into your upper voice and back down the scale to your starting pitch. Focus on moving up and down the musical scale on each vowel sound without any significant deterioration or abrupt shift in tonal quality or color. The sensation of your body carrying the sound should accompany the actively sustained vowel sounds.

Stride-sitting loop (five-note scale) (advanced)

(See Figures 12.46–12.49.)

This exercise consists of three looping actions, the first two performed with an undercurve arm toss, the third with an overcurve arm toss.

■ *Basic exercise*

1 *Stride-sit*: Sit on the floor with the weight of your body equally distributed over your pelvis. Your legs and feet lengthen comfortably in the front of your body in a "V." Your knees are straight but not locked and face the ceiling. Your rib cage and head balance evenly and comfortably over your pelvis. Encourage the sensation of your whole torso lengthening and widening.
2 Crease your thigh sockets, looping your pelvis, rib cage and head over your right leg and foot. As your upper body loops forward, allow your left arm and hand to slide out across the floor along the inside of your right leg.
3 When the loop has completed its full outward trajectory, decrease your thigh sockets so that your pelvis, rib cage, and head loop upward. As your upper body loops upright, your extended left arm is tossed toward the ceiling.
4 Complete the loop by rounding your spine and letting your left arm fall in toward the center of your body.

Repeat the whole looping sequence a second time.

5 Begin the overcurve-arm-toss loop where the undercurve-arm-toss loop ended.

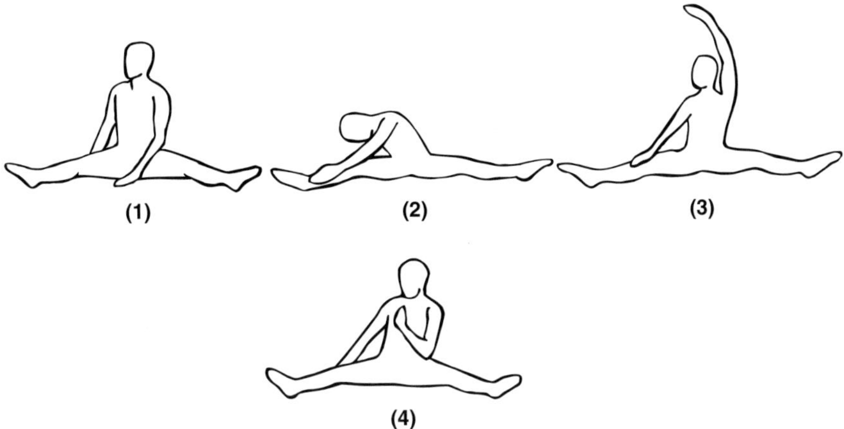

Figure 12.46 Stride-sit loop 1.

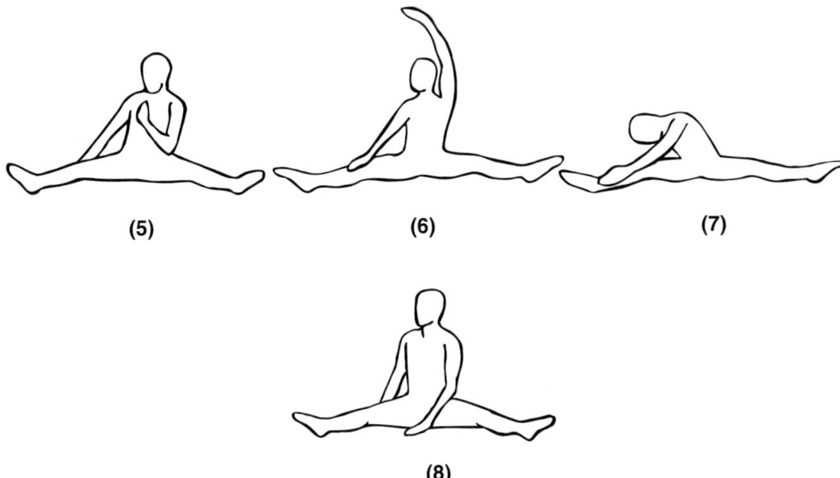

Figure 12.47 Stride-sit loop 2.

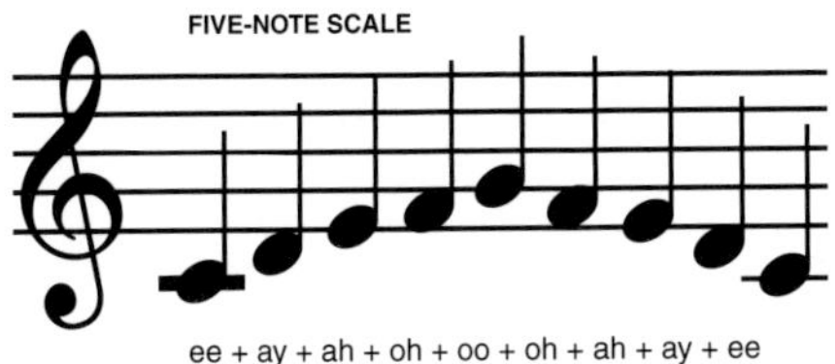

Figure 12.48 Five-note scale.

*EE	AY	AH	OH	OO	OH	AH	AY	EE
1ST UNDERCURVE LOOP			2ND UNDERCURVE LOOP			3RD OVERCURVE LOOP		
FIVE HALF-STEPS UP THE SCALE					FOUR HALF-STEPS DOWN THE SCALE			

* = RECEIVE A NEW BREATH.

Figure 12.49 Five-note scale table.

6 Crease your thigh sockets, looping your pelvis, rib cage, head, and left arm upward.
7 As your upper body continues to loop up and over your right leg and foot, allow your left arm to fall forward along the inside of your right leg near the floor.
8 When the loop has completed its full forward trajectory, decrease your thigh sockets, returning your pelvis, rib cage, head, and arm to their initial starting position.

Repeat the entire sequence looping to the left side. Rest.

◆ *Working with pitch*

Now explore the exercise using a five-note scale (see Figure 12.48). Begin on a comfortable pitch in your middle voice. As your voice progresses through the five-note scale, allow your body to carry the “ee,” “ay,” and “ah” vowel sounds (as in “me,” “may,” and “ma”) on the first undercurve loop, the “oh,” “oo,” and “oh” vowel sounds (as in ‘mow,” “moo,” and ‘mow”) on the second loop, and the “ah,” “ay,’ and “ee’ vowel sounds (as in “ma,” “may,” and “me”) on the third loop as illustrated in Figure 12.49. When the five-note scale is completed, lower the pitch one half step and repeat the looping action on the left side. Repeat several times, moving into your lower voice as far as is comfortable. Then return up the scale to your starting pitch. Rest. Repeat, this time exploring your upper voice. Focus on moving from vowel sound to vowel sound and note to note without any significant deterioration or abrupt shift in tonal quality or color. The sensation of your body carrying the sound should accompany the actively sustained vowel sounds.

◆ *Vowels and consonants*

Explore the stride-sitting loop exercise using various consonant sounds before, after and on both sides of the vowel sounds.

12.3 STANDING EXERCISES

Overview

In a traditional technique class, the lying and breathing exercises and the sitting and sounding exercises remain relatively consistent. The *standing exercises*, however, are always different and constantly evolving. There are two reasons for this: First, your voice and body fail to get a complete workout if too much time is spent learning new exercises. New exercises are not necessarily better exercises. A great deal can be learned by repeating the same well-developed sequence of exercises again and again. Second, it is also important to have some variety. Learning to pick up new combinations of movement, different sequences of vowel and consonant sounds on a variety of pitches in your vocal range, is liberating and keeps your voice and body supple and attentive. With time and experience, the standing exercises can become quite complex and full of adventure.

Unfortunately, most standing exercises are too complex to describe fully in writing. Instead, I will outline a series of guidelines to help you create your own. Additionally, many of the previous lying and breathing exercises and the sitting and sounding exercises can easily be modified into standing exercises. Anyone with an imagination and an intuitive sense of the physical can create a flexible and challenging set of standing exercises.

Guidelines for building standing exercises

Most importantly, the major and minor properties of an expressive action*: energy, orientation, size, progression, flow, direction, speed, weight, control*, and *focus* should guide and direct every aspect of the study when developing standing exercises. They are the essential physical resources when performing any movement exercise.

■ Movement work

Phrasing

When beginning to develop a standing exercise, it is useful to divide the phrase into a series of counts intended for exploration. For example, lets examine a ***4**–3 count phrase.* It is counted as follows: **1**–2–3, **2**–2–3, **3**–2–3, **4**–2–3. The first number is the number of *phrases*, which are separated by a comma and strung together in a sequence—**4**. The second number is the number of counts in each phrase—3. (Many other phrasing options are possible such as: a ***2**–4 count phrase*, a ***6**–3 count phrase*, a ***2**–8 count phrase*. The options are seemingly endless.)

Example

Let's select a ***4**–4 count phrase* for extended exploration. It is counted as follows: **1**–2–3–4, **2**–2–3–4, **3**–2–3–4, **4**–2–3–4.

Stationary, locomotive and gestural movements

There are three basic types of movement that can be explored: *stationary*, *locomotive*, and *gestural*

- *Stationary*: explores movement while standing more or less in one spot.
- *Locomotive*: explores traveling in space. When exploring locomotive movements, the following basic actions may be explored: *step, walk, hop, jump, leap, run*, and *turn*.
- *Gestural*: explores movement of the hand, arm, leg, head, spine, or head that is expressive of a thought and feeling. (Gestural movements may accompany either stationary are locomotive movements.)

Example

Stationary, locomotive, and gestural movement patterns will be explored on each of the four count phrases as follows:
1–2–3–4—stationary + gestural
2–2–3–4—locomotive
3–2–3–4—stationary + gestural
4–2–3–4—locomotive + gestural

Creating phrases

Below is a list of *kits* that may be employed when "filling" phrases with patterns of movement:

- *Direction kit*—When exploring *locomotive movements*, the following directions may be explored: *forward, backward, side, diagonal*, and a *circle*, or *half-circle*.
- *Body region kit*—When exploring *gestural movements*, the following locations may describe the location of the action: *front of the body, back of the body, right or left side of the body, the upper half of the body*, or *the lower half of the body*.
- *Spine kit*—When exploring *stationary, locomotive*, and *gestural movements*, the spine may be moved in the following ways: *arch or round, rotate/twist right or left, bend* or *unbend from side to side*.
- *Action kit*—When exploring *stationary, locomotive*, and *gestural movements*, a verb can be used to describe any of the actions of the body. For example: *point, scoop, reach, press, pull, swipe, rub, stab*, or any other action listed in Appendix II.
- *Physical property kit*—When exploring *stationary, locomotive*, and *gestural movements*, one or more physical properties may be assigned to each of the phrases being explored. For example: *charge/release, contact/withdraw, expand/contract, center/periphery, free/bound, direct/indirect, fast/slow, heavy/light, stable/unstable*, or *sharp/diffused*.

Variations

Any type of movement may be explored, many of which may not be outlined in the basic kits listed above.

Example

The following kits will be explored on each of the *four count phrases*:

1–2–3–4—stationary + gestural

- *Spine kit*: the pelvis initiates a *rounding action* of the spine bringing the head and arms near the feet, and then returns the spine to its upright position.
- *Action kit*: the arms participate in a *scooping-action* as they are lowered to the floor.
- *Physical property kit*: *slow*.

2–2–3–4—locomotive

- *Step kit*: Take four steps forward—one step on each of the four counts.
- *Physical property kit*: *heavy*.

3–2–3–4—stationary + gestural

Same as in the first 4–count phrase above.

4–2–3–4—locomotive + Gestural

- *Spine and action kits*: Same as in the first 4–count phrase above, executed while taking four steps forward.
- *Physical Property Kit*: stable.

● *Breath and movement work*

One of the following breathing actions may be explored during each of the movement phrases:

- *Release*: the *breath falls from the body* on a simple *sigh*—a voiceless "huh" sound. The sighing-action occurs in concert with a releasing-action in the body.
- *Charge*: the *body carries the breath* on a simple *hiss*—a voiceless "sss" sound. This hissing-action occurs in concert with the charging-action of the body.

Example

The following breathing actions will be explored on each of the 4–count phrases:
1–2–3–4—the breath falls from the body
2–2–3–4—the body carries the breath
3–2–3–4—the breath falls from the body
4–2–3–4—the body carries the breath.

◆ *Sound and movement work*

One of the following sounding actions may be explored during each of the movement phrases:

- *Release*: the sound *falls from the body* on a selected vowel sound. The sounding-action occurs in concert with a releasing-action in the body and breath.
- *Charge*: the *body carries the sound* on a selected vowel sound. This sounding-action occurs in concert with the charging-action of the body.

Variations

Any vowel or consonant sound may be explored. Additionally, musical pitches in half steps, triads, five-note scales, arpeggios, or other pitch exercises may also be explored.

Example

The following sounding actions will be explored on each of the 4–count phrases:

- **1**–2–3–4—an "ee" sound as in "me" falls from the body
- **2**–2–3–4—the body carries an "oo" sound as in "moo"
- **3**–2–3–4—an "ee" sound as in "me" falls from the body
- **4**–2–3–4—the body carries an "oo" sound as in "moo."

▲ *Speech and movement work*

One of the following speaking actions may be explored during each of the movement phrases:

- *Release*: the *text falls from the body* on a simple sentence.
- *Charge*: the *body carries the text* on a simple sentence.

Variations

Any type of language is suitable for exploration.

Example

The following simple sentence will be explored on each of the 4–count phrases: "I'm most assured I have not lost my way."

- **1**–2–3–4—the text falls from the body
- **2**–2–3–4—the body carries the text
- **3**–2–3–4—the text falls from the body
- **4**–2–3–4—the body carries the text.

Chapter 13

Language and character exercises

Overview

The following language and character exercises, both simple and complex, are intended to supplement this integrated study of expressive action.

13.1 LANGUAGE

Switching (loves me/loves me not)

Explore the text "Loves me, loves me not." Each time you move from "Loves me" to "loves me not" switch the physical property being explored. For example: "Loves me"—*fast*—"loves me not"—*stable*, "Loves me"—*light*—"loves me not"—*heavy*. Allow the physical properties to shift the manner in which you think and feel about the status of your love life. This exercise can be quite playful and improvisatory. (A copy of the expressive continuum listing the physical properties to be explored is located in Appendix II.)

Articulation tongue twister

Tongue-twister exercises are usually performed in a relatively *fast* and *charged* manner in order to give all the moveable parts of the mouth a thorough and comprehensive workout. However, these fast and energized verbal drills often do little more than integrate the mind and the mouth. The purpose here is to develop articulatory skills when the body is in various physical states, and most importantly playing an expressive action.

Select one of the following tongue twisters:

- Six sick slick slim sycamore saplings.
- A box of biscuits, a batch of mixed biscuits.
- Friendly Frank flips fine flapjacks.
- Vincent vowed vengeance very vehemently.

- Cheap ship trip.
- I cannot bear to see a bear.
- Mrs Smith's Fish Sauce Shop.
- Knapsack straps.
- Lesser leather never weathered wetter weather better.
- Inchworms itching.
- A noisy noise annoys an oyster.
- The myth of Miss Muffet.
- Greek grapes.
- Moose noshing much mush.
- Which witch wished which wicked wish?
- The two-twenty-two train tore through the tunnel.
- Crisp crusts crackle crunchily.
- The Leith police dismisseth us.
- Ed had edited it.
- Quick kiss. Quicker kiss.

Speak the tongue twister aloud multiple times, exploring each of the 20 physical properties of an expressive action. (A copy of the expressive continuum listing the physical properties to be explored is located in Appendix II.)

Dialogue I (actions)

Explore expressive action and language while working with a short scene.

Step 1

Select an action from the list in Appendix II for each line of the scene.

Step 2

Play the scene while exploring the expressive actions you selected. Here's one example among many possibilities:

A: You don't have to explain anything. (*to block*)
B: No, listen, I need to . . . (*to drag up*)
A: Nor should you feel the need to explain anything. (*to gnaw*)
B: We are okay, right? (*to glaze over*)
A: Of course, we're okay. (*to hammer*)
B: I'm just not used to dealing with this. (*to jumble*)
A: No one is. (*to wonder*)
B: This is terrible. What have I done? (*to agonize*)
A: You really have screwed this one up. (*to promise*)
B: I will not accept it. I will not, I cannot, I won't! (*to lash out*)

A: What are you going to do about it, after the fact? (*to stand your ground*)
B: I will celebrate anyway. (*to boast*)
A: You can't be serious. (*to bum*)

(Shultz 2006)

Dialogue II (physical properties)

Explore the physical properties of an expressive action while working with a short scene.

Step 1

Select a physical property of an expressive action for each line in the scene. (A copy of the expressive continuum listing the physical properties to be explored is located in Appendix II.) Spend some time improvising before settling on the specific physical properties in your language study.

Step 2

Play the scene while exploring the physical properties you selected. Here is one example among many possibilities:

A: Where have you been? (*sharp*)
B: Oh, you know me. Around. (*periphery*)
A: I can't believe that you're serious. (*direct*)
B: Well, I am. (*free*)
A: It just doesn't seem possible. (*diffused*)
B: If you think about it though ... it really does make sense. (*slow*)
A: No, I get that. But the timing of everything makes it all the more . . . (*expansive*)
B: Farfetched? (*light*)
A: Implausible, but same difference. (*unstable*)
B: So what? (*contact*)
A: So, you're definitely going to do it? (*heavy*)
B: Absolutely. (*charge*)
A: I can't believe that this is happening. (withdraw)
B: Believe it. (*stable*)
A: How do you manage to always do this? (*release*)
B: Someone has to. (*bound*)

(Shultz 2006)

Dialogue III (monologue)

In the previous exercises, the lines were short and the expressive actions and language met in a simple and orderly line-by-line fashion. In the monologue below, you will explore the manner in which expressive action integrates with the text.

Consider the following interpretive choices:

- Sometimes a simple sentence corresponds directly to the playing of one expressive action.
- Sometimes multiple expressive actions are played in a single longer sentence.
- Sometime expressive actions extend across two sentences or across several phrases (sometimes even marked by a comma) within a sentence.

Step 1

Read the monologue below aloud several times:

> I've been wondering what we were talking about yesterday, and now everything seems perfectly clear to me. Because I keep talking and talking, and you get so tired of listening, you feel like your head will explode. Meanwhile, you've been really busy pretending I'm not here, and that you never met me and that we have no relationship at all. Sometimes when you're silent, not moving but just standing there still and distant, I come closer to you ... so close ... I become you and there is no me. When did you notice me? I mean really notice me. What did you see in me and how did you feel and where were your eyes? I'm your shadow. You move and I move with you. You feel me down your neck ... even when I'm distant. I'm with you even when you're not here and you hate me for it.

Step 2

Explore the monologue on your feet. Read it aloud as you walk around the room. Each time you sense a shift in the thought and feeling of the character, walk in a different direction. A shift in thought and feeling represents a corresponding shift in expressive action. Each time you change direction you will ultimately be asked to change the expressive action that you are playing.

Step 3

Based on your previous exploration, divide the language of the monologue into smaller sections. The smaller sections occur in places where you changed direction in Step 2.

Step 4

Select an action from the list in Appendix II or select a physical property for each section of the monologue. Each smaller section should correspond directly to the playing of a single expressive action. Spend some time improvising before settling on the specific actions in your language study.

Step 5

Explore your choices. Here is one example among many possibilities:

I've been wondering what we were talking about yesterday (*to gain control/bound*) and now everything seems perfectly clear to me (*to forewarn/direct*). Because I keep talking and talking, and you get so tired of listening (*to harden/stable*) you feel like your head will explode (*to recoil/ withdraw*). Meanwhile, you've been really busy pretending I'm not here, and that you never met me and that we have no relationship at all (*to spiral out of control/unstable*). Sometimes when you're silent, not moving but just standing there still and distant, I come closer to you ... so close ... I become you and there is no me (*to haunt/light*). When did you notice me? (*to badger/charge*). I mean really notice me (*to kick/fast*). What did you see in me and how did you feel and where were your eyes (*to aim/sharp*)? I'm your shadow, (*to apologize/release*) you move and I move with you (*to relinquish/heavy*). You feel me down your neck . . . (*to affirm/slow*) … even when I'm distant (*to reel back/contract*). I'm with you even when you're not here and you hate me for it (*to drone on/center*).

Shakespearian sonnet

In the sonnet below, you will explore the manner in which expressive action integrates with the text and the metrical flow of the poetry.

Step 1

Read the sonnet below aloud several times. The natural and consistent flow of the meter is like the pounding of your heart—in five simple beats (di-*dum*, di-*dim*, di-*dum*, di-*dum*, di-*dum*). The last *dum* of the line is given extra emphasis because it is the most important in the poetical pattern.

> Sonnet 27
> Weary with toil, I haste me to my *bed*,
> The dear repose for limbs with travel *tired*,
> But then begins a journey in my *head*
> To work my mind, when body's works *expired*;
> For then my thoughts (from far where I *abide*)
> Intend a zealous pilgrimage to *thee*,
> And keep my drooping eyelids open *wide*,
> Looking on darkness which the blind do *see*;
> Save that my soul's imaginary *sight*
> Presents [thy] shadow to my sightless *view*,

Which like a jewel hung in ghastly *night,*
Makes black night beauteous, and her old face *new.*
Lo thus by day my limbs, by night my *mind,*
For thee, and for myself, no quiet *find.*

Step 2

Explore the sonnet on your feet. Read the sonnet aloud as you walk around the room. Each time you sense a shift in the thought and feeling of the character, walk in a different direction. A shift in thought and feeling represents a corresponding shift in expressive action. Each time you change direction you will ultimately be asked to change the expressive action that you are playing.

Step 3

Based on your previous exploration, divide the sonnet up into smaller phrases. The smaller phrases of the sonnet occur in places where you changed direction in Step 2.

Step 4

Select a verb from the list in Appendix II, or select a physical property of an expressive action for each phrase of the sonnet. Each smaller phrase should correspond directly to the playing of a single expressive action. Spend some time improvising before settling on the specific actions in your language study.

Step 5

Explore the sonnet while playing the expressive actions you selected. (The last word of each line in the sonnet is printed in italics. This is to remind you, once again, that no matter how you choose to phrase the sonnet, the iambic pentameter is driving you forward toward the end of each verse line. Notice that the most important rhyming words are placed at the end of the verse line.) Here is one example among many possibilities:

Sonnet 27
Weary with *toil,* (*to lament/heavy*)
I haste me to my *bed,* (*to luxuriate/light*)
The dear repose for limbs with travel *tired,* (*to stammer/indirect*)
But then begins a journey in my *head* (*to pound/heavy*)
To work my *mind,* (*to pound/fast*)
when body's works *expired*; (*to expire/release*)

For then my thoughts (from far where I *abide*) (*to soar/expansive*)
Intend a zealous pilgrimage to *thee*, (*to soar charge*)
And keep my drooping eyelids open *wide*, (*to droop/heavy*)
Looking on darkness which the blind do *see*; (*to jumble/diffuse*)
Save that my soul's imaginary *sight* (*to race/light*)
Presents [thy] shadow to my sightless *view*, (*to race/stable*)
Which like a jewel hung in ghastly *night*, (*to celebrate/charge*)
Makes black night beauteous, and her old face *new*. (*to contemplate/light*)
Lo thus by day my limbs, by night my *mind*, (*to plod/unstable*)
For thee, and for myself, no quiet *find*. (*to charge/sharp*)

You don't have to label everything

Remember that it isn't always necessary to find a verbal label for every expressive action in a scene. Many times expressive actions fall into place spontaneously and naturally. It is virtually impossible, misguided and pedantic to find a label for every expressive action in a play. Use technique wisely and do not become a slave to it. Trust your impulses and your intuition. When it feels right it most often is right! What is most important is that you know or sense that you are playing a specific and exciting expressive action in each and every moment of the play.

Contemporary language barre

Pair 20 pieces of text selected from 20 different contemporary plays with the 20 physical properties of an expressive action. (You will need to make experiential choices about the language—structure, meaning, and intent—that is appropriate for the physical property selected.) Commit the barre to memory and repeat it as a part of your daily practice. In time, you may wish to change all or some of the language choices for variety's sake.

Here's an example of a contemporary language barre:

Energy: charge

BLANCHE: Why! I've been half crazy, Stella! When I found out you'd been insane enough to come back in here after what happened—I started to rush in after you! ... What were you thinking of? Answer me! What? What?

(*A Streetcar Named Desire*, Tennessee Williams)

Energy: release

HAMM: It's the end of the day like any other day, isn't it Clov?

(*Endgame*, Samuel Beckett)

Orientation: contact

STANLEY: Mr. Whiteside, these gentlemen are deputy sheriffs. They have a warrant by which I am enabled to put you out of this house, and I need hardly add that it will be the greatest moment of my life Mr Whiteside—.... I am giving you fifteen minutes in which to pack up and get out. If you are not gone in fifteen minutes, Mr Whiteside, these gentlemen will forcibly eject you.

(*The Man Who Came to Dinner*, George S. Kaufman and Moss Hart)

Orientation: withdraw

CASY: I ain't preachin' no more much. The sperit ain't in the people no more; and worse'n that the sperit ain't in me no more.

(*John Steinbeck's The Grapes of Wrath*, Frank Galati)

Size: expand

MAGGIE: I tell you I got so nervous at that table tonight I thought I would throw back my head and utter a scream you could hear across the Arkansas border an' parts of Louisiana an' Tennessee.

(*Cat on a Hot Tin Roof*, Tennessee Williams)

Size: contract

SAMMY: I always worry that maybe people aren't going to like me, when I go to a party. Isn't that crazy? Do you ever get kind of a sick feeling in the pit of your stomach when you dread things? Gee, I wouldn't want to miss a party for anything. But every time I go to one, I have to reason with myself to keep from feeling that the whole world's against me.

(*The Dark at the Top of the Stairs*, William Inge)

Progression: center

SISTER ALOYSIUS: I believe this man is creating or has already brought about an improper relationship with your son.

(*Doubt: A Parable*, John Patrick Shanley)

Progression: periphery

EDNA: "The hills are alive with the sound of music" was the first best movie I ever saw and the first best music I ever heard. All I ever wanted to be in life was the star of that show. Someone who sang like a record and ran and twirled in the mountains. Someone so perfect that even the nuns couldn't understand her. Someone who said "Big Deal!" to the Germans and risked her life to save the sad children she was babysitting and then their gorgeous rich handsome father who thought his whole life was wrecked is now so happy and so thankful that he forgets all about his dead wife and then falls madly in love with me.

(*The Good Times Are Killing Me*, Lynda Barry)

Flow: free

LINDA: We're free, We're free.

(*Death of a Salesman*, Arthur Miller)

Flow: bound

HARPER: I WANT TO KNOW WHERE YOU'VE BEEN. I WANT TO KNOW WHAT'S GOING ON!

(*Angels in America*, Tony Kushner)

Direction: direct

EMILY: I don't like the whole change that's come over you in the last year. I'm sorry if that hurts your feelings; but I've just got to—tell the truth and shame the devil . . . Well, up to a year ago, I used to like you a lot. And I used to watch you while you did everything—because we'd been friends so long. And then you began spending all your time at baseball. And you never stopped to speak to anybody anymore—not to really speak—not even to your own family you didn't. And George, it's a fact—ever since you've been elected captain, you've got awful stuck up and conceited, and all the girls say so.

(*Our Town*, Thornton Wilder)

Direction: indirect

MARTHA: You know what's happened, George? You want to know what's really happened! It's snapped, finally. Not me . . . it. The whole arrangement. You can go along . . . forever, and everything's . . . manageable. You make all sorts of excuses to yourself. . .you know . . . this is life . . . the hell with it. . . maybe tomorrow he'll be dead . . . maybe tomorrow you'll be dead . . . all sorts of excuses. But then, one day, one night, something happens . . . and SNAP! It breaks. And you just don't give a damn anymore. I've tried with you, baby . . . .really, I've tried.

(*Who's Afraid of Virginia Woolf?*, Edward Albee)

Speed: fast

DAVE: He loved it, Martha! He ate it up! Get some! Get some a them gooks! Bap-bap-bap-bap-bap-bap! Blow'm away!

(*Strange Snow*, Steve Metcalfe)

Speed: slow

DR CANTWAY: They were both my patients and they were two kids. I took care of both of them ... of both their bodies. . . . And ... for a brief moment I wondered if this is how God feels when he looks down at us. How we are all his kids . . . Our bodies ... Our souls. ... And I felt a great deal of compassion ... for both of them. ...

(*The Laramie Project*, Moises Kaufman and the Tectonic Theater Project)

Weight: heavy

RACHEL: At the funeral, Pa preached that Tommy didn't die in a state of grace, because his folks never had him baptized.

(*Inherit the Wind*, Jerome Lawrence and Robert E. Lee)

Weight: light

HOTCHKISS: How kind of you to say so, General! You're quite right: I am a snob. Why not? ... I am a snob, not only in fact, but on principle. I shall go down in history, not as the first snob, but as the first avowed champion of English snobbery . . . .

(*Getting Married*, George Bernard Shaw)

Control: stable

BERNIECE: I told you I don't play on that piano.

(*The Piano Lesson*, August Wilson)

Control: unstable

EDMUND: Jesus, Papa, haven't you any pride or shame? And don't think I'll let you get away with it! I won't go to any damned state farm just to save you a few lousy dollars to buy more bum property with! You stinking old miser!

(*Long Day's Journey into Night*, Eugene O'Neill)

Focus: sharp

JOAN: What are you doing? Where are you going? What are you doing? You stay right there. Now. What were the two of you doing? I'm just asking a simple question. There's nothing to be ashamed of. (Pause) I can wait. (Pause) Were you playing "Doctor"?

(*Sexual Perversity in Chicago*, David Mamet)

Focus: diffused

BABE: Well, after I shot him, I put the gun down on the piano bench and then I went out into the kitchen and made up a pitcher of lemonade. ... Yes, I was dying of thirst. My mouth was just as dry as a bone. . . . Right. I made it just the way I like it with lots of sugar and lots of lemon—about ten lemons in all.

(*Crimes of the Heart*, Beth Henley)

The sensorial fabric of the text

Some of the language selections listed in this example are longer. Multiple expressive actions will need to be strung together when delivering these longer sections of text. However, each of these expressive actions strung together, all hold in common the single physical property that is intended for exploration. For example a group of *fast*, *heavy*, or *expansive* actions might be strung together in a single section of text. When this occurs this shared physical properties becomes an important part of the sensorial fabric of the text. Pockets of similar reoccurring sensory patterns like this occur in music and art all the time.

Shakespearean barre

Create a barre using speeches from Shakespeare's plays. Commit the barre to memory and repeat it as a part of your daily practice. In time, you may wish to change all or some of the texts for variety's sake. Here's an example:

Energy: charged

HENRY V: Once more unto the breach, dear friends, once more; /Or close the wall up with our English dead.

(*Henry* V III.i.)

Energy: released

ROMEO: It is my lady, O, it is my love!

(*Romeo and Juliet*, II.ii.)

Orientation: contact

MACBETH: Is this a dagger which I see be-fore me, /The handle toward my hand? Come, let me clutch thee!

(*Macbeth*, II.i.)

Orientation: withdraw

IAGO: For that I do suspect the lusty Moor /Hath leap'd into my seat; the thought whereof /Doth (like a poisonous mineral) gnaw my inwards;

(*Othello*, Il.i.)

Size: expand

CRESSIDA: Boldness comes to me now, and brings me heart. Prince Troilus, I have lov'd you night and day /For many weary months.

(*Troilus and Cressida*, III.ii.)

Size: contract

DESDEMONA: I cannot say "whore: It does abhor me now I speak the word;

(*Othello*, IV.ii.)

Progression: center

CORDELIA: Good my Lord, /You have begot me, bred me, lov'd me: I / Return those duties back as are right fit, /Obey you, love you, and most honor you.

(*King Lear*, I.i.)

Progression: periphery

SAMPSON: No, sir, I do not bite my thumb at you, sir, but I bite my thumb, sir.

(*Romeo and Juliet*, I.i.)

Flow: free

PUCK: I go, I go, look how I go, /Swifter than an arrow from the "Tartar's" bow.

(*A Midsummer Night's Dream*, ii.)

Flow: bound

CASSIO: Reputation, reputation, reputation! O, I have lost my reputation! I have lost the immortal part of myself, and what remains is bestial.—My reputation, Iago, my reputation!

(*Othello*, ll.iii.)

Direction: direct

CONSTANCE: Thou art [not] holy to belie me so, /I am not mad. This hair I tear is mine, /My name is Constance, I was Geffrey's wife, /Young Arthur is my son, and he is lost. /l am not mad, I would to heaven I were!

(*King John*, III.iv.)

Direction: indirect

POLONIUS: Marry, well said, very well said. Look you, sir, /Inquire me first what Danskers are in Paris, /And how, and who, what means, and where they keep, /What company, at what expense; and finding /By this encompassment and drift of question /That they do know my son,

(*Hamlet*, II.i.)

Speed: fast

JULIET: Gallop apace, you fiery-footed steeds, /Towards Phoebus' lodging; such a waggoner /As Phaeton would whip you to the west, /And bring in cloudy night immediately.

(*Romeo and Juliet*, III.ii.)

Speed: slow

MACBETH: Tomorrow, and tomorrow, and tomorrow, /Creeps in this petty pace from day to day, /To the last syllable of recorded time; /And all our yesterdays have lighted fools /The way to dusty death.

(*Macbeth*, V.v.)

Weight: heavy

HASTINGS: Woe, woe for England, not a whit for me! /For I, too fond, might have prevented this.

(*Richard III*, III.iv.)

Weight: light

LUCENTIO: Tranio, I saw her coral lips to move, /And with her breath she did perfume the air. / Sacred and sweet was all I saw in her.

(*The Taming of the Shrew*, I.i.)

Control: stable

LEONTES: Is whispering nothing? /Is leaning cheek to cheek? is meeting noses? /Kissing with inside lip? stopping the career /Of laughter with a sigh? (a note infallible /Of breaking honesty)? horsing foot on foot? /Skulking in corners? wishing clocks more swift? /Hours, minutes? noon, midnight? and all eyes /Blind with the pin and web but theirs, theirs only, /That would unseen be wicked? Is this nothing?

(*The Winter's Tale*, I.ii.)

Control: unstable

GLOUCESTER: Thou sayest the King grows mad, I'll tell thee, friend, /I am almost mad myself. I had a son, /Now outlaw'd from my blood; he sought my life, /But lately, very late. I lov'd him, friend,— /Not father his son dearer; true to tell thee, /The grief hath craz'd my wits.

(*King Lear*, III.iv.)

Focus: sharp

GLOUCESTER: Villains, set down the corse, or, by Saint Paul /I'll make a corse of him that disobeys.

(*Richard III*, I.ii.)

Focus: diffused

BOTTOM: When my cue comes, call me, and I will answer. /My next is, "Most fair Pyramus." Heigh-ho! Peter Quince? /Flute the bellows-mender! Snout the tinker! Starveling! /God's my life, stol'n hence, and left me asleep! I have had /a most rare vision. I have had a dream, past the wit of man /to say what dream it was.

(*A Midsummer's Night Dream*, IV.i)

Extended language barres

Select one physical property for extended exploration. (See "switching" exercise in *Chapter 10: Switching for details*, p. 149.) Certain actions will change significantly, expressing new and different thoughts and feelings.

13.2 CHARACTER

While it is commonly recognized that expressive action is essential to creating the authentic expression of feeling, its role in building a dramatic character is less understood. Expressive actions have a special transformative power that is often overlooked: they create character and personality. The personality of an individual can best be understood by examining their actions. Who we *are* is linked directly to what we *do*. We commonly identify character or personality with a series of adjectives—rude, polite, aggressive, shy, funny. However, character is not so much a trait a person possesses as an accumulation of consistent behavior revealed through action.

Suppose three separate drivers are pulled over by a police officer for speeding. The first attempts "to bicker" with the officer: "*I was not going over the speed limit.*" The second attempts "to bluff" his way out of it: *"Good evening, officer, was I doing anything wrong?"* The third attempts "to beg" the officer for mercy: *"But you just can't give me a ticket. You just can't."* The three speeding drivers have three distinct personalities, which are demonstrated in the different expressive actions they play—"to bicker," "to bluff," and "to beg." Their expressive actions trigger our understanding of their character and their personality.

Each of these expressive actions—"to bicker," "to bluff," and "to beg"—could be described in less active terms. The bickering speeder could be called "aggressive"; the bluffing speeder, "slick"; and the begging speeder, a "victim." However, none of these static descriptions provide the actor with anything specific to do. It is not that an actor should never think of a character in static terms. This may be a very useful part of the intellectual and interpretive process. However, until these intellectual ideas about the character reveal themselves in playable expressive actions, they have little power. The personality of the character being played is communicated most directly through a series of structured and selective expressive actions.

Body structure—defined in *Chapter 4: Integration* as "the way we shape ourselves or have been shaped by our life experience"—contributes to an even more detailed understanding of personality and character. Body structures are characterized by modes of expression that are:

- consistently used over time;
- automatic or involuntary; and
- can only be modified through conscious effort.

To some extent, we all have a somewhat *fixed body structure*—a habitual way we like to structure and organize our actions and behavior. Consequently, a person's body structure shapes and influences self-expression, character, and personality. The concept of body structure suggests that character and personality are not simply psychological patterns occurring in the brain but physical patterns living and residing in our bodies. Character, in many ways, is a type of limitation—a habitual manner and method of behaving and moving. A clinically depressed person has a different body structure from that of a paranoid schizophrenic. A light-hearted, easy-going, happy-go-lucky person has a different body structure from that of a stern, straight-laced, mild-mannered person. When playing a character in a play, an actor has to make certain choices about the physical patterns that the character uses to express thought and feeling. This, of course, involves a thorough analysis of the script, but it also requires a type of physical research. Ideally, the actor selects a series of expressive actions that appropriately reflect these limitations.

For example, you could determine that a character like Blanche DuBois in *A Streetcar Named Desire* has a propensity to play *indirect*, *light*, *free*, and *peripheral* expressive actions and a character like Medea in *Medea* has a propensity to play *direct*, *charged*, *stable*, and *heavy* expressive actions. It can be useful to think of character as

Blanche DuBois :

Indirect, Light

Free, Peripheral

Medea:

Direct, Charged

Stable, Heavy

Figure 13.1 Character study.

a type of computer font (see Figure 13.1). Just as these two fonts influence and shape the manner and method in which the words appear on the page, the physical properties of an expressive action influence and shape the character. Remember that while characters do behave in consistent and predictable ways in plays, they also grow, change, and evolve, and sometimes behave erratically and unpredictably. Ultimately, the actor's physical work on character must be rooted in a thorough understanding of the script.

Physical task

Build three different characters by exploring three physical properties. (Spend some time improvising before settling on the parameters of your specific character study.)

Step 1: Prompt

- Character 1: *fast, contact, stable*;
- Character 2: *direct, bound, slow*;
- Character 3: *heavy, unstable, center.*

Step 2: Basic exercise

Complete the following physical activity as you explore the physical properties of each of the three characters.

- Open door.
- Enter room.
- Close door.
- Call out, "Is anybody home?"
- Discover that no one else is home.
- Cross to counter.
- Set down groceries.
- Take off coat.
- Cross to chair.
- Place coat on back of chair.
- Return to counter.
- Start to unpack groceries.
- Find something to eat in the grocery bag.
- Find newspaper in the grocery bag.
- Cross to chair and table.
- Read and eat.

"Being brilliant"

Using the three physical properties selected for each of the three characters above, prepare the monologue below three times, as each of the three characters you have developed:

> Would you like to be brilliant? Not just ... I don't mean just "outstanding." I mean the sort of thing that would separate you, really separate you from others. Just: Would you like to be brilliant? A reservoir? a flood? With a kind of light inside you that other people ... do you know what I am saying? found hard to look at—see, understand. Like a certain pain. Like fire. Brilliant. Even if it meant . . . well, alone: being alone. More than graceful. More than funny. More than very good, competent. Like fire. Like light on snow. Brilliant. So intense that ... I mean really: don't you think we slow ourselves down for other people? Haven't you ever thought that? What if either of us, you or I, never stopped ourselves, never slowed ourselves, allowed resistance? Can you imagine the light, the velocity we might ... I want to be brilliant—at at least one thing. Don't you want that too? Don't you think you could be? Don't you think you could startle something in the world? I want to be amazing; I think you could be amazing. I am trying, please, to think about things. That's all. I am trying to think. I see things happening. I see a doorway. I'm at a door. Ready to walk in or out of. . . some house. You see: I see things getting very ... choices. Yes. We are talking choices. And I'm not settling.
>
> (Kranes, 2011)

To help you in these character studies, ask two essential questions:

1 *Are the three physical properties of an expressive action fully integrated in the body as you perform the physical task?* For example, if you are consciously focusing on moving *slowly*, *stably*, or *directly*, the physical properties have probably not been fully integrated in your body.
2 *Do you "feel yourself" as a different person?* This is a subjective question, but useful nevertheless. Character transformation is successful when you feel you are moving and behaving as if you are somebody else. This can only be determined by felt experience. The "feeling of a character" is like the "feeling of a perfume." Just as different perfumes smell different, your three different characters should feel different.

Epilogue

Artistic expression and aesthetics

Most American actor training programs are committed to training actors for what they nobly refer to as the professional theater. In addition to offering acting, voice, movement, and play-reading classes, a great deal of time is also spent sharing the secrets of show business. The students learn all about résumés, headshots, casting calls, agents, unions and how to survive in New York, Los Angeles or Chicago. Many maintain this "business" training is essential and all-important, as if the commerce of theater were a complicated and sophisticated subject.

In fact, theater is a surprisingly simple business, especially compared with computer technology, pharmaceuticals, aerospace, the stock market, or the insurance trade. Because of recent advances in technology, other industries have experienced profound and revolutionary changes, while the business of acting has remained relatively unchanged for centuries. Most of what the ambitious and determined actor needs to know about the commerce of theater can be gleaned from reading any one of several very good books currently available on the subject.

While teaching students that theater is a business is widely accepted, teaching them that it is an art is too often ignored. Too little time is spent preparing actors to be artists or even talking about the function and purpose of art. This short chapter is in no way an exhaustive study of the actor's art. It is a primer that I hope will answer some important questions, challenge some old ideas, and most important, stimulate more discussion on this much-neglected subject.

Science and art

Articulating the purpose and function of art is a tricky business. Nonetheless, a preliminary understanding of art can be gained by distinguishing it from its complement, science. Art refers to the creative contribution of poets, musicians, dancers, actors, novelists, painters, and so on. Science in its broadest sense refers to any systematized or structured method of knowing—not only the natural sciences (biology, chemistry, and physics) but also the social sciences (sociology, psychology, anthropology, and even history).

Science and art provide two different perspectives of our world. Science seeks to develop our intellectual appreciation for how the world works. Art, on the other hand, seeks to develop our appreciation of sensory experience. When our senses are educated, our understanding of emotion and feeling is simultaneously strengthened and enhanced. Developing sensitivity to human feeling is a central aim of almost all artistic creation.

Most individuals have a great appreciation for the purpose and importance of science. However, they are hard pressed to articulate an intelligent or remotely compelling justification for the purpose or importance of art. When pressed they invariably resort to the need for entertainment or escape. Art is responsible for feeding and developing the spirit in the same way that science feeds and develops the mind. Science in America thrives and is well funded, while art programs falter, underfunded and under attended. Unfortunately, Western culture has traditionally rewarded thinking and devalued sensing and feeling.

At the university in which I teach, undergraduate students are required to take one course in the fine arts and six in the sciences. When a moment is set aside to teach art, the senses are rarely educated. In most classrooms in the US, art is taught like a science. Scientific methods of identification and classification are applied indiscriminately to the study of art, music, poetry, theater, and dance. Students spend hours memorizing dates, movements, titles, historical perspectives, and biographical data. Students are taught to think about works of art but not to feel them. Rarely are the subjective aspects of viewing a painting, listening to music or watching a play celebrated or encouraged.

A balanced world requires individuals balanced in thinking and feeling to people it. In recent history, the attention and celebration of the sciences has been greater and more profound than at any time in history. Each new scientific discovery poses a new set of ethical and moral questions that present tough choices that have serious consequences. What do we do with our nuclear waste? Should we genetically alter our food? Do we want to know if we have the gene for Alzheimer's disease? It is not simply enough to have the technology to do these extraordinary things. These questions have no rational, logical, scientific answers. They are human questions. The answers are intuitive, a product of felt experience, requiring a logic of the spirit and a wisdom of the heart.

The world's most complicated ethical, moral, and spiritual issues are explored in great works of art. All the while a great work of art is entertaining us and providing us with pleasure, it is subtly and indirectly preparing us to answer complicated moral and ethical questions. Most of the lay population's ethical and moral education about the intellectual advances of the world's leading scientists and thinkers comes from popular films, television, novels, and plays. Genetics, disease, history, women's rights, racism, homosexuality, space travel, environmental issues, and so on all receive a thorough and important human treatment in art. Art puts science in a palatable wrapper so that even those unschooled in the ways of scientific thought can grapple with complex human issues.

Art explores the sciences from a human perspective. Popular movies like *Jurassic Park* explain to the nonscientific world the dangers of mixing genetic engineering and theme park entertainment. Ibsen taught his generation the important role heredity and environment play in determining human destiny. Generations have learned more about English history from the plays of Shakespeare than from any history book. Jerome Lawrence and Robert E. Lee challenged the nation to examine evolution—a tough issue at the time and again today—in their dramatic exploration of the Scopes "monkey" trial, in the play *Inherit the Wind*. Science is the objective study of serious subjects. Art is the subjective study of serious subjects. Scientists and artists are equally important. A culture with strong science and strong art has nothing to fear from its technological advances. A culture with strong science and weak art has everything to fear.

A socialist and a capitalist go to a production of *Death of a Salesman*. Afterwards, they have an intellectual discussion about the play. The socialist views Willy Loman as a victim of capitalism, free enterprise, profit, and a false American dream. The capitalist views him as a lazy, unethical liar—a silly dreamer and a blowhard who would rather talk than work. The capitalist and socialist have very different intellectual ideas about the play. However, when they put their intellectual ideas aside and begin discussing the way the play made them feel, both the socialist and capitalist acknowledge that they were moved by a sense of compassion for the desperate, lonely, and isolated Willy Loman. Perhaps this common compassion can pave the way for them to synthesize their seemingly irreconcilable philosophical differences. What is most important about good theater is not the differing thoughts, interpretations, and intellectual biases we bring to it but its power to unite every observer emotionally and even spiritually. To truly understand theater—or any work of art—we must turn our discussion away from what we *think* and begin to discuss how the work of art makes us *feel*. Ultimately, a work of art cannot be appreciated in light of the intellectual baggage that we bring to it, but in light of its direct appeal to our feelings. Most important, what a work of art makes us feel can sometimes change the way we think. This is art's greatest and most profound achievement.

Significant form

The actor, like all artists, is a form maker. Painters create visual forms by arranging pigment on canvas. Musicians organize pitch and rhythm into musical forms recognizable as melody. Dancers organize shifts of weight into the physical form of a dance. Actors organize the voice and body into meaningful forms of expression that reveal the life of the character they are portraying. A work of art, like many other things, can be either *significant* or *insignificant*. When the artistic creation is well done, the work of art possesses *significant form*.

Significant forms are intense, appealing, commanding and profound. Any time that we are captivated in the theater, struck by a painting, or moved by a piece of music, we have encountered significant form. Aesthetic philosopher Susanne K. Langer defines significant form "as the essence of every art; it is what is meant by anything we call "artistic"(1953, 24).

The creation of significant form is primarily a product of selection, of conscious and unconscious choices by the artist. A work of art achieves significance when the raw materials of the artist's craft are organized and structured in a skillful and meaningful way. The painter selects paint, color, brushes, brush strokes, and a canvas; the musician selects the appropriate key, time signature, and musical notes; the dancer selects a sequence of rhythmically organized weight shifts and gestures; and the actor selects a unified series of expressive actions that reveal the life of the character.

It is difficult to describe in words what makes a work of art significant. Before the advent of modern art, all significant art was simply called beautiful. Art was considered a study of the beautiful, and the art objects created were also beautiful. Though the term beautiful is applied less frequently to contemporary works of art, the concept of beauty is central to an understanding of significant form. Human beings possess an extraordinary aesthetic appreciation for the beautiful. Our fascination with mountains, fireworks, flowers, starry nights, rainbows, and sunsets all reflect a celebration of the beautiful. Painted houses, furniture groupings, fashion, gardens, parks, makeup, and hairstyles demonstrate the human creatures seemingly illogical need to perpetuate the beautiful. The fine arts—music, dance, painting, poetry and theater—are codified aesthetic extensions of this obsession with the beautiful.

In the twentieth century, insightful artists began to find new subjects of beauty in unfamiliar places; the term beautiful became inappropriate and fell out of fashion. It is hard, in the traditional sense, to describe *Waiting for Godot*, *No Exit* or *Marat Sade* as beautiful. Indeed, much of modern and postmodern art, while possessing a unique and special appeal, seems to defy the traditional beautiful label. When the term beautiful failed to satisfy, it was difficult to find new language that could adequately describe the import of modern art. Some art critics avoided the problem altogether and simply asserted that the import of great art was beyond description. Others sought to create new terms.

The seemingly ambiguous term *suchness and otherness* is a fine example of this new terminology. A work of art is said to possess *suchness and otherness* when its import is so great that the spectator is convinced its brilliance and depth is "something other than" and "like no such thing" experienced before. Art objects with suchness and otherness undoubtedly possess significant form. Similarly, scholar and philosopher F. S. C. Northrop (1962, 189–90) replaced the imprecise and seemingly inappropriate term beautiful with *radical, empirical immediacy*. It took Northrop three very erudite words, and undoubtedly a great deal of sound thinking, to articulate precisely what makes a work of art significant. Nonetheless, Northrop's *radical, empirical immediacy* is aptly coined. Significant art is radical, possessing boldness—a rebellious and revolutionary quality. Empirical suggests a direct appeal to the senses. A significant work of art is a celebration—an exploitation of and sometimes an assault on the senses. Immediacy refers to the commanding presence of a well-constructed work of art. Significant art attracts, invites, and demands attention. While any term attempting to articulate what makes a work of art great may fail to satisfy, the terms *suchness and otherness* and *radical, empirical immediacy* are very useful in clarifying what makes a work of art significant.

Contemporary actor training in America would benefit greatly from a responsible discussion of the importance of significant form. The legacy of Stanislavski in America has resulted in an unprecedented call for truthfulness and honesty—a type of everyday realism, a slice of life. Actors practice emotional substitution, create voluminous life biographies for the characters they play, personalize and ask, "What would I do if I were in this situation?"—all in search of a honest and truthful performance. Though this quest for truthfulness was well intended and useful, the effort was not without its shortcomings. In some circles a naively realistic approach to acting has emerged, rendering style destructive, heightened language unnatural, largesse of expression taboo, voice and movement training inessential, and character transformation unnecessary. Absurdly, actors are encouraged to simply be themselves.

Certainly, the actor's work must be truthful, plausible, and most important authentic, but beyond that it must be exciting, vital, and dynamic. What is commonly rewarded in many acting circles, as truthful and honest work is often pedestrian, mundane, and sometimes even boring. Not everything that is truthful is necessarily artful. If it were, there would be art all around us. Rarely—and perhaps thankfully— is everyday life exciting, structured, or stylized enough to be worthy of the label theatrical, significant, or artful. A mature discussion of acting requires that we move beyond truth and believability and also include in our aesthetic criteria a newfound appreciation for significant form. The actor's primary responsibility is not merely to live truthfully in imaginary circumstances but also to live artfully in imaginary circumstances.

Real and imaginary feelings

The type of feeling experienced by the actor is of a different kind and nature than the type of feeling experienced in daily life. These two distinct types of feelings are identified by various terms: psychological feeling and aesthetic feeling, subjective feelings and objective feelings, imaginary feelings and real feelings. Regardless of the terminology, the assertion is that there is a distinction between the type of emotional experience present in daily life and the kind of emotional experience present in a work of art (Hornby 1992, 117–30). Some art critics go so far as to suggest that the feelings experienced when viewing a work of art are not so much ones own personal feelings; but rather, the feelings that belong to the art object itself. A significant work of art, when viewed without personal entanglement, arouses feelings that are uniquely its own.

In saying this, I have probably offended many readers, who will have rushed to the conclusion that I am suggesting that acting is merely artifice and technical demonstration: "Acting must be real." "I am my character." "I only draw on my personal experiences." Suggesting that the actor experiences a special type of feeling is in no way meant to diminish or lessen its importance. A great deal of sound thinking suggests that there is a special type of feeling reserved solely for artistic expression.

You and a friend go to see a movie. You are both emotionally moved by the movie and leave the theater with tears running down your faces. On your way out of the theater, you encounter a friend who is going to see the next showing. She asks, "How was the movie?" You respond, "Wonderful! Wonderful! It was one of the best movies I ever saw" Your weeping friend, on the other hand, says nothing and hurries toward the car. On the way home, your friend is especially quiet. To break the silence you ask, "Did you like the movie?" Your friend responds by stating that he does not want to talk about it.

The most important distinction between you and your friend's experiences is one of perspective. Your imaginative feelings allowed you to experience the movie. His real feelings interrupted and distorted his perceptions of the movie. Perhaps, it closely mirrored a personal problem he was currently experiencing, reminded him of a traumatic childhood experience, or even evoked new concerns or fears of which he was previously unaware. Your friend did not experience the imaginative world of the film, because he was caught up in the drama of his own life. If asked about the film, it is doubtful whether he could provide any objective response at all. Of course, you must not diminish the importance of your imaginary feelings simply because they were different from your friends. The tears streaming down your face during the movie were quite real. They were powerful and authentic. However, they had no real bearing on the outcome, course, or direction of your life. You could feel them completely and freely without consequence or fear. Because you were able to make an aesthetic distinction between your real life and the pretend life of the movie, you were able to enjoy these feelings, no matter how sad, horrible, or depressing they might have been, and learn from them.

If we put aside all the romantic talk about the necessary emotional turmoil of the truly committed actor, we should agree—at least on some level—that there is a difference between our real feelings and those of the characters we play. The stereotypical method actor with his illicit personalization and compulsive quest for real feeling may have created an emotional response that interferes with or blocks the feelings contained in the play itself. A very wise instructor of mine would frequently comment, "I wasn't aware the play was about you." I have never forgotten this cryptic statement. It was meant to challenge the imagination.

A Practical Handbook for the Actor states, "The actor's job is not to bring the truth of his personal experience to the stage, but rather to bring the truth of himself to the specific needs of the plays" (Burder et al. 1986, 94). Susanne K. Langer goes so far as to suggest that the truth the artist may be seeking may transcend the self:

> Even the artist need not have experienced in actual life every emotion he can express. It may be through manipulation of his created elements that he discovers new possibilities of feeling, strange moods, perhaps greater concentration of passion than his old temperament could ever produce or his fortunes have yet to call forth.
>
> (1953, 374)

The job of the actor is not to reduce the complexity of the character to the confines of limited personal experience, but rather, to allow the character to expand the actor's own human potential. The problem with real feelings is that they are subjective. When an actor's real feelings are substituted for those of the character being played, the play becomes muddied and distorted. Just like your friend who could not objectively experience the movie, actors who are overcome with their personal feelings often lose all objectivity about the quality of their performance. Real feelings are difficult to shape and focus into meaningful and significant form. They are usually beyond control. The mistake is to assume that because real feelings are powerful and truly fell they are artistically satisfying for the audience. When an actor is entangled in personal feelings, the audience members are often duped into paying more attention to the actor than to the character being portrayed or to the play. Some actors, unfortunately, have reduced some of the theater's greatest plays to a petty exploration of whatever trivial personal entanglement happens to be occurring in their own lives. When great actors build great characters, they are undoubtedly drawing upon their past personal experiences, not for the purposes of finding real feelings, but for a deeper understanding of their imaginary ones. The best acting is not a validation of one's own life but transcendence into a larger and deeper understanding of the human condition.

Smart actors with emotional stability and longevity recognize that all the world is not a stage. The actor's personal life is not the theatrical equivalent of the dancer's ballet barre and the violinist's musical scales. Fortunately, the talented actor can transcend, through strong technique and a powerful imagination, any personal limitation and embrace any character or experience conjured up by even the most inventive playwright.

The distinction between imaginary and real feelings is not always as apparent in practice as it is in theory. Distinguishing real and imaginary feelings is not meant to deny that in the process of training or in rehearsals imaginary feelings can revert to or become confused with real feelings. The fine line between real and imaginary feeling can easily become blurred or disappear altogether. Just as it is possible to view a movie that hits too close to home, it is possible to stumble onto imaginary feelings in rehearsal that cannot be disassociated from real ones. This is often the case, particularly in the initial stages of the actor's development, when the necessary sophistication to navigate the emotional instrument has not yet been developed. The occasional confusion of real and imaginary feeling is a part of the process of learning and a hazard of the profession. Even the most skilled actors can on occasion find themselves in real emotional trouble. What is important and necessary is that the actor, the director, the other actors, or the acting teacher recognize that the imaginary process has reverted to a real one and that responsible and conscious choices need to be made about how to proceed. Actors are always dancing a fine line between the real and the imaginary

Pure form

When an actor's technique rises to the level of sophistication where personal feelings are not confused or muddled with those of the character, an extraordinary thing takes place. The actor, without recourse to personal limitations, is able to tap into and unlock the pure form of human feeling. Pure form is a highly specialized type of feeling that requires a selflessness and "egolessness" rarely exhibited in Western acting. The Hindus identified this highest type of metaphysical feeling as *rasa*:

> This last they call rasa; it is a state of emotional knowledge, which comes only to those who have long studied and contemplated poetry.
>
> (Langer 1953, 323)

Rasa is the Hindu understanding of *pure form*. Pure form occurs when the actor becomes selfless. Ironically, the deepest and most profound expression of feeling occurs not through getting into the self but by transcending the self. Ultimately, pure form provides the actor with a boundless and limitless range of expression. This egoless and selfless form of expression cannot occur without technique. All good technique, through the process of repetition, discipline, and dedication, results in a type of self-transcendence that triumphs over personal limitations, obstacles, inexperience, and idiosyncrasies. Good technique puts the actor in touch with the perfect self.

Yoshi Oida, the famous Japanese actor, in his own way touches on pure form and the egoless actor in his book *The Invisible Actor*:

> For me, acting is not about showing my presence or displaying my technique. Rather it is about revealing, through acting, "something else," something that the audience does not encounter in daily life … . For this to happen, the audience must not have the slightest awareness what the actor is doing. They must be able to forget the actor. The actor must disappear. In Kabuki theatre, there is a gesture, which indicates "looking at the moon," where the actor points into the sky with his index finger. One actor, who was very talented, performed this gesture with grace and elegance. The audience thought:" Oh, his movement is so beautiful!" They enjoyed the beauty of his performance and the technical mastery he displayed. Another actor made the same gesture, pointing at the moon. The audience didn't know whether or not he moved elegantly; they simply saw the moon. I prefer this kind of actor: the one who shows the moon to the audience. The actor who can become invisible.
>
> (1997, xvii–xviii)

When the actor's expression finds pure form, its impact has a consistent and universal appeal. All in the audience observe with clarity and complete human understanding the same unselfish, archetypal human truth. Something great is attained when an actor moves beyond mundane and muddied everyday feelings and embraces without resistance the pure form of feeling. We see feeling with a greater precision than ever possible in the context of daily living. This selfless rendering of pure form is at the heart of the emotional education of the actor, the audience, and our culture.

Appendix I

Expressive continuum

EXPRESSIVE CONTINUUM	
PROPERTY	**SENSORY ELEMENTS**
Energy	Charge←--→Release
Orientation	Contact ←--------------------------------------→Withdraw
Size	Expand ←--→Contract
Progression	Center ←--→Periphery
Flow	Free←---→Bound
Direction	Direct←--→Indirect
Speed	Fast←--→Slow
Weight	Light←---→Heavy
Control	Stable←--→Unstable
Focus	Sharp←---→Diffused

Appendix II

Actions

Below is an exhaustive list of actions that may be used as prompts for expressive actions. The list may be more comprehensive than practical, and some may assert that many of the actions listed are virtually unplayable. However, the list of actions is meant to spark the imagination of the actor rather than curtail it. Surprisingly many gifted actors select the seemingly most difficult or unlikely of actions and organize them into meaningful and productive expressive actions.

A

to abandon
to abduct
to abhor
to abide
to abolish
to absorb
to abuse
to ace
to accelerate
to accept
to access
to acclaim
to accommodate
to accost
to address
to adhere
to admire
to admit
to admonish
to adopt
to adore
to adorn
to advance
to advert
to advise
to advocate
to afflict
to affirm
to aggravate
to agitate
to agonize
to agree
to aid
to aim
to alarm
to alert
to alienate
to align
to allocate
to allot
to allow
to allude
to allure
to ally
to amaze
to amble
to amuse
to angle for
to announce
to anoint
to annihilate
to annoy
to answer
to antagonize
to anticipate
to apologize
to appeal
to appraise
to approach
to approve
to arbitrate
to argue
to arm

to arouse
to arrange
to ascertain
to ask
to aspire
to assail
to assent
to assess
to assign
to assist
to assure
to atone
to attest
to attract
to audition
to avenge
to awaken
to award

B

to back away
to back down
to back off
to back out
to back up
to bail
to balance
to balk
to ban
to bandy about
to banish
to bank on
to bar from
to bargain
to barge in
to bark
to barrel along
to barter
to bask
to bat around
to batten down
to battle
to bawl out
to bay
to beam
to bear
to bear down
to bear out
to beat
to beat about
to beat down
to beat up
to beckon
to beef up
to beg
to beguile
to bellow
to bequeath
to beset
to besiege
to besmirch
to bestow
to bet
to bias
to bicker
to bind down
to bitch
to bite
to blab
to blame
to blank out
to blanket
to blast
to bless
to blitz
to block
to blossom
to blot out
to blow up
to bluff
to blurt out
to blush
to boast
to boil
to bolt
to bomb
to bombard
to bone up
to boogie down
to book up
to boost
to boot
to booze it up
to borrow
to boss
to bother
to bottle up
to bounce
to bow down
to bow out
to bowl over
to box in
to brace for
to brace up
to brag
to brainwash
to brave out
to break
to break away
to break down
to break through
to break up
to breeze along
to breeze in
to breeze through
to bribe
to brief
to brighten up
to brim over

to bring about
to bring around
to bring into line
to bring out
to bring up
to bristle
to broach
to brush aside
to brush away
to brush off
to brush up
to bubble over
to bubble up
to buck for
to buckle down
to bulldoze
to bully
to bum around
to bum out
to bumble through
to bump
to bump along
to bunch
to bundle
to bungle up
to burden
to burn
to burst
to bury
to bust out
to bust up
to bustle about
to butt in
to butt out
to butter up
to button one's lip
to buzz along
to buzz off

C

to cage
to cajole
to calculate
to call
to call down
to campaign
to cancel
to capitalize
to capitulate
to care about
to care for
to carp
to carry on
to carve out
to cast aside
to cast away
to cast down
to cast off
to catch off guard
to cater
to caution
to cave in
to celebrate
to cement
to censure
to center on
to challenge
to change
to channel
to charge
to charm
to chart out
to chase after
to chase away
to chat
to chatter
to cheat
to cheat on
to check
to check out
to check over
to cheer
to chew out
to chew over
to chicken out
to chide
to chill out
to chime in
to chip away
to chisel
to choke
to choose
to chop
to chortle
to chow down
to chuck away
to chuckle
to chug along
to chum up
to churn out
to circle
to cite
to claim
to clam up
to clamor
to clamp down
to clash
to clasp
to claw
to clear
to cleave
to click
to climb
to cling
to clip
to cloak
to clock
to clog
to close
to closet
to cloud

to clown
to clue in
to clunk
to cluster
to clutch
to clutter
to coach
to coalesce
to coast along
to coax
to coerce
to coil
to collaborate
to collapse
to collect
to collide
to collude
to come around
to come at someone
to come between
to come clean
to come down on
to come over
to come through
to commend
to comment
to commiserate
to commit
to commune
to communicate
to commute
to compare
to compel
to compensate
to compete
to compile
to complain
to compliment
to comply
to compress
to compromise
to compute
to con
to conceal
to concede
to conceive
to concentrate
to concern
to condemn
to confer
to confess
to confide
to confine
to confirm
to confiscate
to conflict
to conform
to confront
to confuse
to congratulate
to conjure
to connect
to connive
to consecrate
to consent
to consider
to console
to consort
to conspire
to constrain
to construct
to construe
to consult
to contend
to convalesce
to converge
to converse
to convert
to convey
to convict
to convince
to cook up
to cool down
to cool off
to cooperate
to coordinate
to cop out
to cope
to cork up
to correspond
to cough up
to counsel
to cover
to cover up
to cower
to cozy up
to crack down
to crack up
to cram
to crash
to crave
to crawl
to creep
to cringe
to criticize
to cross
to crouch
to crow
to crowd
to crown
to cruise
to crumple
to crunch
to crusade
to crush
to cry
to cuddle
to cue in
to curse
to cuss out
to cut
to cut down

D

to dab
to dabble
to dally
to damn
to dance
to dangle
to dart
to dash
to dawn upon
to daydream
to deal
to debate
to deceive
to decide
to deck out
to declare
to decorate
to dedicate
to deduce
to deduct
to deface
to default
to defect
to defend
to defer
to define
to deflect
to defraud
to deign
to delegate
to deliberate
to delight
to deliver
to delude
to deluge
to delve
to demand
to demonstrate
to demote
to denounce
to dent
to deny
to depart
to depend
to deposit
to deprive
to descend
to describe
to desert
to design
to designate
to despair
to despise
to detach
to detect
to deter
to detract
to develop
to deviate
to devote
to dicker
to dictate
to diddle
to die
to differ
to differentiate
to diffuse
to dig
to dig down
to digress
to dilly-dally
to dip
to direct
to disagree
to discipline
to disclose
to disconnect
to discourage
to discriminate
to discuss
to disembark
to disengage
to disentangle
to disguise
to disgust
to dismiss
to dispatch
to display
to dispose
to dispute
to disqualify
to dissociate
to dissolve
to dissuade
to distance
to distinguish
to distract
to dive
to diverge
to divide
to divorce
to divulge
to divvy
to dodder
to dodge
to dole out
to doll up
to doom
to dose
to doss
to dote
to draft
to drag
to drag down
to drag up
to drain
to drape
to draw apart
to draw out
to draw together
to dream
to dredge
to drift
to drill
to drip
to drive

to drive out
to drone
to drop
to drown
to drown out
to drum
to duke out
to dwell on

E

to ease
to eavesdrop
to edge around
to egg on
to eke out
to elaborate
to elbow
to embellish
to emblazon
to embroil
to empathize
to empower
to enable
to encourage
to endeavor
to enforce
to engage
to enlighten
to enlist
to enshrine
to ensnare
to entangle
to entertain
to enthrall
to entice
to entrap
to entreat
to entrust
to envision
to envy
to erase
to erupt
to escape
to escort
to establish
to estimate
to evict
to exact
to examine
to exceed
to excite
to exclude
to excuse
to exhort
to exile
to exonerate
to exorcise
to expand
to expect
to expel
to expend
to experiment
to explain
to explode
to expostulate
to express
to extend
to extol
to extort
to exult

F

to face
to fade
to fail
to faint
to fake
to fall
to fall apart
to fall in love
to fall into trap
to falter
to familiarize
to fan out
to fancy
to fashion
to fault
to favor
to fawn over
to fear
to feel out
to fence in
to fend for
to fess up
to feud
to fiddle
to fidget
to fight
to figure on
to find out
to finish
to fink on
to fink out
to fire at
to fish
to fix up
to fizzle out
to flag down
to flake out
to flame up
to flap
to flare
to flash
to flatten

to flee
to flick
to flicker
to flinch
to fling
to float
to flog
to flood
to flop
to flounce
to flow
to flow over
to flub
to fluctuate
to fluff
to flunk
to flush
to flutter
to fly
to foam
to focus
to fog up
to foist
to fold
to follow
to fool around
to force
to forewarn
to forgive
to fortify
to foul up
to fraternize
to freak out
to freeze
to freshen up
to fret about
to frighten
to fritter
to front for
to frost over
to froth up
to frown
to fumble
to fume
to fuss

G

to gag
to gallivant
to gallop
to gamble
to gang up
to gape at
to gasp
to gather
to gawk
to gaze
to gear up
to generalize
to get a grip
to get a rise out of
to get in one's face
to get off your chest
to get on one's case
to get on the good side
to get out of a mess
to get out of a jam
to giggle
to give
to give out
to give up
to glance
to glare
to glaze over
to gleam
to glean
to glide
to glisten
to gloat
to glory
to gloss over
to glow
to glower
to glut
to gnaw
to go against
to go all out
to go along
to go into orbit
to go on and on
to go out of bounds
to go out on a limb
to go overboard
to go to pieces
to goad
to gobble
to goof around
to goof off
to goose
to gore
to gorge
to gossip
to grab
to grant
to grapple
to grasp
to grate
to greet
to grin
to grind
to gripe
to groan
to groom
to groove
to grope
to gross out
to ground
to grovel
to grow
to growl
to grub
to grumble
to grunt
to guard
to guess

to guide
to gulp
to gum up
to gun down
to gush
to gussy up
to guzzle down
to gyp out

H

to hack
to haggle
to hail
to ham up
to hammer
to hand out
to hand over
to hang around
to hang back
to hang in
to hang on
to hanker
to harbor
to harden
to hark
to hark back
to harken
to harness
to harp
to hash over
to hassle
to haul
to haul off
to have it out
to head off
to head out
to heal
to heap
to hear
to hear out
to heat up
to heave
to hedge
to help
to hem in
to herd
to hesitate
to hew down
to hide
to high pressure
to hike up
to hinder
to hint
to hire
to hiss
to hit
to hit below the belt
to hit on
to hit up
to hitch
to hoard
to hobnob
to hold against
to hold back
to hold down
to hold in
to hold off
to hold out
to hold up
to holler
to honor
to hoodwink
to hook
to hook up
to hoot
to hop
to hope
to horse around
to hound
to hover
to howl
to huddle
to hum
to hunch over
to hunger
to hunker
to hunt
to hurl
to hurry
to hurt
to hush
to hustle
to hype
to hypothesize

I

to ice up
to identify
to idle about
to idle away
to idolize
to illuminate
to illustrate
to imagine
to imbue
to immerse
to impale
to impart
to impel
to impinge
to implant
to implicate
to impose
to impress
to inch
to incite
to incline

to include
to indicate
to indoctrinate
to induce
to indulge
to infatuate
to infect
to infer
to infest
to infiltrate
to inflict
to inform
to infringe
to infuse
to ingratiate
to inhibit
to initiate
to inject
to inoculate
to inquire
to insinuate
to insist
to inspire
to instigate
to instill
to instruct
to insure
to interfere
to intermingle
to interpret
to intertwine
to intervene
to interview
to intimidate
to intoxicate
to intrigue
to introduce
to intrude
to inundate
to invest
to invite
to invoke
to iron out
to isolate
to issue
to itch

J

to jab
to jabber
to jack around
to jack up
to jam
to jangle
to jazz up
to jeer
to jerk
to jest
to jet
to jibe
to jimmy
to jockey
to join
to joke
to jolt
to jostle
to jot
to judge
to juggle
to juice up
to jumble
to jump
to justify
to jut out

K

to keel over
to keep
to keep after
to keep down
to keep from
to keep up
to kick
to kick around
to kick aside
to kill
to kink up
to kiss
to kiss off
to klutz around
to knock
to know about
to knuckle
to kowtow

L

to label
to labor
to lace into
to ladle out
to lag behind
to lam into
to lament
to languish
to lap

to lapse
to lash
to last
to latch
to lather
to laugh
to laugh off
to launch
to lavish
to lay
to leach
to lead
to leak
to lean
to leap
to learn
to lease
to leave
to lecture
to leer
to legislate
to lend
to lengthen
to level
to levy
to liberate
to lick
to lie
to lift
to light
to lighten
to liken
to limber up
to limit
to line up
to linger
to link
to liquor up
to list
to listen
to litter
to liven up
to load
to loaf
to loan
to lob
to lobby
to loiter
to loll
to long for
to look
to look away
to look down
to look forward
to look over
to loom
to loosen
to lop off
to lope along
to lord over
to lose
to lounge
to luck into
to lull
to lumber along
to lump together
to lunge
to lurch
to lure
to lurk
to lust
to luxuriate

M

to maintain
to make a pass
to manage
to maneuver
to map out
to mar
to march
to mark
to marvel
to mash
to masquerade
to measure
to meddle
to mediate
to mellow out
to melt
to mention
to mess
to mess around
to mess up
to mill around
to mingle
to minister
to mislead
to moan
to model
to monkey around
to mooch
to moon over
to mope
to motion
to mourn
to mouth off
to move
to mow down
to muddle along
to muddy up
to muffle up
to mull over
to murmur
to muscle
to muse
to muss up
to muster up
to mutiny
to mutter

N

to nag
to nail
to name
to narrow down
to needle
to neglect
to negotiate
to nest
to nestle
to nibble
to nick
to nip
to nod
to nod off
to nominate
to note
to notify
to nudge
to number
to nurse
to nuzzle

O

to object
to obliterate
to obsess
to offend
to offer
to ogle
to ooze
to oppose
to opt
to ordain
to order
to orient
to oscillate
to oust
to overflow

P

to pace
to pack
to pad
to paint
to pal around
to palm off
to pan
to pander
to panic
to parade
to pardon
to pass over
to pat
to patch up
to pattern
to pave
to pay back
to peck
to peek
to peel back
to peep
to peer
to peg
to pelt
to pen up
to penalize
to penetrate
to pep up
to pepper
to perch
to percolate
to perform
to perk up
to permit
to persecute
to persevere
to persist
to persuade
to pester
to peter out
to petition
to pick
to pick apart
to piddle
to pile on
to pilfer
to pin
to pinch
to pine after
to pine away
to pivot
to plague
to plaster
to play
to play along
to play around
to play down
to play into
to play up
to plead
to please
to pledge
to plod
to plonk
to plot
to plow
to pluck
to plug
to plummet
to plump down
to plunge
to plunk

to point
to poison
to poke
to polarize
to polish
to ponder
to pontificate
to poop out
to pop out
to pop up
to pore over
to portion out
to portray
to pose
to possess
to postpone
to posture
to pounce
to pound
to pout
to practice
to praise
to prance
to prattle
to pray
to preach
to preface
to prefer
to prejudice
to prepare
to prescribe
to press
to pressure
to presume
to pretend
to primp
to probe
to proceed
to prod
to prohibit
to promise
to promote
to prop up
to prostrate
to protect
to provoke
to prowl
to prune
to pry
to puff up
to pull
to pull together
to pump
to punch
to punish
to purge
to purr
to purse up
to push
to push ahead
to pussyfoot
to put off
to put on
to put over
to put up
to putt
to putter
to puzzle

Q

to quail
to quake
to quarrel
to question
to quibble
to quiver
to quiz

R

to race
to rack
to radiate
to rag on
to rage
to rail
to railroad
to rain down
to raise
to rally
to ram
to ramble
to rank
to rant
to rap
to rasp
to rate
to rattle
to reach
to rear back
to reason
to reassure
to rebel
to rebuke
to recall
to recede
to reckon
to reclaim
to recognize
to recoil
to recommend
to reconcile
to recover
to reel back
to reflect
to refrain

to refresh
to reign
to rejoice
to relax
to relinquish
to remark
to remember
to remind
to reminisce
to repel
to report
to reprimand
to reproach
to request
to resign
to rest
to retaliate
to retire
to retreat
to retrieve
to revel
to revenge
to revolt
to reward
to rid of
to rifle
to rip
to ripen
to rise
to rival
to roam
to roar
to rob
to rock
to rocket
to roll
to romp
to root for
to route around
to rub
to ruffle
to rule
to ruminate
to rummage
to rumple
to run
to rush
to rustle

S

to sack
to sacrifice
to safeguard
to sag
to sail
to salute
to salvage
to satiate
to satisfy
to saturate
to saunter
to save
to savor
to scale down
to scamper
to scare
to scatter
to scoff
to scold
to scoop
to scoot
to score
to scour
to scout
to scowl
to scramble
to scrape
to scratch
to scream
to screw around
to scrounge
to scrub
to scuff
to scuffle
to scurry
to scuttle
to seal
to seam
to search
to secure
to seduce
to seethe
to seize
to serve
to settle down
to shake
to shear
to shelter
to shield
to shift
to shine
to shiver
to shock
to shoo
to shoot
to shore up
to shoulder
to shout
to shove
to shovel
to show off
to shower
to shriek
to shrink
to shrivel
to shroud
to shrug
to shudder
to shuffle
to shush
to simmer
to sink
to skid
to skim
to skip

to skirmish
to slack
to slam
to slant
to slap
to slash
to slice
to slick
to slide
to sling
to slink
to slip
to slither
to slobber
to slosh
to slouch
to slug
to slump
to slur
to smack
to smash
to smear
to smile
to smirk
to smooth
to smuggle
to snap
to snarl
to snatch
to snazz
to sneak
to sneer
to sniff
to snitch
to snoop
to snort
to snuggle
to sob
to sparkle
to spatter
to spaz
to speculate
to spew
to spice
to spin
to spiral
to spit
to splash
to splatter
to splinter
to splurge
to sponge
to spoon
to sport
to spout
to sprawl
to spray
to spread
to sprout
to spruce
to spurt
to sputter
to spy
to squabble
to squander
to squash
to squeak
to squeeze
to squint
to squirm
to squirt
to stab
to stack
to stalk
to stall
to stammer
to stamp
to stampede
to stand
to star
to stare
to stash
to steal
to steam
to stimulate
to sting
to stir
to stoop
to store
to storm
to stow
to strain
to strand
to strap
to stray
to stream
to stretch
to stride
to strike
to strip
to strive
to stroll
to struggle
to strum
to strut
to stumble
to submit
to sulk
to summon
to surge
to surrender
to swab
to swallow
to swarm
to sway
to swear
to swear off
to sweep
to sweeten
to swell
to swerve
to swindle
to swirl
to swish
to switch
to swoon
to swoop
to sympathize

T

to tag
to taint
to take
to talk back
to tally
to tamp
to tamper
to tangle
to tinker
to tap
to target
to tattle
to taunt
to tax
to tear
to tease
to tempt
to tend
to terrify
to test
to testify
to theorize
to thrash
to threaten
to thrill
to throw
to thrust
to thud
to thumb
to tick
to tickle
to tidy up
to tighten
to tilt
to tinker
to tip
to toddle
to topple
to torment
to torture
to toss
to tote
to toughen
to tout
to tower
to trace
to trade
to train
to tramp
to trample
to transfer
to trap
to tremble
to trick
to trifle
to triumph
to trot
to tumble
to tussle
to tweak
to twiddle
to twinkle
to twist

U

to unify
to unite
to unleash
to urge

V

to value
to vanish
to vary
to veer
to venture
to verify
to vie
to visit
to visualize
to volunteer

W

to wade
to waffle
to wage
to wager
to wait
to wallow
to waltz
to wander
to wangle
to ward off
to warn
to wash
to wave
to weave
to weep

to whack
to whine
to whip
to whirl
to whisk
to whisper
to wiggle
to wimp
to win
to wink
to wish
to withdraw
to wither
to wobble
to wonder
to worry
to wrangle
to wrap
to wrench
to wrestle
to wriggle
to wrinkle
to writhe

Y

to yak
to yammer
to yank
to yearn
to yell
to yield

Z

to zig-zag
to zing
to zip

Bibliography

Ackerman, Diane (1991) *A Natural History of the Senses*. New York: Vintage.

Albee, Edward (1962/2003) *Who's Afraid of Virginia Woolf*. New York: Scribner.

Alderson, Richard (1979) *Complete Handbook of Voice Training*. New York: Parker.

Anderson, Virgil A. (1977) *Training the Speaking Voice*. 3rd ed. London: Oxford University Press.

Aristotle (1996) *The Nicomachean Ethics*. Hertfordshire, UK: Wordsworth Editions.

Barry, Lynda (1993) *The Good Times Are Killing Me*. New York: Samuel French.

Beckett, Samuel (1958) *Endgame and Act Without Words*. New York: Grove Press.

Best, David (1974) *Expression in Movement and the Arts*. London: Lepus Books.

Burder, Melissa and Lee Michael Cohn, Madeleine Olnek, Nathaniel Pollack, Robert Previto, and Scott Zigler (1986) *A Practical Handbook for the Actor*. New York: Vintage.

Celichowska, Renata (2000) *The Erick Hawkins Modern Dance Technique*. Hightstown, NJ: Princeton Book.

Charlie Rose: The Brain Series (2009) Television Program. United States: Public Broadcasting Service: 22 December.

Charlton, W. (1970) *Aesthetics: An Introduction*. London: Hutchinson University Library.

Chekhov, Michael (1953) *To the Actor*. New York: Harper & Row.

Cohen, Bonnie Bainbridge (1993) *Sensing, Feeling, and Action*. Northampton, MA: Contact Editions.

Cory, Gerald A. Jr and Russell Gardner, Jr (2002) *The Evolutionary Neuroethology of Paul Maclean*. Westport, CT: Greenwood.

Csikszentmihalyi, Mihaly (1990) *Flow: The Psychology of Optimal Experience*. New York: Harper & Row.

Damasio, Antonio (1994) *Descartes' Error: Emotion, Reason, and the Human Brain*. New York: Penguin.

—— (1999) *The Feeling of What Happens: Body and Emotion in the Making of Consciousness*. New York: Harcourt, Brace.

—— (2003) *Looking for Spinoza*. London: Vintage.

Dewey, John (1934/1980) *Art as Experience*. New York: Perigee.

Douglas, Stanley (1950) *Your Voice: Applied Science of Vocal Art*. New York: Pitman.

Eagleman, David (2011a) Incognito*: The Secret Life of the Brain*. New York: Pantheon Books.

—— (2011b) "The Mystery of Expertise." *The Week*, 30 December–6 January 2012, pp. 49–50.

Fry, D. B. (1979) *The Physics of Speech*. London: Cambridge University Press.

Galati, Frank (1991) *John Steinbeck's* The Grapes of Wrath. New York: Dramatist Play Service.

Goleman, Daniel (1995) *Emotional Intelligence,* Kindle Version, accessed 20 August 2010 from Amazon.com. New York: Bantam.

—— (2011) *The Brain and Emotional Intelligence: New Insights*. Northampton, MA: More Than Sound.

Grotowski, Jerzy (1968) *Towards a Poor Theatre*. New York: Simon & Schuster.

Harrop, John (1992) *Acting*. London: Routledge.

Hawkins, Erick (1964) *The Body Is a Clear Place*. Princeton, NJ: Princeton Book Company.

Henley, Beth (1986) *Crimes of the Heart*. New York: Viking.

Hornby, Richard (1992) *The End of Acting*. New York: Applause.

—— (1997) *Script into Performance: A Structuralist Approach*. New York: Applause.

Inge, William (1945) *The Dark at the Top of the Stairs*. New York: Dramatist Play Service.

Internet Encyclopedia of Philosophy (refereed), 8 July 2005, University of Tennessee at Martin, United States, accessed 9 September 2011, http://www.iep.utm.edu/embod-cog/.

Johnson, Mark (2007) *The Meaning of the Body*. Chicago: University of Chicago Press.

Kahneman, Daniel (2011) *Thinking, Fast and Slow*. New York: Farrar, Straus and Giroux.

Kaufman, G. S. and Moss Hart (1939) *The Man Who Came to Dinner*. New York: Dramatist Play Service.

Kaufman, Moises and the members of Tectonic Theatre Project. (2001) *The Laramie Project*. New York: Dramatist Play Service.

Keleman, Stanley (1979) *Somatic Reality*. Berkeley, CA: Center Press.

Kepner, James I. (1993) *Body Process*. Santa Cruz: CA: Gestalt Press.

Kranes, David (2011) *David Kranes: Selected Plays*. "Park City Midnight" (Act One: *Future Tense*). San Diego, CA: Level 4 Press.

Kushner, Tony (1993) *Angels in America*. New York: Theatre Communications Group.

Laban, Rudolph Von and F. C. Lawrence (1950/1971) *The Mastery of Movement*. Boston: Plays Inc.

Langer, Susanne K. (1942/1993) *Philosophy in a New Key*. 3rd ed. Cambridge, MA: Harvard University Press.

—— (1953) *Feeling and Form*. New York: Charles Scribner's Sons.

—— (1957) *Problems in Art*. New York: Charles Scribner's Sons.

—— (1964) *Philosophical Sketches*. New York: Mentor.

Lawrence, Jerome and Robert E. Lee (1979) *Inherit the Wind*. New York: Bantam.

LeDoux, Joseph (1998) *The Emotional Brain*. New York: Simon & Schuster.

Linklater, Kristin (1976) *Freeing the Natural Voice*. New York: Drama Book.

McKinney, James C. (1994) *The Diagnosis and Correction of Vocal Faults*. Nashville, TN: Genevox Music Group.

Mamet, David (1978) *Sexual Perversity in Chicago*. New York: Grove Press.

Marrone, Robert (1990) *Body of Knowledge: An Introduction to Body/Mind Psychology*. New York: State University of New York Press.

Metcalfe, Steve (1983) *Strange Snow*. New York: Samuel French.

Middendorf, Elsa (1990) *The Perceptible Breath*. Paderborn, Germany: Junfermann-Verlag.

Miller, Arthur (1949/1976) *Death of a Salesman*. New York: Penguin.

Miller, Richard (1996) *The Structure of Singing*. Belmont, CA: Wadsworth.

Moore, Sonia (1960) *The Stanislavski System*. New York: Viking.

Northrop, F S. C. (1946) *The Meeting of East and West*. New York: Macmillan.

—— (1962) *Man, Nature, and God*. New York: Simon & Schuster.

Oida, Yoshi. (1997) *The Invisible Actor*. London: Routledge.

O'Neill, Eugene. (1956) *Long Day's Journey into Night.* New Haven, CT: Yale University Press.

Passons, William R. (1975) *Gestalt Approaches in Counseling.* New York: Holt, Rinehart and Winston.

Reichmann, James B. (1985) *Philosophy of the Human Person.* Chicago: Loyola University Press.

Richards, Thomas (1995) *At Work with Grotowski on Physical Actions.* London: Routledge.

Rosen, Richard (1995) "Urdhva Dandasana: Raised Staff Poise." *Yoga* Journal. July.

Rosenberg, Jack Lee, with Majorie L. Rand and Diane Asay (1985) *Body, Self, and Soul: Sustaining Integration.* Atlanta, GA: Humantics.

Ryle, Gilbert (1949) *The Concept of Mind.* London: Hutchinson.

Schechner, Richard (1973) *Environmental Theatre.* New York: Hawthorn.

Shanley, John Patrick (2005) *Doubt: A Parable.* New York: Theater Communications Group.

Shaw, George Bernard (1970) *The Bodley Head Bernard Shaw: Collected Plays with Their Prefaces.* London: Bodley Head.

Shultz, Jonathan (2006) Open-Ended Scene. Unpublished.

Skinner, Edith (1990) *Speech with Distinction.* Revised by Timothy Monic and Lilene Mansell. New York: Applause.

Smith, Edward W. L. (1985) *The Body in Psychotherapy.* Jefferson, NC: McFarland.

Stanislavski, Constantin (1936/1984) *An Actor Prepares.* New York: Routledge.

—— (1961) *Creating a Role.* New York: Theater Arts.

Sweigard, Lulu E. (1974) *Human Movement Potential.* New York: Harper & Row.

Todd, Mabel E. (1937) *The Thinking Body.* Princeton, NJ: Princeton Book.

Tormey, Alan (1971) *The Concept of Expression: A Study in Philosophical Psychology and Aesthetics.* Princeton, NJ: Princeton University Press.

Turner, J. Clifford (1950) *Voice and Speech in the Theater.* London: Pitman House.

Wilder, Thornton (1938/2003) *Our Town: A Play in Three Acts.* New York: Perennial Modern Classics.

Williams, Tennessee (1947/1995) *A Streetcar Named Desire.* London: Heinemann Plays.

Wilson, August (2007) *The Piano Lesson.* New York: Theatre Communications Group.

—— (1954) *Cat on a Hot Tin Roof.* New York: Dramatist Play Service.

Zarrelli, Philip B. (1995) *Acting (Re)considered: Theories and Practices.* London: Routledge.

Index

Taylor & Francis

eBooks

FOR LIBRARIES

ORDER YOUR **FREE 30 DAY** INSTITUTIONAL TRIAL TODAY!

Over 23,000 eBook titles in the Humanities, Social Sciences, STM and Law from some of the world's leading imprints.

Choose from a range of subject packages or create your own!

- Free MARC records
- COUNTER-compliant usage statistics
- Flexible purchase and pricing options

Benefits for your user

- Off-site, anytime access via Athens or referring URL
- Print or copy pages or chapters
- Full content search
- Bookmark, highlight and annotate text
- Access to thousands of pages of quality research at the click of a button

For more information, pricing enquiries or to order a free trial, contact your local online sales team.

UK and Rest of World: **online.sales@tandf.co.uk**

US, Canada and Latin America:
e-reference@taylorandfrancis.com

www.ebooksubscriptions.com

A flexible and dynamic resource for teaching, learning and research.